When Ocean

Ernest F. Crocker holds the following degrees: Bachelor of Medicine and Bachelor of Surgery (MBBS), Bachelor of Science (BScMed), Fellow of the Royal Australasian College of Physicians (FRACP), Diploma of Diagnostic Ultrasound (DDU), Fellow of the Australasian Association of Nuclear Medicine Specialists (FAANMS).

Dr Crocker's Australian MBBS degree is the equivalent of the Doctor of Medicine (MD) degree in the United States of America.

'Dr Ernest Crocker has delivered another amazing read in his new book, *When Oceans Roar*. I was greatly encouraged and inspired by the powerful true stories of present-day believers who overcame great challenges, calamities and cruelty, and others who responded to God's invitation to advance in the kingdom of God. This is a book that offers hope to the helpless, and help to the hopeless. If you enjoy being inspired and encouraged, you will enjoy *When Oceans Roar*.'

Randy Clark, DMin, Founder and President, Global Awakening and the Apostolic Network of Global Awakening

'You'll not be able to go on with life as usual once you've read this inspiring book! The author has travelled the world over and pulled together a compilation of real life heart-rending stories and testimonies of ordinary folk like you and I. There are stories of those who became heroes with remarkable transformations and there are others whose names will never even be remembered. But they all had one thing in common, they knew who they believed and they were persuaded that God had the power to do what He had promised (Rom. 4:21). They believed that though oceans roared He was and is the Lord above all! There are stories of miracles, martyrs and phenomenal transformations. As you read of the remarkable faith of those who gave their lives for his glory, men and women "of whom the world was not worthy" [Heb. 11:38], you too will be changed!'

Brian and Candice Simmons, The Passion Translation

'This book chronicles stories of the remarkable way God works in the lives of His people. It will encourage people of faith, and inspire them to worship. It will challenge those with an open mind to consider the claims of Jesus Christ.'

Dr Michael Spence, Vice Chancellor, University of Sydney

'Dr Ern Crocker has a powerful message to share! After many years in the medical profession, Dr Ern has so much experience and expertise. It's so important in these troubling times that we hear from medical experts about how miracles still happen today! After interviewing Ern on Historymakers radio and following his adventures on social media, I'm keen to see how this next book will impact people's lives. We need to get this book into the hands of many people far and wide so that this life-changing message can be heard. Dr Ern is a true blue Aussie Historymaker. I pray that this book blesses everyone who reads it!'

Pastor Matt Prater, New Hope Brisbane, Historymakers Radio and TV

'In a world of increasing identity confusion, Ern Crocker will take you around the globe introducing you to people from all stations in life who have found what it means to be a child of God. Not childish, but genuine sons, both male and female, who have discovered that the whole of creation groans awaiting them to step in to the trust, love, and connection, that eventually moves mountains.'

Tom Hallas, Asia and Pacific Field Director, Youth With A Mission;
Member, YWAM International Elders Group

'For those readers who have read Dr Crocker's first book, *Nine Minutes Past Midnight*, you will find a very similar, unique style in the author's approach in this book. He introduces you to very interesting people that have crossed his path as he follows God. I have travelled with Dr Crocker and have seen his unique God-given skill of sensing when quiet-spoken servants of God have a story to tell about the faithfulness of God. In addition, I have observed him interview them in a very unassuming way that releases amazing stories that glorify the living God. You will read profound stories of encounters with Christ from different personalities that say yes to the Father as they walk out His call on their life. In addition, the author will help you see the scriptural principles that these lives signify. Let the same Spirit that raised Christ from the dead speak to you through the pages of this book. Let this not be just a book of others' encounters with God, but let it be a book that results in an encounter for you with the Father.'

Donald R. Tredway MD, PhD, Emeritus Professor and Chairman, Department of Obstetrics and Gynecology, Oral Roberts University and University of Oklahoma, Tulsa, Oklahoma; former Vice President & Head Clinical Development Unit for Metabolic and Reproductive Endocrinology, EMD Serono, USA (Merck KGA, Germany)

'I love watching the ocean with each day changing with high then low tides, sand formations and sea life constantly changing. The title of the book, *When Oceans Roar*, perfectly describes how God moves and works. No situation or day is ever the same. He roars (speaks and moves) in our lives. We see how God works one way in one situation and then another way in another situation. He's not boxed in. Ern provides stories that God's plan will get done no matter what our response may be. We read of examples of people falling on their *faith* not their *face*. You will see throughout this book what King Solomon said after all his ups and downs, successes and disappointments throughout his life – "Now all has been heard; here is the conclusion of the matter: fear [reverence] God and keep his commandments" Ecclesiastes 12:13 [NIVUK].'

Peter Irvine, Co-founder Gloria Jean's Coffees, Australia; author and keynote speaker

'This book is a true reflection of the courageous faith in Jesus that I have always known when it comes to my uncle. Through so many storms that we as a family have navigated together, he has always maintained a solid and unshakeable faith, knowing and believing that Jesus is in complete control, and that He holds the wheel. I pray (and I know) the words in this book will help you also find a courageous

faith in Jesus, as you step out of the boat into whatever situation you find yourself in today.'
Matt Crocker, Worship leader and songwriter, Hillsong Church and Hillsong United

'Dr Ern Crocker, in *When Oceans Roar,* generously shares of his own life and is able to help us gain deep insight into the lives of others. He paints a rich portrait of lives joyfully lived with Jesus at their centre. He shares his own personal experiences and those of family and friends, of many Australian colleagues and stories from extraordinary overseas friends. He often returns to the important question of identity, reinforcing that much will perish yet there is eternal significance in a relationship with Jesus. A gifted storyteller who inspires . . .'
Michael Burke, MBBS, FRACGP, PhD; Chair, HealthServe Australia

'Dr Ern Crocker writes with intelligent researched succinctness. Grappling, as a man of medicine, with observable outcomes seemingly unrelated to medical interventions, he persuades us with stories, testimonies if you will, of what can only be miracles of transformation and healing. With the gentle logic of both observation and interview we are persuasively guided into the world of the supernatural. Not bad for a doctor of medicine, not bad for God. Both find comfortable harmony in this well written book. I love reading stories of healing written by doctors. This one, however, is special.'
David Crabtree, Senior Leader, DaySpring Church, Castle Hill, NSW

'Dr Ernie Crocker's second book, *When Oceans Roar*, is a fantastic read and I highly recommend it. Sharing stories from refugees, missionaries, professors, generals and everyday people, Crocker engages the reader from start to finish with stories of unwavering faith leading them on a wonderful journey of growth and servanthood. Crocker displays raw humanity intertwined with his own experience, creating an inspirational must read book that at times brought me to tears.'
Professor John Boyages, author and Professor of Breast Oncology, Macquarie University

'In this uplifting and challenging book, Dr Ernest Crocker writes as a skilled physician and fellow pilgrim. He aptly stitches together stories of people's lives of Faith. Courage meets great darkness and is matched by greater Light – the thread of sustaining hope in a loving and good God – no matter the circumstances. As a faithful custodian of these stories he is not afraid to lay all the facts on the table and is meticulous in his desire to be factual and compassionate. This book remains faithful to hope and the strength of the legacies left behind. Legacies bought with the lives of these people.'

Christie Buckingham, Senior Pastor, Bayside Church,
Melbourne, Australia

When Oceans Roar

**Powerful true stories of courageous faith
and changed lives**

Dr Ernest F. Crocker

Authentic

.   22 21 20 19 18 17 16   7 6 5 4 3 2 1

First published 2016 by Authentic Media Limited,
PO Box 6326, Bletchley, Milton Keynes, MK1 9GG and
Authentic Media Limited, PO Box 185, West Ryde NSW 2114, Australia.
authenticmedia.co.uk

British Library Cataloguing in Publication Data

A catalogue record for this book is available from the British Library.

ISBN: 978-1-78078-160-0
978-1-78078-161-7 (e-book)

Some names have been changed to protect the privacy
and security of those involved.

Cover design by Jennifer Burrell, Fresh Vision Design
Printed in the UK by CPI Group (UK) Ltd, Croydon CR0 4YY

Copyright acknowledgements

10,000 REASONS
WRITTEN BY
JONAS MYRIN / MATT REDMAN

To my parents, Doreen and Ern, who taught me
by example what it means to live by faith
and to trust in a God who never fails.

Acknowledgements

I am deeply indebted to the many who have made this book possible.

To the doctors, colleagues and friends who shared their stories, sometimes at great personal risk, to allow us to see for ourselves how faith in God can overcome the most difficult of life's situations.

To Feby Chan and the family and friends of Andrew Chan and Myu Sukumaran. I saw God lift their boys victoriously beyond the transient and the constraints of this temporal world in which we live. I have witnessed the direct impact of their legacy on thousands of lives in Bali, Australia and in the world beyond.

To Gladys Staines and daughter Esther who willingly shared their story of tragic loss but also of great victory as they allowed God's grace to carry them through a raging tempest.

To my own family members, and especially Naomi and Mike with whom we shared the perilous voyage of Elliott the Brave.

To Paul and Rob Bootes and members of the Authentic Media team for their encouragement and professional support.

To Sheila Jacobs, for her most valued editorial advice and assistance.

To Liz West, for her constant encouragement, and advice.

To those who have given time and consideration to provide endorsements. They have done so from positions of influence, responsibility and experience of God's enduring presence in their lives.

To my wife, Lynne, my finest critic and greatest supporter. Without her encouragement this book may never have been written.

To God, who has never failed to provide and who never will. I have sometimes questioned His methods but never His purpose or resolve.

Contents

The LORD also will roar from Zion, And utter His voice from Jerusalem; The heavens and earth will shake . . .

(Joel 3:16)

Preface

In *Nine Minutes Past Midnight* I shared my experience as a young doctor searching to reconcile my medical training with my Christian faith. I openly challenged God that if He heals today He should prove that to me within seven days. Such was my desperation. The very next night I attended a house call where a heart attack patient died before my eyes. My efforts at resuscitation were not effective in saving her. But as I knelt by her side there came an inner voice saying, 'Now's the time, now's the time.' I prayed and her life was fully restored.

In this book I relate my continuing experience as a Christian doctor who has witnessed the wonderful ways in which God may intervene in the lives of doctors, their patients, families and friends. I have learned to stand down from my own expectations and ambitions that I might step up into His purpose for my life. My learning curve has been steep and there have been many times that I have stumbled. However, day by day, I am able to draw upon the empowering presence of God's Spirit in my life. And perhaps my most important discovery has been to find true identity as a very much-loved son of Father God rather than in my own pursuits.

I have been fortunate to share my journey with many co-travellers, and their experiences have expanded my expectation of the manner in which God intervenes when we allow Him to do so. Their stories are also told in these pages. Many have passed through deeply troubled waters. Yet God's steady hand over the storms of their lives has allowed them to travel on unharmed and profoundly strengthened.

The philosopher John Paul Sartre has said that 'no finite point has meaning without an infinite reference point'. Likewise, the stories of people's lives are mere anecdotes of wasted time unless they are anchored in truth. They are mere scratchings on a stone unless that stone is Jesus. At this point they become testimonies and as such are powerful beyond understanding. They also become spiritual weapons: 'And they overcame him by the blood of the Lamb and by the word of their testimony' (Rev. 12:11).

During my career as a Christian doctor I have moved on from a childlike perception of 'Gentle Jesus, Meek and Mild' to a personal relationship with Jesus the warrior king. To an experience of one who demonstrates His power and unrelenting love. To one who touches humanity at its greatest point of need, one who cannot be limited, one who overturns the traditional and sets the agenda. He did not come into the world to found a church 'but to proclaim a Kingdom',[1] an unshakeable Kingdom.

Though oceans may roar, He is Lord above all. His name is Jesus and at His name every knee shall bow. And as I write this morning, the words of C.S. Lewis ring loud and clear: 'God whispers to us in our pleasures, speaks in our conscience, but shouts in our pain: it is His megaphone to rouse a deaf world.'[2]

Peter Hitchens, interviewed on national television in Sydney, was asked the following question: 'Which so called dangerous idea do you think would have the greatest potential to change the world if it were implemented?'[3] His response:

'The most dangerous idea in human history remains the belief that Jesus Christ was the Son of God and rose from the dead. That is the most dangerous idea that you will ever encounter.'

'But you can't leave it there,' said the moderator. 'Why dangerous?'

'Because it alters the whole of human behaviour and all of our responsibility. It turns the universe from a meaningless chaos into a designed place where there is justice and hope. And therefore we all have a duty to discover the nature of that justice and to work towards it. It alters us all. If we reject it, it alters us all as well. It is incredibly dangerous. That is why so many people turn against it.'

As you prayerfully read this book, you will be drawn to make personal decisions, which carry the potential to change your life. But tread warily. As much as this is a standing invitation, it may never present itself to you again.

> You are a letter of Christ . . . written not with ink but with the Spirit of the living God, not on tablets of stone but on tablets of human hearts.
>
> (2 Cor. 3:3, NIV)

Introduction

Every happening, great and small, is a parable whereby
God speaks to us, and the art of life is to get the message.
Malcolm Muggeridge

'I've had some chest pains lately, doc. Never had 'em before but they
seem to happen when I'm stressed.' The man was in his mid-forties.
He wore jeans, a blue singlet, his head was shaved and he sported
several tattoos and body piercings. He looked to be fairly fit but this
was no guarantee against coronary artery disease.

After taking a history and determining that he carried several risk
factors for ischaemic heart disease, I prepared him for the exercise
bike. He quickly became short of breath and his blood pressure began
to fall. I terminated the study immediately and decided to perform
echocardiography.[1]

'Just sit here quietly while we set up,' I encouraged him. But I was
concerned and kept a weather eye on him. As we prepared I noticed
that he was reading a book.

'What are you reading man?'

'The Bible. I read Psalms, Matthew, Luke, John. They were good.
Read Ecclesiastes too. Didn't understand that one at all.'

'Have you been reading the Bible for long?'

'Oh yes, me and me missus, we sit on the bed at night and read the
Bible together.'

'Do you go to church?'

'No, doc, don't go to church.'

'Are you a Christian, then?'

'Oh no, doc, no way.'

Now totally confused, I had to ask the final question: 'Why not?'

'Doc, you wouldn't understand. You don't know what I've done . . . I'm not worthy.'

The call of God is upon all of us. We may suppress it, we may try to ignore it. We may bury it with a busy lifestyle. But eventually it will resurface, rear up and demand attention.

It has been said that every man, woman and child has a God-shaped vacuum in their life, a vacuum which must be filled. There are many ways that we may try to achieve this. Sometimes by acquisition of material possessions, by success in business, the pursuit of love or the attention of others, and sometimes by service to others or pursuit of knowledge. All of these may temporarily satisfy, but in the long-term will fail miserably.

Planted deep within the heart of every nation is the concept of eternity and of the existence of a supreme being. Noted author and scholar Don Richardson in his book *Eternity in Their Hearts*[2] described how cultures through history have held to the concept of a single creator God. That deep conviction over many centuries prepared hearts to receive the concept of a Christian God and to receive the message of forgiveness and salvation through Jesus Christ. Unanswered questions from generations past were often answered by the message of Christianity.

Author and historian Emeritus Professor Geoff Blainey is listed as one of Australia's 100 living treasures. In April of 2013 I attended a library evening at the Australia Club in downtown Sydney to hear Blainey discuss his recent book *A Short History of Christianity*.[3] In this book, Blainey traces the path and impact of Christianity through recorded history.

He spoke of his own Christian heritage. His parents were devout Methodists, and as a child he attended church services and Sunday school.

At the conclusion of his address I asked him this question: 'Has the research and writing of this book had a personal impact on your life?'

His response was evasive. He confessed as much. But it was clear that with passing years he had developed a positive and growing interest in Christianity.

I would not venture to comment on where Professor Blainey stands in respect of a personal faith, but am confident from his written and spoken word that he believes that faith in a Christian God has played a most positive role in the development of civilisation.

Peter Craven, reviewing Blainey's book for *The Australian* said: 'He sees Christianity as the most distinctive and most civilising thing we have in the West. And it's hard for anyone who has ears to hear not to be moved by his quiet but testamental conclusion:

> The debate about Christ's message and influence will continue. Long after we are all dead and the 21st century is lost behind passing clouds, the fascination with him will persist: and many will still see him as triumphant.[4]

There is no hiding from God no matter how high the wall of scepticism may be that we build around ourselves. The British journalist, war correspondent and agnostic Malcolm Muggeridge was a well-known satirist and media personality. As a young man he was drawn towards Communism. Travelling to Moscow in 1932, he became correspondent for the *Manchester Guardian*. During World War Two he served in the British Intelligence Corps as a Lieutenant and in 1942 became a member of MI6. But none of his pursuits satisfied his needs and during that time he attempted suicide on at least one occasion.

In later years he embraced Christianity, finding freedom of expression of his new faith in God through the Catholic Church. During his life he had contributed richly to world literature and debate. But in consideration of his many years spent as an agnostic he entitled his two-volume autobiography: *Chronicles of Wasted Time*.[5]

The brilliant intellectual Christopher Hitchens was an avowed atheist his entire life. His last book, *Mortality*, chronicled his journey through terminal malignancy. The book was published by his wife after his death. The final chapter is a series of disconnected statements and jottings made by Hitchens in his final days. One cannot read too deeply into the final thoughts of this dying man, but attention is drawn to the statement: 'If I convert, it's because it's better that a believer dies than that an atheist does.'[6]

The call of God may come upon us in the context of a Christian family or church fellowship. It may echo down the years as the plaintive cry of a mother for her lost child. It may blaze out of utter darkness as a blinding light, which cannot be ignored. Saul, struck down by a great light on the Damascus road, responded to the awesome presence of God with the words: 'Who are You, Lord?'[7] Thomas in the darkness of doubt was swept back into reality by the gaping wounds on Jesus' hands. His response: 'My Lord and my God!'[8]

Samuel, who did not know the Lord at all, was called by Him in the darkness of his room whilst he slept. His response: 'Here I am.' But after the third call he replied, as must every man, woman and child summoned into the presence of Almighty God:

'Speak, for Your servant hears.'[9]

As a doctor, I meet people daily in crisis. Some are Christians, some not. Many I venture to say are lazy atheists[10] and others have never experienced the practical outpouring of God's love on their lives. Yet all of these people have one need in common. They need hope for the future, and hope to build their lives on. I have not subsequently seen my young patient with the cardiac problem. His management needs will be met by others. But I pray regularly that the Spirit of God will lead him into a new life of promise and hope.

Hope is the light that guides our path through the day and the dark hours that follow. It is an 'anchor of the soul, both sure and steadfast, and which enters the Presence behind the veil, where the forerunner has entered for us, even Jesus' (Heb. 6:19).

The important thing about an anchor is that it holds the whole boat. Hope supports the whole person, body, mind and spirit. And Romans tells us that hope never disappoints, or as *The Message* puts it, never leaves us 'feeling shortchanged' (Rom. 5:5).

In recent years, I have known and worked with men and women who felt the call of God on their lives in the most perilous of circumstances. Their actions placed them at great personal risk. Yet they discovered that only a relationship with God would fill the aching void that overwhelmed their lives. They found hope in Jesus Christ. Their experiences enrich my life. Here are their stories.

Part I

Facing the Impossible

Preface to Chapter 1

A doctor is faced daily with human crisis. Only this week I attended a man with terminal prostate cancer and with a second primary tumour in his brain. His family members were devastated. They related how they had recently lost their sister to breast cancer and that one of them also had a breast tumour. They were wracked with fear and the prospect of imminent loss.

I was able to share with them a promise given me by Pastor Narelle Crabtree of Dayspring Church some years ago that 'when God is in the room there is no room for fear'. That promise is something to hold on to in the darkest hours. The words are as links in a chain to hold fast to in the tempest of the night until morning comes.

I am often asked how I protect myself from the trauma of these extreme situations.

Doctors must remain objective, compassionate and professional. To do this they place a protective shield around themselves. There are various means of achieving this. I find my strength by allowing the Spirit of God within me to love that person and with the understanding that Jesus is able to meet their deepest needs. I find great comfort and strength in the verse:

> I have set the LORD always before me; Because He is at my right hand
> I shall not be moved.
>
> Ps. 16:8

Yet there are times when the crisis is so close and personal that it challenges me profoundly. Such was the situation with my niece's son, Elliott. Yet God used that time not only to intervene in a miraculous way but also to fulfil His purpose far beyond the immediate. Here is his story.

1

The Incredible Journey of Elliott the Brave

'Can you come? Can you come quickly?' I had missed the first call a few seconds earlier. But the immediacy of the second prompted me that something was wrong.

'He's not doing well, Ern. Can you come, now?'

It was my brother, Tony, on the line.

It had been a fairly quiet afternoon at the nuclear medicine rooms at Penrith, and I was looking forward to leaving a little early.

My niece's son, Elliott, at 6 weeks of age had just that week been diagnosed with a severe congenital heart problem. He had coarctation, a narrowing of the major artery from the heart, causing blood to be shunted back through his lungs, and he also had a VSD.[1] This morning, surgeons at the Royal Alexandra Hospital for Children had operated to correct the situation.

'It's a serious condition,' they had warned, 'but one that we have dealt with many times before. We are cautiously optimistic. But be prepared, we are going to leave his chest open for a few days, just in case.'

Last evening we had met as family and friends in the paediatric cardiology ward to pray over young Elliott. He gazed up at us; a complete innocent, cradled in his father's arms as we prayed, and our hearts went out to him and his parents. There was a quiet confidence that all would be well.

But such was not the case. Surgery had been successful, the coarctation had been corrected and the VSD closed. But three hours later at 4 p.m. without warning and for no obvious reason, Elliott's heart simply stopped beating. He was given twenty-five minutes of cardiac

massage by the ICU[2] doctors but with no response. The ECMO by-
pass machine continued to perfuse his tiny body but his heart remained motionless.[3] His parents were advised of the gravity of the
situation and family and friends hurried to the hospital in support.

I called my wife, Lynne, who was in downtown Sydney, and asked
her to pray. Independently we made our way to the hospital, each
adding our prayers to those who were already praying for the life of
young Elliott. As Lynne drove through the Sydney Harbour Tunnel,
she recalls the tears running down her face as she prayed audibly for
the life of this little boy. But as she emerged into daylight at 4:26
p.m. precisely, something changed. 'Something shifted,' she said, 'and
I knew that he would be all right.' It was just as Rees Howells had
discovered: that there comes a time in prayer when the tide changes
and we know that there has been a breakthrough.[4]

Arriving at the Children's Hospital we found family and friends
crowded into a small waiting room in the ICU. The mood was sombre. There were tears, there was silent contemplation. Some prayed,
some were immersed in their cell phones, texting. Prayers and best
wishes rained in from around the world.

'Jesus Culture are praying,' said Matty, Naomi's brother.[5] The strain
told on the parents' faces. Naomi was in tears; Michael sat quietly,
trying to come to grips with the situation. This was not what he had
expected. Where was the happy, content little boy of yesterday?[6]

I prayed silently. What words could I bring? Elliott had embarked
on an incredible journey, one fraught with danger. And we would
travel with him. We were all passengers. A number present were from
the Hillsong musical team. Michael himself was soon to produce the
Hillsong Live DVD for 2014.

The words that came had been given to Matty and his friends as
they co-wrote a recent song:

> You call me out upon the water
> The great unknown where feet may fail
> And there I find You in the mystery
> In oceans deep, my faith will stand.[7]

It was going to be a long journey and a rough one but one, we prayed, that would lead to a safe haven.

'Would you like to see him?' they asked. With my brother, Tony, I made my way along the corridor into a room that looked something like a set from *A Space Odyssey*. Doctors and nurses busied themselves monitoring and adjusting sophisticated equipment and there on a plinth in the centre lay tiny Elliott, dwarfed and almost completely obscured by banks of monitors and other sophisticated electronic gear. I could not help but notice that his arterial monitor indicated no pulse pressure. It was a flat red line.

But he was stable on by-pass. The doctors said they would monitor him over the next forty-eight hours and that there would be no more interventions for the time being.

Saturday passed, and then Sunday. No change. The flat red line continued. An echocardiogram showed that the main chamber of Elliott's heart was enlarging and this would make it more difficult for the heart to pump.[8]

It was decided to perform an angiogram on the Monday morning. Imaging the passage of dye as it passed through the heart, the great vessels and coronary arteries might give some clue as to why the heart was not functioning.

Monday (Day 4).

Breakthrough! The angiogram showed normal flow but best of all, the left ventricle was beginning to show early signs of contraction. Great news! 'But keep praying,' we urged one another. The Bible says to pray when the rains come that they might continue.[9] Often we pray in times of need but fail to prevail in prayer as we see the answers evolve. There was a long way to go.

We took turns praying over Elliott, and Michael set up an iPod close to his head, which played quiet worship music. There was an ambience of peace and God's presence around that bed. Cards, love letters, small toys festooned the bed. Prayers and best wishes continued to flood in.

But that night, more bad news. Elliott was beginning to hemorrhage into his chest. He was losing 58 mls of blood per hour, a lot for a little boy of 3 kilograms. The surgeon knew that he would have to operate that night to save Elliott's life. To the astonishment of parents watching over their own children in the ICU, a team of twenty assembled around the tiny boy at 11 p.m. There were surgeons, anaesthetists, perfusionists, ICU staff, residents and nurses. Eventually a tiny tear was found in the aorta. This was not able to be patched but was repaired and the bleeding halted. Elliott's condition was stabilized. The team disbanded, returning to their homes at 2 a.m. They had done a great night's work.

There was not much sleep to be had that night. I sensed in my spirit a tension between hope and despair, between healing and demise, between God's will for this little boy and the alternative, which was unthinkable. We have all experienced this at some time but often don't understand the root cause. This has been called 'spiritual warfare' and I discovered that night the term to be a total misnomer. It is a battle between good and evil, which takes place in our hearts, our minds and our spirits, and which taxes every element of our being.

But I remembered something else that my friend General Ajai Masih had told me. He called it 'battle inoculation'.[10]

'When a soldier goes into battle he is terrified,' he said. 'But when that first bullet flies past his head, he falls to the ground and lies there thinking, "I'm alive, I'm alive!" He picks himself up, his fear is overcome and he goes for it, boots and all.' And so I discovered it was with warfare in the spiritual realm.

Wednesday (Day 6).

Elliott's arterial blood pressure was 70/60 and his heart rate 126, quite remarkable for a little boy who for almost three days had no pulse pressure at all. A text message from Naomi's mother that morning:

'Our dear Elliott "The Brave" is stable today! Please keep praying! Your hands of prayer over this little boy's heart have carried him!'

At such times it is vital to look up to the only one who can help. In 2 Kings 4 we read how Elisha's servant rose up early to find that the city was surrounded by an army with horses and chariots. 'What shall we do?' he asked. Elisha replied:

> 'Do not fear, for those who are with us are more than those who are with them.' And Elisha prayed, and said, 'LORD . . . open his eyes that he may see.' Then the LORD opened the eyes of the young man, and he saw. And behold, the mountain was full of horses and chariots of fire . . .
>
> (2 Kgs 6:16,17)

Thursday (Day 7).

We gathered at Starbucks in the hospital lobby that afternoon recalling the events of the past days. Naomi and Michael had not left the hospital since day one and were physically and emotionally drained. Elliott had been taken down to the OR.[11] The surgeon was to adjust the flow in the by-pass machine and we eagerly awaited news. But then at 5:25 p.m. word came down from a nurse in the ward.

'Great miracle news!'

An hour later we were to hear that he had actually been taken off the ECMO machine and that he was maintaining his own blood pressure.

'He should be out of the Intensive Care Unit within the week,' they said. Again they remained 'cautiously optimistic' but were 'amazed how quickly he had recovered'.

I saw Elliott later that afternoon. This was indeed a remarkable journey. His blood gases were good. His pulse pressure was rising. 'Steady as she goes,' I thought.

Friday (Day 8).

Elliott was progressing well. I was amazed how the evolving events had caught the imagination of so many: Narelle wrote: 'Good news! Praying! Elliott and his family are very much on my heart and in my prayers. And I don't even know them. I feel this great love for them all . . . guess that's what the Father does when He puts something on your heart!'

At my Wednesday morning men's group, builders in yellow fluorescent jackets, IT guys, businessmen, industrial manufacturers and retirees cheered as they saw a photo of Elliott the Brave gazing at the wide world, engaging his mother's eyes.

'You know,' said my friend Kel, 'this little boy has been my total focus for the past two weeks, and I don't even know him. This has been an absolute celebration of God's grace and goodness.'

Saturday (Day 9).

Elliott was continuing to make good progress off by-pass. This morning the surgeon would close his chest wall, which had been open for a week. I entered this comment in my personal notes:

> Ships Log HMAS COURAGEOUS: Nine days out of port. Calmer waters after the storm but still quite squally. Cargo secured, running repairs to be made today. Slight change in course. Set mainsail for home.

The chest wall was closed at 8 a.m., twenty stitches in all. The doctors would start to reduce sedation.

From day 10 to 21, Elliott became progressively stronger and more aware of his surroundings as sedation was slowly wound down. On day 10 he began to move his feet and made efforts to breathe for himself. His blood pressure was 90/52.

By day 11, both eyes were open and blood pressure 110/70. We read in Acts 12 how Peter was released from prison when 'constant' prayer was offered to God by the church. We began to understand that prevailing prayer would be vital to see this journey through.

By day 14 Elliott was awake, smiling and lifting his arms to his mum and dad, and on day 15 they saw the scar for the first time. His mother, Naomi, who had been through such turmoil over the preceding weeks and with Michael had seen the hand of God move in a mighty way, put it simply: 'Well, if you're going to go through something like that, you better have something to show for it.'

On day 23 the stitches were removed and on day 25 Elliott was discharged home a happy, smiling, alert little boy. Surgery had been a total success.

I have chronicled the events that occurred as a doctor might record progress notes. It is a hard habit to break after forty-five years in medical practice. The days were as stepping stones from a dark place. Yet the days and dates in themselves were as mere 'scratchings on a stone'[12] soon to be washed away with time. The stone however, never changes. That rock is Jesus and the name of Jesus is powerful over all.

Some have called the events that transpired a miracle. Others have called it a miracle of modern medicine. I would call it both. My experience as a doctor has revealed to me that modern medicine is a gift of God. My definition of modern medicine is 'our progressive understanding of God's creation and our increasing ability to intervene to monitor and modify its welfare as He allows us to do so'. It was humbling for me as a doctor to observe the dedication, the level of expertise and the hours of constant effort by the medical staff of that paediatric unit. We were deeply blessed by their actions and are wholly grateful.

But, you might ask, why was little Elliott healed in such spectacular fashion? Was it because so many prayed? Was it because of the faith of his mum and dad? Was it simply to be an example of God's healing power? No, the answer goes far beyond. We have seen families united. We have seen people's faith reignited. We have seen non-believers for the first time stand in awe of the power and the presence of God. We have seen churches pull together to pray for the life of this little boy. To our amazement we have seen complete strangers from around the world stand united in a common cause. Best of all we have witnessed again the truth of words humbly offered by Graham Cooke:[13] 'God is the kindest person I know.'

Whether one person prayed or a thousand, the prayer would have been answered. God had His purpose in this healing and it went far beyond the immediate. The implications of these past weeks will be felt for generations.

One day shortly after surgery, Elliott's dad and I shared a cup of coffee.

'You know,' he said. 'I just long for the day when I can stand in the yard of our new home and watch Elliott mow the lawns.'

'One day,' I said, 'you'll do just that. He may slip off his shirt and somebody ask, "What's that scar on your chest, bro?" His answer may well be: "That's a badge that I wear to remind me of the day God intervened to give me back my life."'

The storms of life may occur suddenly and without warning. We may find ourselves completely overwhelmed and out of control. My friend Ginny[14] found herself in such a storm off the African coast in March 2007 whilst circumnavigating the world in a 13 metre catamaran. Here is an extract from her log:

Position 0100 local time Mozambique, S 26° 10', E 33° 15'. Quite suddenly we found ourselves in the middle of severe weather, with winds that had been building up into early 30s (knots that is) waves about 3–4 metres.

By 1800 things were so bad we had no choice, if we were to save ourselves, but to allow the boat to drift at the mercy of the storm. Let me tell you what this is like and what we have done. It is difficult to describe the sea state.

There is such a fury of wind and breaking sea it is like living in the worst surf zone. The roar of the wind and sea and loud hiss and sloshing of water is terrifying if you concentrate on it. The whole boat vibrates in the high wind gusts and as waves hit us every article in cupboards smashes together. A few things have crashed to the floor and books fallen from their shelves. I have had my ear plugs firmly in to avoid being overcome by fear and earlier played Billy Joel loudly to cheer us up. I am not able to watch the waves break on us. Some are as tall as 3 or 4 stor[e]y buildings. They lift and gently lower us but occasionally one has tons of white water being pushed along its front, like a monstrous bulldozer pushing dirt and racing along at about 25kn speed. These dump gallons of water over the boat and push us around. At times visibility is limited because of spume and spray filling the air.

When Peter stepped out of the boat and into the storm he placed his trust in Jesus.[15] So must we. When he looked to the waves he was overcome and began to sink. But when he looked away from the tempest and fixed his eyes on Jesus he was saved, along with the boat and his friends. Jesus *is* that safe haven. There is . . . no other name.

Author's note

On 29 October 2014 I received an urgent note from a dear friend, a local school headmaster, one I had known for many years.

'We have been praying for a young couple,' he said. 'They have been blessed with a twin pregnancy. But at 24 weeks they are faced with a formidable challenge.'

One of the twins was not thriving and the doctors had suggested cord occlusion to protect the second healthier twin. This meant that the smaller twin would perish but the healthier one survive . . . possibly.

'They are reluctant to take this action,' he said, 'and would prefer to pray for a miracle that both twins might survive.'

I was privileged to review the ultrasound findings and advised them that they were receiving the very best of medical care. Whatever their decision, Lynne and I would stand by them in prayer.

Two weeks later I received a second note. The young couple had decided to proceed without intervention. If the twins were to survive to thirty weeks they would be delivered. 'We continue to pray for God's miraculous intervention,' they said, 'and trust His mercy and grace.' I forwarded them a draft copy of our own experience with Elliott the Brave with the prayer that this might comfort and strengthen them through their own stormy passage.

And then, two weeks later, a third note. The twins had been delivered that day, Justin weighing 1.2 kg (2 lb 9 oz) and Charles, 629 g (1 lb 6 oz). Boys and mother were doing well.

But one week later the news was not good. Young Charles had been transferred to Westmead Children's Hospital for urgent surgery. It seems that he had bowel complications. We met with family that night, locked arms and prayed for safe deliverance for the tiny boy. At operation the next day, a perforation was found in his small intestine. This was repaired and he would remain in the NICU[16] for ten weeks.

But there was more to come a week later, 'We are at Westmead Children's Hospital right now. Tomorrow morning young Charles is to have surgery to close a hole in his heart. Justin is here too. He has lung issues. We continue to pray that God will give us grace to walk through even these most difficult circumstances.'

At surgery, the hole in Charles's heart was able to be repaired and ten days later the word came through.

'Both babies doing well. Praise God and have a Merry Christmas.'

I was beginning to understand that when we are to face difficult issues, God often prepares the way and provides the means. There are ledges and crevices in the rock of His presence that allow us to hold on and to stand fast even under the most extreme circumstances. Our experience with Elliott the Brave would be a powerful help to those in similar need.

And then I began to understand why God had sent me down to Melbourne earlier that year to learn first-hand of an event that would challenge and shape my own certainties and that would prepare Lynne and I for the months ahead.

I will call upon Your name
Keep my eyes above the waves
My soul will rest in Your embrace
I am Yours and You are mine.[17]

Preface to Chapter 2

> *Truth divorced from experience will always dwell in the*
> *realm of doubt.*
>
> > *Henry Krause*[1]

Despite the words of his trusted friends, it was not until Thomas was able to place his hands into the wounds of the risen Christ that he was able to believe. His response: 'My Lord and my God.' We live in a material world, one of doubt and scepticism, one where not only proof but experience is required for belief.

On Saturday, 12 April this year I flew from Sydney down to Melbourne to speak with a doctor friend who had related to me one of the most remarkable accounts of God's intervention that I had ever heard.

The Virgin flight down was mercifully short but cramped and noisy and I was weary after a busy week in the surgery. But as I flew home that night, I knew that it had all been worthwhile. The account that I had received first-hand from the doctor who had been there, who had experienced and bore witness to it all, was extraordinary.

The following events took place in a remote area of Arnhem Land in Northern Australia on 26 February 2014. Out of respect for the doctor's ongoing work and in respect of the local aboriginal people, I have not identified personalities or given the exact location of where these events occurred. Yet I have verified the details and state them now as fact.

2

Resurrection 2014: An Easter Story

*I am the resurrection, and the life. He who believes in
Me, though he may die, he shall live.*

(John 11:25)

A brooding presence descended over Macassin Well in a remote village of the Gulf country of far Northern Australia. It was the last week
of February 2014, just four weeks ago as I write.

Kelly, with five of his young friends, made their way down to the
billabong after school. They were local aboriginal children. Kelly, the
oldest, was 11. They often played and fished there, and occasionally
Christian missionaries would gather with them to tell stories of Jesus
and to pray for their needs. But today was different. It was 32 degrees
centigrade and steamy at the very peak of the wet season and their
single purpose was to find relief in the cool waters.

There was no danger of crocodiles as the water hole was located
near the middle of the village. But the pool was said to be the home
of a blind dreamtime serpent with a very nasty disposition indeed.[1]
The Japanese had bombed the pool during World War Two and the
dark waters of the deep crater were said to be the home of the serpent.

'I'd been swimming there a few days earlier,' said Dr Paul, 'and the
boys had told me about the big scary snake that lived under the water.
It was a bit risky to swim there, they said, but it made it all the more
exciting.'

As they waded into the water, Kelly's friend felt something soft
underfoot. Reaching down the boys discovered a motionless form,

which they dragged from the water. Before them, to their horror, encased in mud, lay the body of a small child.

Screaming, they ran from the scene, haunted by the spectre of the drowned boy. Finally, at a respectable distance, they stopped. Kelly climbed a tree and looked back only to see the body sliding back down under the dark waters. Summoning courage, they ran back to the water hole and dragged the small form once again up onto the muddy bank. Kelly's heart was racing as he knelt down beside the lifeless boy. But then, something remarkable happened. As he knelt, a calming presence came over him. These were Christian kids known to the doctor, and were much aware of the Spirit of God. Kelly remembered that he had seen CPR demonstrated on television. Bravely he began to administer CPR as best he could remember, while the others knelt in the mud and prayed.

Water flooded from the little boy's mouth and within minutes he coughed and gasped for air, but remained deeply unconscious.

'The noise of the shouting alerted a local woman who had been looking for her daughter and also a nurse who was out walking at the time,' said Dr Paul. 'They saw the boys kneeling around the body of the small lad, one giving CPR, and began praying for him too. The woman had been praying and fasting over the area for a week. She had felt uneasy in her spirit, as though something was about to happen. The day before she had found men gambling there. She told them about the snake and they took off.'

The nurse rolled the little boy onto his side into the recovery position and called for the ambulance on her cell phone. The child was quickly transported to the clinic.

Dr Paul was in his office when the ambulance arrived. 'We were finished for the day and about to leave,' he said. 'There were just three or four of us left.'

'Quickly, come down to the trauma room,' said the nurse, 'there's a kid that needs your help urgently.'

'We ran down,' he said, 'and there we saw Billy. He was very small and covered in mud. He had a pulse. Don't remember what his blood pressure was but he was deeply unconscious. When I applied painful stimuli he flinched on one side of his body. But the other side seemed paralyzed. We cannulated him and gave him oxygen. His saturation was about 90 per cent on oxygen.[2]

'At first his pupils were unequal but then they became fixed and dilated and for two hours while we waited for a medical flight to transport him to Darwin there was no response to light, no pupil response at all. The medical flight was on its way with a specialist paediatric trainee but it looked as though we would lose him.'

Everything that could go wrong did go wrong. No one had turned the lights on at the airport. The trolley with the resuscitation gear and monitors was jammed in the air ambulance and it took about half an hour to get it out. By this time it was about 8 p.m.

The children who had prayed for young Billy had followed the ambulance to the clinic. They were deeply distressed and thought that they had done something wrong.

'They were scared little kids who thought they were in trouble,' said Paul. 'There they were in the clinic surrounded by parents firing questions at them and demanding answers.'

The plane was further delayed and the family asked if they could come into the room to pray for Billy before his evacuation to Darwin.

'There must have been thirty people in the room,' said Paul, 'children and adults, and it was only a small resuscitation room. They laid their hands on Billy and prayed for Jesus to "wake him up". Then they went out.'

It was then that it happened. Billy opened his eyes.

'*Amala, Bapa* [Mother, Father],' he cried.

'Suddenly he was back with us,' said Paul. 'His pupils were normal again. He had no weakness and was quite animated. He wanted to empty his bladder and tried to get out of bed.

'"Let me go to the toilet," he said. But he was all hooked up to monitors and drips.'

Young Billy was finally transferred to the hospital at Darwin. After three days he was discharged, perfectly well. He had suffered no brain damage and is now reunited with family.

Kelly was lauded as a local hero, given a bravery medal and interviewed by the local press.[3]

Friends and family rejoiced.

'God has crushed the head of the serpent,' they said.

'Leading up to these events there had been a real sense of joy in that community and an understanding that Jesus was setting people free,' said Paul. One of the Christian women had a vision of a cross coming down from heaven covered in flowers, so she made an exact replica of what she'd seen in her vision and set it up on the beach. Each night the local Christians would meet there to worship.

'After clinic I would go down there to meet with them,' said Paul. 'We would pray and sing till after midnight. There was preaching on the goodness of God, that He loves us and sets us free with gifts of healing, restoration and freedom. There was a real hope that the light of God would break through the darkness.

'The kids up there take spirituality deadly seriously,' he said. 'They learn to be quite independent early in life. Even a 2-year-old might be asked his opinion. So when kids make up their mind about God, their parents respect that decision. And if kids believe in healing or miracles or angels, then that is respected. Children up there see angels all the time. The supernatural world is very close to these people. They have visions and dreams on a regular basis.'

This was not the first time that Paul had seen the power of God exercised in his medical practice. A week before Billy's return to life, Paul had visited an old aboriginal man.

'We sat down on his verandah,' said Paul. '"I'm glad you came today, doc," he said, "I've got a really sore leg. I was going to come to the clinic today but it was too painful. I just couldn't walk."'

Paul looked at the man's foot. 'It was classic gout,' he said. 'A big, hot swollen joint. I said, "Let's just pray about it in Jesus' name." Right then the pain, the temperature and the swelling disappeared before my very eyes. I was shocked. I'd never seen anything like this before.'

Paul grew up in Albany on the southern coast of Western Australia. As a boy he attended church with his family and at university was actively involved with the evangelical Christian movement on campus.

'I didn't believe in healing till a year ago,' he said. 'I was hardened. I was cynical. After you've done ten years in a teaching hospital you get hardened to anything and everything and life in general.

Then, just eighteen months ago, Paul's life changed forever when he developed community-acquired septicaemia. He enjoys shooting, hunting and fishing and at the time was shooting geese in a big wetland in the Northern Territory when he cut his foot.

'I thought nothing of it at the time,' he said, 'but it went on to cellulitis. I started a course of antibiotics from the clinic. But lymphangitis spread up my leg and I developed a fever and rigors.[4] This happened over the weekend and by Monday morning I was really ill. I went back to the clinic. There was a visiting doctor there that day. She took one look at me and called for a critical-care medical flight. I went downhill very rapidly and became hypovolemic. They filled me up with fluid and evacuated me to Darwin. But by the time I arrived at Darwin I was fluid overloaded and went into pulmonary oedema. I became hypotensive and my CRP was very high 250.[5] I was really septic and man, I thought that I was going to die. My kidneys were failing and my creatinine was 230.[6] The pain in my joints was excruciating. I had headache and photophobia.[7] When I reached the hospital they thought I was dead as I had the sheet pulled over my face to protect my eyes from the light.

'"Someone in the village has cursed you," they said. I felt that I was under real spiritual attack. So I cried out to Jesus to heal me. My fever fell. My symptoms resolved, my kidney function returned and I was completely healed. That was the turning point in my life. I could have died. But I was healed. I was alive! I thought, "This is real. I've got to start making every day count. I should be doing more, maybe selling my possessions and giving the money to the poor."

'Then God started opening doors. I was adopted into an aboriginal family. I resigned my job in the hospital and used my savings to live in the community. I did an external language course and worked part-time as a doctor to keep up my registration. I had been a Christian for many years but when the sickness took hold of me and I nearly died, that was a real wake-up call. I realized that I had never seen miracles and that I wasn't experiencing the joy and peace of the Holy Spirit in my life. Doors started to open. Every step I took led to ten more.

'The last ten months have been an amazing journey. I've seen God's Spirit move in a wonderful way. Last year I spent six months on the road with a group of young Christian aboriginal men and women. We went through all the communities from Aurucun to Cape York and saw God's hand move every step of the way providing for our financial needs, our health. That's when I started speaking in tongues and seeing miracles for the first time in my life. I saw God using the most unlikely people, the unloved, the dispossessed, the uneducated, the little boys who knelt in the mud and prayed for a miracle. Can you picture them? Can you? Watching the gift of life being returned to their friend. Some had been abused, some abandoned by their parents.

'Jeremiah 29:11 has special relevance to these people,' he said.

'For I know the plans I have for you,' declares the LORD, 'plans to prosper you and not to harm you, plans to give you hope and a future.' (NIVUK)

'To offer that hope, that promise to an indigenous community, is wonderful,' he said. 'There may be 70 per cent unemployment and 50 per cent school attendance. There may be sexual abuse, alcohol abuse. To go in there and love these people, to give them a hug, a meal, even a lift, that's tangible evidence of love. One of my friends had a vision of spot fires of the Holy Spirit starting in every community and burning brightly and of seeing the glory of God cover Australia and the world.'

I looked him straight in the eye. 'Who are you, Paul?' I asked.

'I am God's son,' he said. And he meant it.

In 1979 a great revival took place amongst the aboriginal people in the same area as these events that occurred just a few short weeks ago. It has been well documented by a number of historians, and many personal testimonies have been recorded. One week before the revival a local man reported that:

At an all-night prayer meeting at 4 am the Spirit came. How did they know? Because a cloud came from the east and rested upon them and they were in the mist of God's presence and they became cold, which in a hot climate is the way the Spirit graciously presents Himself.[8]

I found it interesting and somewhat ironic that the man who reported this in 1979 had the same surname as the little boy who was raised and who appears to be a member of that extended family.

Many testimonies resulted from that revival. One such was given by Willy, a timid aboriginal man who had spent a lot of time in jail for drunkenness. The revival not only dried him out, but made a man of him as well. In a simple, moving testimony to his Church, he gave the glory to Jesus:

'I'm Willy,' he said. 'A lot of people think I'm rubbish. I'm not rubbish anymore; I've got Jesus Christ inside of me.'[9]

I am sitting at my computer completing this account over the Easter weekend 2014. How gracious of God to give me such a story at this time when our focus is on the death and resurrection of Jesus Christ and the forgiveness and new life that He brings to all who call on His name.

Little Billy was raised just a few weeks before Easter, just as Lazarus was raised by Jesus shortly before His own death and resurrection. Jesus' own words written at the beginning of this chapter were a promise to Mary. His words immediately following in verse 26 are a challenge to all: 'And whoever lives and believes in Me shall never die. Do you believe this?'

And what of the little children who exercised their faith in a God whom they believed could save their friend under the most difficult of circumstances? They demonstrate to all that unless we become as little children we can never enter into or fully experience the promises of the kingdom of God.

And Dr Paul? His life has been changed forever. Having almost lost his life to septicaemia while working with the aboriginal people of the Northern Territory, he regained it when he called out to God to save him. His hope, his expectation, his relationship with God has changed for all time.

For whoever desires to save his life will lose it, but whoever loses his life for My sake will find it.

(Matt. 16:25)

Author's note

I had heard little of Dr Paul since our meeting, but had been aware of his continuing work amongst the indigenous people of far Northern Australia. But then in January 2015 I received this note from Paul telling a remarkable story:

'God has been touching the hearts of people up here,' he said. 'Since we spoke last we've seen Christmas come and go. My friend Dave and I are now spending four weeks at a community near Gapuwiyak, as God has opened a door here with new opportunities.

'As with many other people in Australia,' he said, 'Christmas meant little to the people in Gapuwiyak. It was just a story they had heard in part or seen on TV. A few were going through the motions of playing an old album of Christmas carols over and over again. But to others it was just another ceremony to get through, along with the dozens of funerals, initiations and smoking rituals throughout the year.[10] Jesus was just one of a host of totems who was worth acknowledging in the seemingly never-ending cycle of appeasing the deities. Very few children received presents and many parents continued their hard-core habitual card-playing.

'Fortunately, God had other ideas and gave us the fun job of handing out bags of candy to the kids and screening *The Grinch Who Stole Christmas*. We watched as God's grace and mercy was lavished on the people and as parents and children laughed and played together. The Word of God was preached and many card players on the street that night heard of God's love and forgiveness.

'Over Christmas a lot of the young guys hit the grog and a big fight broke out. One man was stabbed and left to die, bleeding on the side of the road. The next day payback came into play and the feuding families took things to the next level.[11] There were men walking around with spears and iron bars. Another fight broke out and a sombre mood fell across the community as families hunkered down for the inevitable "war" to follow. I went bush to pray, but Dave got a word from God that said,

'"Fear not for I am with you. You will walk where angels fear to tread."

'Later that night instead of war there was the sound of singing in the camp. Dave walked to his friend's house to find the likely lads not fighting but dancing and praising God to the sound of gospel music! The worship continued and the spirit of payback and revenge dissipated as men fell to their knees, humbled before a God of mercy and grace. That mercy came running one Christmas morning 2,000 years ago when the love of God was poured out upon a dying world in the form of a little baby boy. The true light that brings life had come into the world.'[12]

And so the year of 2014 became an Ebenezer, a rock, a landmark in our lives. It began with the resurrection of a small aboriginal boy in a remote area of Northern Australia just before Easter. This prepared us for our own journey with young Elliott the Brave in the darker days of winter that followed. And as Christmas approached, we rejoiced with others as we saw two premature twins healed and restored and as we remembered the birth of another small child, the Prince of Peace.

You may be facing an impossible task, something that has you completely beaten. Maybe it's a health issue, finances or a family matter. In the next chapter I introduce you to two of my friends, people who faced the impossible head-on, and won. Two single women against the world. And they did it by faith in God.

Preface to Chapter 3

Just a routine operating day in a Sydney teaching hospital, really. The surgeon scrubbed before operating on a man with a foot hopelessly scarred and contracted as a result of diabetic neuropathy. His surgical assistant, an older lady with sparkling blue eyes, would advise, bringing years of practical experience to bear.

The young intern was confused.

'Who was that woman?' he later asked.

That lady was Dr Grace Warren AM, SPk, MD, MS, FRACS, FRCS, FAOrthA, DTM&H(Syd), co-author of the seminal publication: *The Care of Neuropathic Limbs: A Practical Manual.*[1]

There are some very special people in this world. They might have written Bill Bright's *Come Help Change the World* if only Bill hadn't written it first. On 4 July this year I was privileged to spend time with two of them. Grace I had known for years but Jo I had not met before. She was a special surprise. I brought camellias from my garden. But the radiance of these two ladies far outshone my gift.

3

Mission Impossible

Only the impossible is worth the effort.
Jeanette Winterson[1]

It was a bright Wednesday morning as I made my way to the home of Dr Grace Warren in the leafy Hills district of Sydney. I found her cottage nestled comfortably in an English-style garden. The morning sun played on her face as she welcomed me with a broad grin and a friendly kiss.

We sat in her living room drinking freshly brewed tea and cookies. I glanced around. The walls were festooned with photographs, letters from world leaders, quotes and prestigious awards including the 'Star of Pakistan', which she had received for humanitarian services over a thirty-seven-year period. And there in the corner was a photo of her shaking hands with Lady Di in Nepal.

At 86, Grace is remarkable. She continues to drive a small red hatchback with an unrestricted licence and practices surgery one day per week at Westmead hospital, one of Sydney's premiere teaching hospitals.

'My father was killed when I was five in the first civil aviation accident in Australia,' she said, 'leaving my mother with four kids to bring up. He had been a pioneer missionary in Northern Australia where he ran the work at the Roper River mission and later on Groote Island.

'We were a 'can-do' family,' Grace mused. 'When Dad was at Roper River the Bishop of Darwin came to visit. He broke a wheel of his car. So dad cut a piece of timber from a tree trunk, fashioned a new wheel and fitted it to the axle. It served admirably for a long time. My brother David, an engineer, inherited this do and adapt attitude,' she said. 'He invented the black box flight recorder in the 1950s now fitted to so many planes.[2] I wondered if this had been in response to his father's untimely death.[3]

'I began to understand that my gift also was to make do with what I had, and to achieve what couldn't be done,' she said with a chuckle. 'If they said it couldn't be done, then I made sure that I did it.' I was familiar with Grace's laugh. But it was more than a laugh. It was a challenge. It put things into perspective, her perspective and, as I was to discover, God's perspective.

After her father's death, the family moved to Sydney.

'My schooling was very disrupted,' said Grace. 'In the first year I attended six schools.' Eventually, with financial assistance from family friends, she was enrolled at St Catherine's, Waverley, the oldest Anglican private school in Australia.

'I still have my report from year four,' she said, 'saying that I wouldn't pass the school leaving certificate because of poor writing and spelling. And yes, I did fail, but then in a second attempt I passed with a "lower" in French.'

At graduation, Grace was awarded a Commonwealth scholarship to study medicine at Sydney University.

'I have no idea why they put me into medicine,' she said. 'But by the time I graduated in 1954 I desperately wanted to become a surgeon. The Royal Australasian College of Surgeons would have no part of it. They simply did not accept women. The hierarchy of the college told me so in no uncertain terms.'

'So here was something that couldn't be done that had to be done?'

'Absolutely!' she said. 'So I studied obstetrics at the Queen Victoria Hospital in Melbourne and then moved on to a registrar position at Geelong hospital where there were some really good surgeons. While I was there, a boy came in with a head injury and started to fit. I called the surgeon on call.'

'"Have you ever done a burr hole, Grace?" he asked. "You better go ahead and I'll come in as soon as I can."

'As soon as I opened the dura,'[4] said Grace, 'the boy stopped convulsing. The surgeon later told me that he had never done a burr hole either.'

Hearing this story brought back vivid memories of my country term as a resident at Bathurst District Hospital, west of Sydney. I was required to escort a young woman who had fallen from a horse and sustained a head injury to Royal Prince Alfred Hospital in downtown Sydney. Thirty minutes after setting out, the patient's condition deteriorated and she lost consciousness. We radioed ahead to the nearest hospital for someone to be available to perform burr hole decompression. But when we arrived there was no one available with expertise. By the time a surgeon arrived, it was too late and the patient perished. If only I'd had surgical training at that stage perhaps I could have saved that life just as Grace did.

After Geelong, Grace studied linguistics and tropical medicine. She had received an urgent call to Korea to relieve a doctor, Helen McKenzie. 'So there I was in South Korea,' she said, 'three years after graduation. And I had to perform surgery as well as do obstetrics. Two years later I was invited to Hei Ling Chau (literally the Island of the Happy Spirit) in Hong Kong as a locum. To my delight, I discovered that they had a reconstructive surgery programme for patients with leprosy. An American plastic surgeon had taught the physician in charge, Doug Harmond, how to do a couple of procedures. So Doug taught me what he knew and the rest I got from the books. And, would you believe it, one year later I was invited to Taiwan to teach fully qualified American plastic surgeons how to do tendon transplants. I had only qualified as a doctor in Jan '54. If I'd stayed home and studied I wouldn't even have completed basic surgical training.

'Let me tell you a wonderful story,' she said. 'In 1973 I visited the leper colony at Moloka'i, a Hawaiian Island off the coast of Honolulu. I learned of Father Damien who had worked there with leprosy patients in the nineteenth century.[5] A photo showed him with a nodular face. "That's the face of lepromatous leprosy," I thought, "of a patient who's had the disease for at least twenty years." But at the time of the photo he'd only been on the island for five. He was from Belgium and he'd been working in Hawaii as a priest for quite a while. I knew that there were patients with leprosy scattered throughout Hawaii. He had obviously caught it before coming to Moloka'i. But he knew if they found him out he would be sent to Moloka'i in disgrace. So when the suggestion came that he should go there as a volunteer, he accepted.'

Sometime later, Grace was working in Jerusalem when one of her friends in Hawaii sent her further news of Father Damien. 'One Sunday morning before church,' she said, 'he had spilled boiling water on his foot while making a cup of coffee. People were astounded to see that he felt no pain. His foot was quite numb. Just an hour later he commenced his sermon with the words "We lepers". To that point no one had realized that he had leprosy.'[6]

There was a knock at the door and Grace paused. I glanced through the curtains to see an older lady bent over a walking frame.

'Oh, you'll want to meet Jo,' said Grace.

'Not now,' I thought! I had planned to spend uninterrupted time with Grace. But I was wrong, big time. God had set this up. I was just beginning to understand that this book I was writing was like a giant jigsaw puzzle. Completed, it would display a life-changing panorama to its readers. God had given me some fascinating pieces to work with. And now the image was beginning to emerge. Both Grace and Jo were key pieces in the puzzle.

Jo is a small, animated lady with gentle brown eyes and a strong Southern accent. A US citizen, she was born in a small town in east Texas in 1925. 'We lived on the poor side of town,' she said, 'just across the Sabine River from Louisiana. It was Cajun country and more people spoke French than English. My dad, a French immigrant, was a tailor. Mom was of English descent. She had worked as a school mam in the wild west of Wyoming before she met Dad. My parents deprived themselves to raise us kids through the depression years. We had no telephone and we never took family holidays. Dad finally bought an old car. But he had no idea how to drive and white-knuckled it most of the time. Whenever we went out as a family we seriously wondered if we would survive the journey.

'I was a tomboy,' she said, 'often in fights at school, and I liked nothing better than to go barefoot and play cowboys with the local kids. My happiest days were when we went by streetcar to the park and I got to ride the pony.'

At age 11, Jo attended a vacation Bible school run by the Presbyterians, where she heard a woman talk about caring for sick kids.

'Maybe I could be a doctor,' she thought, 'maybe even a missionary doctor.'

'Don't hitch your wagon to a star, Jo,' said her schoolteacher. 'You'll only be disappointed.'

Graduating from high school in 1943, Jo worked at an oil refinery in Port Arthur, Texas. It was wartime and her plan was to save a little money to study nursing at Galveston and, after that, to study medicine. During her three years of nurse training she majored, as she put it, in 'social growth' rather than academic achievement. 'Galveston was a port city,' she said, 'and there were plenty of sailors to be entertained. I learned social graces and the facts of life.' After nursing, she enrolled in Medicine at the University of Texas. By this stage she had her mind set on becoming a doctor – and a missionary doctor at that.

'As a child, my understanding of Christianity was that it was all about doing good, period,' she said. 'But there had to be more to it than that. Surely there was a purpose to life, and to me it must satisfy three criteria: It must be absolute truth, it must be available to everyone and it must be life-changing. The grace of God finally zapped me when I was in medical school,' she said, 'and it was then that I became a Christian.' A visiting speaker at the Intervarsity Fellowship touched Jo's heart with the verse:

> For by grace you have been saved through faith, and that not of yourselves; it is the gift of God, not of works, lest anyone should boast.
>
> (Eph. 2:8,9)

'That night,' she said, 'I prayed: "God, I know these things about You in my head but help me to know You in my heart." And He did.

In Jesus I found a person, not an abstract truth. He was the answer to my quest. He *was* absolute truth.'

As a young girl, growing up on the poor side of town and with little encouragement from family or friends, everything had been a battle for Jo. But here was something new. And it was wonderful. In a personal relationship with Jesus Christ she would strive no longer, but allow God to direct her life.

After graduation Jo found that she was not accepted as a doctor. She would take a history and examine the patient who would then say, 'When do I get to see the real doctor?'

'It was frustrating for a young woman such as myself,' she said, 'but good for my pride.'

With her new faith, she began to search for direction. What was God's plan for her life?

'I learned,' she said, 'that there is no magic formula for determining God's will. Some people need a verse to confirm their decisions. Others use sanctified judgement.' Eventually, after pursuing several avenues of interest and making various applications, she was accepted for service by the Sudan Interior Mission. As a young, single woman not long out of medical school, she would be the only doctor in a remote hospital in Somalia. The dream that she had held since a child was about to materialize, despite discouragement from her teacher and others. And it was happening not of her own effort, but by virtue of her new identity as a child of Father God.

In 1960 Jo stepped from a plane in Mogadishu in Somalia. 'It was like stepping into a sauna,' she said. 'And I knew that it wouldn't take long to sap my energy. But my reaction turned to prayer. "You challenged me to trust you for the impossible, Lord,"' she prayed, '"so this is one of the tests I must face for survival in this land."'

I decided to press further and addressed them both.

'Have there been times in your medical careers when you've been pushed to the limit and you've just had to ask God for help, times when you've had to depend on Him completely?'

'Just getting into some places was difficult,' said Grace, 'and dangerous. I often went to Jerusalem to work in the leprosy hospital and from there down to Gaza. In fact, I operated at the military hospital in Gaza. One of my friends in Jerusalem was a Scottish physiotherapist. She had become friends with a Muslim physio in the West Bank and arranged for me to visit Ramallah to teach hospital staff. So we dressed in our best Arab garb and went to the Arabic gate in Jerusalem. As my friend had managed to learn some Arabic, we were able to catch an Arabic taxi. We drove through the checkpoints without interrogation, quite illegal, of course, at that time. At the hospital they hastily opened the door, let us in and closed the shutters.'

God opened many doors for Grace: into Burma, Pakistan, Cambodia, Thailand, Hong Kong and other countries, twenty-six in all. There she trained other people to carry on the work that she had pioneered using whatever resources were available, demonstrating her can-do attitude and her practical faith in God. Officially retiring from full-time overseas work in 1989, she turned her attention in Australia to the care of patients with diabetic neuropathic limbs, publishing the definitive work *The Care of Neuropathic Limbs: A Practical Manual* at age 70, with the assistance of Professor Sydney Nade of Sydney University.

But Grace's biggest battle had been in becoming a surgeon in the first place. The powers that be in the Royal Australasian College of Surgeons would simply not countenance the idea of training a woman. Yet in 1972, eighteen years after graduating as a doctor, Grace was awarded the degree of Master of Surgery by Sydney University and in 1977 she was elected as a Fellow of the Royal Australasian Colleges of Surgeons. In 1983, she was made a Fellow of the Royal College of Surgeons of England and in 1987 gained a Professorship of the Royal College of Surgeons.

I turned now to Jo. 'How on earth did you survive, as a single woman and new graduate in that hospital in Somalia? You were the only doctor.'

'My reaction was "God help me" because I *wasn't* a trained surgeon,' she said. 'But in Somalia either I operated on them or they died. Their Muslim thinking was "If God wills I will get better". But if I was to operate on them and they died then I'm out!' she said (drawing the side of her hand across her throat twice). 'That was Sharia law.'

'Often they would refuse surgery for their wives,' she said. '"If God wills she will get better," they would say. If not, then they could easily get another. That wasn't really important. But if a man came in requiring surgery that was another story. If at all possible I would refer him down to the capital city hospital, but if it was life-threatening I would offer to operate then and there. They would say "Unto Allah I'll get better" and they would actually crawl out of the hospital on all fours rather than have a foreign woman operate on them.'

But there were times when Jo had no choice. It was a matter of life or death. And sometimes she had to perform surgery that was far beyond her. 'So I would get the books out,' she said. 'Where do I start? What do I do? There was one man I remember with bowel obstruction. There were no X-rays or other tests to help. Nothing! I had only two years of general residency training and just a few weeks of surgical assisting. But before that I had been a scrub nurse and that helped me most of all.

'Either I operated or they died. That was the frustration that I faced.

'You spend your life training. You're there to help the people and they say, "No, we'll take him home to die." If I operated and he died, it was my fault. That was blood money. My blood. That was the law of the land, Sharia law, the law of the country, just that. "You've spilled our father's blood, we spill your blood. We kill you." We lost a lovely young doctor from Tamworth country, New South Wales, a young guy just a couple of years out of medical school. Our leader in the capital city was also murdered.'

One of the most disturbing problems that Jo faced was the management of women who had undergone female circumcision. The clitoris and other tissues had been cut away with an unsterile blade and the genitals skewered with a large thorn, resulting in terrible complications. 'Sometimes they would come to the hospital with scar tissue that was bone hard, begging for help,' she said. 'I would operate but my attempts were often unsuccessful. It was after one such episode that my friend at the hospital wrote home, "Our doctor cried last night."'

'How do you handle fear and danger, Jo?' I asked.

'On my knees. The radical Islamist sees it as his divine right to do away with you as you are hindering the cause of Islam.'

'Have you been personally threatened?'

'Yes, I have. On one occasion a father hammered on the door of the OR with a big stick while I was operating on his daughter. She was diabetic and had an infected hand, which had to be drained.'

'"Don't cut her. I'll kill you if you do!" he shouted.

'*Ancha*, Allah [If God wills], she'll get better, without that '*gala*' [Christian deceiver] cutting on her.'

'Come on, Sheik Abdi,' said the hospital staff. 'Leave them alone. Doctor is only trying to help your daughter.'[7]

'Jo, how can you possibly share God's love with these people?' I asked.

'We did it through caring,' she said. 'Get to know them and allow them to trust you. Share with them honestly. They say, "Why did you come here from America? Why would you do that? Why do you sit up all night with our women in labour? Why, why?" But this, of course, is a biblical principle. Jesus did just that. He shared with the multitudes and demonstrated His love by feeding and healing them. He shed tears of compassion over them.'

I sat facing Grace and Jo, in awe of what I had heard and marvelling at the manner in which God had empowered them both and worked through them.

'Who are you, Grace?' I asked.

'I'm God's servant number one. Whatever He's wanted, wherever He's wanted to send me, that's OK by me.'

'Who are you, Jo?'

'I'm in Christ. That's my bottom line, in Christ. When the Muslims threatened me, called me *gala* [infidel] and *sharamut* [prostitute] and wanted to kill me, that was OK because, as I said, I'll be with the Lord.'

It was late that evening after dinner. I sat contemplating the events of the day when the phone rang. It was Grace and there was a note of urgency in her voice. 'When I was at school,' she said, 'we had to recite the "King's Prayer" as an elocution exercise. You know, the one spoken by George VI at the outbreak of World War Two, the one about placing your hand into the hand of God. Well, I decided that I would take God's hand. That's when I committed my life to Him. Unless you take the hand of God you'll never know the heights to which He'll lead you. Heights never considered, let alone anticipated. And remember,' she continued, 'wherever He leads, He equips us for the journey. He provides the wherewithal, money, ability, whatever. That's worked with me in twenty-six countries around the world.'

Just as Father Damien identified with those whom he served with the words 'We lepers', so Grace and Jo have identified with those faced with impossible obstacles such as disease, social isolation, poverty and broken lives. They have faced deprivation, opposition and the threat of violence. But with each problem there has been a promise; and with that promise, a provision. By finding identity in God as their Father they found purpose, direction and the power to succeed.

'Place your hand into the hand of God,' said Grace, referring to the King's Prayer.

Those who have read my first book, *Nine Minutes Past Midnight*, will know that I also have held fast to the words of the 'King's Prayer' over many years. God's hand has led me through times of trial and triumph. I have been especially aware of his presence in areas of outreach in China and North West Cambodia and during a Force 10 gale off the coast of Antarctica. But also in the context of my home and my practice of medicine. I have yet to find a 'better way'.

For with God nothing will be impossible.

(Luke 1:37)

Author's note:

On a sunny afternoon in 1973, Jo Anne Ader, aged 54, married Australian businessmen Bill Dennett in Addis Ababa. They could not have come from more different backgrounds. Marriage had been the last thing on Jo's mind and was yet another challenge. 'Bill and Jo, a couple of great characters, became a couple of great character,' said Gordon Stanley, Director of Missions Interlink (NZ). Their faith and determination to make their marriage work and to combine their gifts to God's Glory makes inspiring reading. Their story is written in their autobiography: *Unusual Marriage* (SPCK Australia, 2006).

Dr Grace Warren continues to inspire generations of people seeking the will of God. Her secret: by maintaining a close relationship with God; by regarding Him as her closest friend and allowing Him to lead; having taken His hand, she has never let go.

Her story is written in her autobiography: *Doctor Number 49* (SPCK Australia, 1973).

Preface to Chapter 4

The play *Art*, by Yasmina Reza, tells the story of a man, Serge, who bought a painting. It was a 1.5 × 1.2 metre canvas of a white field . . . no detail, just a white field. He invited his friends to view the painting. They were at first surprised, then critical, and could see no value in his investment. In the final scene, Serge took a felt-tip pen and handed it to his friend Marc. With some trepidation Marc approached the canvas. He drew a diagonal line from the top left-hand corner to the bottom right.

On that line he drew a man on skis. Marc then approached the front of the stage.

> Marc: Under the white clouds, the snow is falling.
> You can't see the white clouds, or the snow.
> Or the cold, or the white glow of the earth.
> A solitary man slides downhill on his skis.
> The snow is falling.
> It falls until the man disappears back into the landscape.
> My friend Serge, who's one of my oldest friends, has bought a painting.
> It's a canvas about five foot by four.
> It represents a man who moves across a space and disappears.[1]

Life is both transient and fleeting. We are that man on skis who appears for a short time. Whether we reach out and touch eternity will depend upon whether we anchor ourselves to the infinite.

4

Reaching Out, Touching Eternity

When patients face surgery, they must be preoperatively assessed to exclude underlying conditions such as heart disease or lung and kidney problems which may place their lives at risk beyond the procedure alone.

The man before me was to have a total hip replacement. Years of hard physical work had taken their toll. His right hip was now bone on bone and there was only one solution, surgery. He was animated, Maltese and about 65 years of age. He stood boldly upright, feet apart, grasping his wife's hand. His daughter stood close by in moral support.

'I've come for a heart scan,' he announced.

I took a brief history and was about to lead him away when his wife took my arm.

'Ask him,' she said. 'Ask him about what happened. Ask him about the aneurysm.'

I had no intention of exercising a man with an aneurysm, so I sat him down.

'Three years ago,' he said, 'I was rushed to Westmead hospital by ambulance with severe pains in my stomach. The emergency room doctors diagnosed a leaking aortic aneurysm.[1]

'"It's serious," they said, "and you'll die if we don't operate straight away."

'Doctor, on the operating table my heart stopped beating three times. I was unconscious, of course, but I saw myself sitting on a large rock overlooking the ocean in my country of Malta. I recognized the place immediately. As I sat there, a bright light appeared before me. It was blinding. As I watched it began to grow smaller and to take on the form of a face. It was Jesus, doctor, and he said to me in Maltese,

"What are you doing here? We're not ready for you yet." And then He said,

"Go back. We'll call you when we're ready."

The man was resuscitated and surgery was successful. He spent many weeks in intensive care and then several more in the general wards before discharge. But his life would never again be the same.

As a young medical student I was assigned, with my group, to a city hospital to gain surgical experience before final exams. On the first morning we assembled at the main entrance to be greeted by the chief of surgery, a red-faced, balding man of about 50 with a comb-over and heavy horn-rimmed glasses. It was a Catholic hospital, and proudly so, and the surgeon from the outset declared his Irish-Catholic heritage. We were asked to identify ourselves and, as we did, he seemed disappointed that none of our names hinted of Irish descent, until finally the last student stepped forward.

'Healey, sir.'

The surgeon beamed.

'I'm Presbyterian, sir,' said Healey with a straight face, resuming his position military-style.

With exams rapidly approaching, we soon developed a rigorous study regime. This was often interrupted by one particular student riding his motorcycle up and down the hallway of the student quarters, supposedly to release stress – also, on one other occasion, when we carried a student's bed to the middle of a nearby football field while he was having dinner with a lady friend. We lived to regret our actions. When he returned at 2 a.m. to discover the deed, he turned his ghetto blaster to full volume, locked it in his room and promptly went home. There was no sleep that night.

Most evenings after dinner we would study for several hours, quiz each other over a coffee, then jog around the nearby football field before showering and retiring at about 10:30 p.m. But one night we were summoned to the ER[2] at around 9 p.m. A man had been admitted with a leaking abdominal aortic aneurysm. We examined the patient briefly. He was in severe pain and although IV fluid was being pumped into several veins, the emergency staff were having trouble maintaining his blood pressure. A normal abdominal aorta is approximately 2 centimetres in diameter below the renal arteries. This mans was greater than six and a small tear had developed. The house doctor contacted the vascular surgeon as a matter of urgency, ordered blood and alerted the OR.

The surgical registrar gave us a quick heads-up on what was to happen but warned us that the expected mortality approached 25 per cent.[3]

The vascular surgeon from St Vincent's Hospital was a highly respected man. He assessed the patient and straight away had him transferred to the operating room. It was the custom of this particular surgeon to have classical music playing quietly in the background while he operated. Nothing too rousing, just gentle strains to calm the operating room staff and create a peaceful ambience.

The patient was prepared and the surgical team began the mammoth task of repairing the man's aorta. All seemed to be going well. There was an air of optimism and impending success. The staff were buoyed along by the music piped throughout the OR. But then it all went dreadfully wrong. The man began to bleed torrentially. The haemorrhage was finally controlled, but the patient was in shock and within minutes went into cardiac arrest. The team struggled to save the man's life. But all was in vain and, despite their efforts, he perished.

The equipment was turned off. Nobody spoke. Only the music continued. Finally the surgeons, the anaesthetist and the nursing staff departed and I found myself alone, eyes fixed on the motionless form now shrouded on the table before me. The music continued almost as an ode to the sanctity of life now departed. It echoed down the darkened halls through the open doors, into recovery and beyond. I recall the torrent of emotion that flooded over me as I came face to face for the first time with a patient's death and wondered where had God been. Why had He not intervened to save this man's life?

I have pondered this event for many years. It is not one that will fade from my memory or my emotions. However, I have come to understand that God is fully aware of every day of our lives.

And in Your book they all were written, The days fashioned for me, When as yet there were none of them.

(Ps. 139:16)

How we spend those days, the paths we follow and the commitments that we make are entirely of our own choosing. However, when we become Christians we enter into God's plan and purpose. His plan will be achieved whatever. His purpose requires our participation. We have just a few short years to make that commitment. That decision will determine the course of our lives and where we spend eternity.

Here were two men of similar age, both with the same potentially fatal condition, a leaking aortic aneurysm. One survived, one perished. The Maltese man who had recounted to me his near-death encounter had become a Christian through this experience. God had a plan for his life and it would not be cut short by an unforeseen medical emergency. God had the number of his days. And God used that event to change the future quality of his life.

'He has always been a good man and a fine husband,' said his wife. 'But now he is more than that. He has a sense of humour, a sense of destiny, he is not fearful of death and he loves to tell people of his experience with the Lord.'[4]

He passed his heart test with flying colours and went on to have successful hip surgery.

I have no idea whether the man who perished was a Christian. The fact is that God had the number of his days also. He had a plan for his life and a standing invitation to come 'home' one day. I can only hope that within his three-score years he chose wisely.

My friend Nicole is a vivacious young general practitioner from New Zealand, the land of the long white cloud. She has spent much of her time providing medical aid in Vietnam but also operates as a busy family doctor in Queensland. She recently told me of an experience with one of her patients.

The patient before her was an attractive young lady. Long fair plaits and fine facial features betrayed her northern European heritage. She had brought her young son to see the doctor. He had an earache and high fever. Life had not recently been good for this young family. Only weeks before, husband Rudy had lost his job and that same week, on the Friday, had been diagnosed with lung cancer.

Nicole examined the young boy, wrote a prescription for antibiotics and handed it to his mother. She took the script eagerly and headed for the door.

'How's Rudy?' asked Nicole.

'He's in the OR right now and I've just been called by the hospital. He's in a critical condition. As they were trying to remove the tumour they've cut his pulmonary artery and they can't stop the bleeding.'

Nicole was gobsmacked.

'And you're here?'

'Well, I had to bring my boy, he was so ill.'

Nicole took her hand. 'Let's pray for Rudy right now.'

Six weeks later Rudy walked into Nicole's surgery.

She had checked his discharge papers. They had indeed lacerated his pulmonary artery. 'He had lost "mega litres" of blood.' Furthermore, the histology had not been as predicted. Instead of an operable primary lung lesion, the malignancy had proven to be a metastasis[5] from an adrenal tumour.

'As far as I knew Rudy had not been a Christian,' she said. 'But now he was a different man. There was softness about him. Through that close encounter with death he had given his heart to the Lord. He'd had a revelation of Jesus and become a Christian.'

'Life is incredible now,' he said. 'Even if I only have weeks or months to live.'

Rudy and his wife decided to go back to Poland for chemo and radiotherapy.

A few days before their departure they came back to see Nicole.

'Did you tell Rudy that we were praying for him during surgery?'

'No, I forgot.'

They told of their last meeting with the surgeon: 'Rudy,' he said, 'you had a one in a million chance of surviving. Someone must have been praying for you.'

Nicole laid hands on him and prayed. 'The presence of God was tangible,' she said. 'You could feel it.'

A few days later Rudy came back for a final consultation.

'Nicole,' he said, 'the pain is almost gone. All I've needed is paracetamol. You know, even if I'm not healed physically, I *am* healed, I *am* whole. I just want to enjoy as much time with my family as I can. My 10-year-old boy has been asking me to build him a tree house for years now. We're going back to Poland and I'm going to build that tree house.'

And when Rudy does go home, what will he leave behind? More than a tree house. He will leave a living memory to his wife and son that will buoy them on as they adjust to life without him. And the sure knowledge that he found purpose and fulfilment in the precious time that he had with them. He will leave the example to his son that he was man enough to stand down from his own pursuits and to step up into the peace and wholeness that God had for him.

Rudy was going home, somewhat prematurely, but he *was* going home. That's what counted. After all, his Father was waiting for him.

I came to Jesus as I was,
Weary and worn and sad;
I found in Him a resting-place,
And He has made me glad.[6]

Part II

Finding True Identity

Preface to Chapter 5

It is a sad fact that today too many people practise a third-person brand of Christianity. They relate to God objectively as one to be observed, obeyed and revered, as one who is remote and approachable only in crises. This may apply to other world religions, but not to Christianity.

A friend once said to me, 'You must have tickets on yourself, Ern, if you regard God as your personal friend.' Well, I have news; God is my best friend, one who never leaves my side, one who never fails. In every circumstance, He is my silent partner. In Him I live, I move and have my being.[1] It is because of Him that I have a reason to get out of bed in the morning. It is because of Him that I can face each day without fear and with hope and expectation.

Over the years I have come to know Jesus as Saviour and friend, to know God as my loving Father and the Holy Spirit as my comforter, advocate and strengthener every moment, every day.

But to develop such a relationship I first needed to understand my true identity. It was only then that I was able to relate to God in a personal way.

In the chapters that follow, I trace my own path to identity and the lives of others who sometimes, in the direst of circumstances, have discovered their true identity as a child of God. As my North Korean friend confided with tears in his eyes: 'God is my love dad.'

5

Finding True Identity

I will also give him a white stone with a new name
written upon it which no man knows except the man
who receives it.

(Rev. 2:17, PHILLIPS)

'You've had some bad days lately, haven't you, Geoff?'

Geoff nodded. He was a big man in his mid-50s, but slouched down in the chair opposite he looked quite diminutive. Tears welled in his eyes.

'Well, I want to tell you, Geoff, today is a good day.'

Clinical medicine is all about news. Good news, bad news. 'Don't give me any bad news, doc, I just don't need any more bad news.'

Geoff had come to me for an isotope bone scan. His urologist had confirmed that he was in the early stages of prostate cancer. His numbers were good, PSA 4, Gleeson score 7,[1] but his doctor needed to know whether there had been any spread to bone before he could plan therapy. Happily, Geoff's bone scan showed no sign of metastases.[2]

As a doctor I am aware that health plays a major role in the make-up of our personal identity. I am also aware that good health can be snatched away in a moment and with it goes security and often a sense of identity.

We build our identities from many areas of life: profession, family, church and club affiliations, even the cars we drive and the football teams that we support. But these identities are fragile and often transient. They can be snatched away without warning, leaving us void and empty. When I resigned from my position as Director of Nuclear Medicine and Ultrasound at Westmead hospital to enter private practice, I experienced this myself. Not only had I lost my position, but also my professional identity. In just a few days I went from a budget to a bank facility, from being a sought-after speaker to 'Didn't you used to be?'

There followed a period of confusion and deep soul-searching. But during that time God spoke to me in an extraordinary way and said, 'You are Ern Crocker, very much loved son of the Father.' That recognition and understanding changed my life. 'Much loved son of Father God' became my prime identity and my personal badging.[3]

I found that strength flowed from my new identity and that I was able to enter into and meet all circumstances with a completely changed attitude: challenges, good times and bad, knowing that God's presence was with me by adoption as His son.[4] Even in the busy daily routine, people knew that the way in which I practised medicine was an extension of my personal identity, profoundly influenced by my relationship with my Father. In the same way you, too, can walk boldly into every situation, supported by the empowering presence of God's Holy Spirit.

It is only recently that I recognized that Christ experienced that same sense of son-ship when John baptized him. As the Holy Spirit alighted on Him God said, 'This is My beloved Son, in whom I am well pleased' (Matt. 3:17). He walked up onto dry land having accepted the proclamation of His identity in God. This would lead Him all the way to His Calvary road of ministry and beyond.

'Much loved son of Father God' are the words the Holy Spirit whispered to me so many years ago now. It is often not until we find that identity that we find lasting contentment, true purpose and hope for the future. That identity is also our fall-back position when things go pear-shaped or when doubt creeps in. Loss of health, retrenchment, bereavement, are just some of the crises we may face. But if we are firmly rooted in God's love we will not be shaken. God's love for us will always remain. Nobody and nothing can take that away.[5]

In *Nine Minutes Past Midnight* I wrote of my friend Brad, a family doctor in San Diego.[6] As a young man he was unable to find purpose or identity. Everything was a battle. Nothing he did ever seemed quite good enough. But, as he said, he 'had a heart for God'. One morning, as he walked through a beautiful garden near his home, he remembers praying: 'It doesn't matter, God, what I do. I just need to be sold out to You. Don't care whether I'm a plumber or a doctor, I'd just give up everything for You.'

On fourteen occasions he applied to medical schools for admission and fourteen times he was rejected.

'My grades were OK,' he said, 'but for medical school you need stellar grades. I had a GPA of 3.6. I needed 3.7 or better.'[7] Eventually Brad was invited to enrol in the medical school at Loma Linda when one of the first-year students withdrew.

After graduation he trained in family medicine and in 1996 went with a group of specialist physicians to Central Asia to train Soviet doctors in family medicine.[8] During that time, Jim, a retired US military officer, came into the clinic.

'He was ashen grey and complained of chest pain,' said Brad, 'I couldn't find anything wrong with him. His EKG [ECG] was fine.'

The next morning in the shower, God spoke to Brad and said, 'Jim has a dissecting thoracic aortic aneurysm.'

Brad called him urgently. 'Meet me in cardiology, now!'

Ninety-six thousand dollars later, Jim returned from Germany with a new aortic valve and an aortic graft.

'He didn't just survive,' said Brad. 'He thrived.'

Brad was deeply moved as he related this story. 'He's the Great Physician,' he said, or, to use his own words, 'the King Rat'. 'I'm just His assistant. He said to me,

'"I'm going to use you, Brad, to help achieve My purposes here on earth."'

Now firmly established in his identity, Brad practises family medicine in San Diego. He is secure in the knowledge that he is a very much loved son of Father God, the Great Physician. Each morning he prays, 'What new thing do You have for me today, Lord? What do You want to teach me today?'

If we are not able to claim identity as a child of God, then sadly our default becomes 'not worthy to be Your son', which was the cry of the prodigal son. But God is always willing to accept us, no matter how unworthy we may consider ourselves to be. When the prodigal son returned home after wasting his inheritance, his father ran to him and embraced him. Then he gave him three gifts: a ring, a robe, and sandals. The ring represented his restored authority, the sandals, his humanity, and the robe symbolized his new identity.[9] So we, too, receive that robe of identity once we receive Jesus into our heart and allow God to be our loving Father.

Our perceived identity is often tied into the way we see ourselves or as we imagine others see us. But true identity is only revealed when we see ourselves as God sees us. My friend Paul is a Christian psychiatrist who worked for many years in a women's prison in Georgia. Over 90 per cent of the inmates had been severely abused, most sexually. Some had been shot up with heroin as children and sold into prostitution. All were addicted to something and involved in prostitution or, as he put it, 'in toxic relationships with abusive men'. As you might expect, all of these women had poor self-esteem and poor self-image. Paul told them that they had been looking into the wrong mirrors all their lives. They needed to look into the face of Jesus and see themselves as He saw them. Those that were able to do so found that the love of Jesus lifted them out of despair and established a new identity as very much loved daughters of Father God.

The Scriptures tell us that Mary Magdalene was severely oppressed both mentally and spiritually by demons. Jesus cast out those demons which had held her captive for so many years. What she then saw in the Lord's eyes transformed her life miraculously. It was she who remained at the foot of the cross and was the first to see Him risen. Her life was restored and transformed. So many women in the world today have been stripped of their humanity, of their identity and authority by virtue of gender alone. Yet in God's eyes they are

His precious daughters. He alone is able to restore them completely in one loving act of grace when they are able to call Him Father. Selwyn Hughes notes[10] that four women are mentioned in the genealogy of Jesus. They include Tamar, Ruth, Rahab the prostitute and Bathsheba. Each, he says, was foreign, immoral or undesirable from her actions. Yet each knew the redemptive power of God to the point where they were incorporated into the very genealogy of Christ.

Having established a primary identity as a child of God, we should then understand that we also possess secondary identities based on our abilities, our talents, experience and life circumstance. We may excel at some particular sport; we may be gifted at teaching, at playing a musical instrument, or have business skills. These characteristics contribute to our secondary identities. They may be learned or be part of our natural make-up. How and when we apply them will determine our success in earthly pursuits. Our primary identity is unshakeable. It can never be snatched away. But secondary identities are constantly changing.

As life progresses, our secondary identities may need to adapt according to the challenges to which we are called. As Graham Cooke says, our identity in Him may be extended from time to time according to the need to which we are called.[11] For example, Dr Jo, whose story is told in this book, was called as a single woman to be a nurse, then a doctor, then to take control of a remote hospital in Somalia, then later again to marry and assume the responsibilities of a mother and wife. My friend Paul, in a chapter to follow, was gifted in maths and became an Oxford Don, but later found himself stepping down from that exalted academic position to minister to street kids and later pastor a church in Sydney on the other side of the world.

We must decide how to use our talents. We can apply them as we best see fit and meet a measure of success, or we can let God direct our lives. There is a good analogy to becoming a member of a football team. We can play like children all running around trying to kick the ball, or we can join the major league where each person is strategically placed according to his or her specific abilities to achieve a team purpose and to win the game. If we imagine that God is the captain of that team and allow Him to lead and locate us, we can accomplish so much more.

In the preface to this book I quoted the philosopher John Paul Sartre as saying that 'no finite point has meaning without an infinite reference point'. Likewise, the stories of our lives are mere anecdotes of time, soon to be forgotten unless they are anchored in truth. Jesus said: 'I am the way, the truth, and the life. No one comes to the Father except through Me' (John 14:6). When we accept Him at His word and commit ourselves to Him, then our lives take on eternal significance as they are grafted into His plan and purpose.

We have a responsibility to use the gifts and talents that we have. But sometimes it is those very gifts and talents that prevent us from moving ahead to achieve our potential. They are the starting point. But we can become dependent and secure in them, failing to recognize that there will be new challenges, which may present themselves at 30, 40, 60, even 70 years of age. If we accept these challenges, they extend us and enrich our lives.

Some of these challenges may indeed be daunting and lead us into areas that we might not have previously considered. In the past two years I have participated in medical outreach teams on the Thai Cambodian and Vietnamese borders and visited inmates of Kerobokan prison in Bali and had the opportunity of speaking at the chapel service there run by one of the Bali 9. As we grow in trust and in expectation of how God may use us, so these opportunities present themselves.

As Christians, we never retire. God has a plan for every day of our lives. And as we grow older, our talents and abilities are often modified by our physical abilities and our schedule. My father, as a young man, was busily engaged as a Christian businessman in the Gideons and in Christian businessmen's associations. He was a lay preacher, a youth leader and was engaged in prison ministry. As he got older and became less mobile, he spent time visiting those in need, especially the housebound and people in hospital. He became active in the healing ministry of his church. When this became impossible he wrote letters, and when his vision failed because of macular degeneration, he called people on the phone. He lived to 91 years of age and on the day before he died he called my sister Rose to his bedside.

'I told the nurse about Jesus,' he said. 'Do you think she heard me?'

To continue the analogy of the football team, God may say: 'You've been an excellent fullback for many years but I want you to be a winger. I am going to make you fast.' (Or maybe 'a goalie' or defender.) So . . . 'I am going to teach you to defend, be a striker, I want you to shoot the goal to bring the game home'.

These times of change come to all of us, and when they do we must often learn to *stand down* before we can *step up* into that new role. This may mean standing down from strengths and giftings so that He can re-equip us for the task ahead. In my own case, as a doctor I had to surrender my rationalism before God could show me how He is able to intervene in the healing process. This was a difficult process for me, but in so doing I was able to discover how faith and rationalism can find mutual acceptance.

When we accept Jesus into our hearts and find our identity as a son or daughter of Father God, then Christ lives through us, extending His love to those around us. Paul said:

'It is no longer I who live, but Christ lives in me' (Gal. 2:20). I once asked my father how I could love someone who has gone out of his way to hurt me or make life difficult for me. His answer: 'Allow Christ to love them through you.'

Eric Liddell is well known as the Scottish athlete who refused to run in the 100-metre qualifiers at the 1924 Olympic Games in Paris as they were to be held on a Sunday. He was heavily criticized but deeply respected for taking this stand. Later in those games he won the gold medal in the 400-metre event and returned to England a hero. Years later, as a missionary in China during World War Two, he was placed into a Japanese internment camp where he became a servant to all and was greatly loved. Shortly before the end of the war, he died of a brain tumour. The day following his death, one of the men within the camp, not a religious man, was heard to say, 'Jesus Christ used to live in this camp, but He died yesterday.'

I once knew a man called Bob, Uncle Bob we called him, a thundering man with a raw sense of humour. There was never any doubt when he was around. Growing up as an only child he had a rather lonely childhood but, as a young man, married a gracious and loving lady. Sadly, they were unable to have children.

Bob had a background in accounting and worked as a relief branch manager for one of the 'big four' banks. His professional life consisted of moving from town to town providing leave relief for resident managers. As such, he never built or owned a house or had anywhere that he called home. He never started a business, joined a club, wrote a book or even had a Facebook page. He attended church and was obsessed with ritual: the ribbons, the seasons and the creeds, but never really understood what it was all about. Eventually he developed prostate cancer and on his deathbed scornfully refused prayer from my father. He had been in some respects a difficult man, and at his funeral the pastor who had never met him in life had to be reminded of his name and experienced some difficulty in knowing what to say about him.

His wife is now also gone and he is essentially forgotten, except by me. It is almost as though he never lived. Yet it is my belief that God had a plan for that man's life. The tragedy is that he never found it, that he never found true identity and that he never experienced an empowering relationship with God as his loving Father.

I recently heard an interview with an overseas refugee. After entering a country illegally, he had been placed in a camp with other new arrivals. Here he eventually met his wife and had a family, and his children now have their own small ones. He has lived his entire adult life in an internment camp with no country to call his own and no guaranteed future. He has lived a life in limbo.

My question to you before reading on, is this:

Who are you . . . really? Have you ever seriously considered your true identity before? Are you able to call Him Father?

Preface to Chapter 6

Read now the story of David Claydon, a man born with no name, with no known birth date and no nationality. Yet God knew him and had a plan for his life.

> For He shall give His angels charge over you,
> To keep you in all your ways.
>
> In their hands they shall bear you up,
> Lest you dash your foot against a stone.

(Ps. 91:11,12)

6

The Man with No Name – But Known Unto God

*Because he has set his love upon Me, therefore I will
deliver him;
I will set him on high, because he has known My name.*
(Ps. 91:14)

The front door was guarded by the largest and most beautiful cymbid-
ium orchid that I had ever seen. Bracts of luminescent ivory blooms
swayed in the cool morning breeze.

'We keep giving them away,' said Robyn, 'but they just keep
growing.'

The orchid was symbolic of this couple's life. It was rare, exotic,
and beautiful. David and Robyn had given themselves unselfishly to
others over a lifetime, but the more they gave away the more they
thrived.

Lynne and I had driven to Hornsby Heights, north of Sydney, to
verify a remarkable story related to me by my friend Dr Russell Clark.[1]
It seems that David had been delivered from near-certain death at the
hands of Congolese soldiers during his time as a missionary in Africa.
I needed to check details.

We settled into comfy chairs armed with strong brewed coffee and
Robyn's specialty, a lemon lime slice.

'The story *is* remarkable,' he began. 'But that was not the first time
that God rescued me and please understand, my life to that point had
not been easy.'

I was soon to discover that this was an understatement of mammoth proportions.

David was born in Bethlehem sometime in 1936 by his reckoning. His parents, British citizens, had been killed in crossfire between the Zionists, British and Palestinians and all records regarding his birth, family and citizenship had been destroyed by bombing. A fair-skinned boy with red hair he had no name, no birth date and no family. He was totally without identity and as such became a ward of the Bethlehem Orphanage on the road between Bethlehem and Jerusalem.[2] Arabic became his first language.

With the coming of war, the German matron was interned and the orphanage closed. Lora Claydon, an Australian social worker, was assigned the duty of finding homes for the children. Most were taken in by Arabic families but David, the only white boy, and who was suffering from measles and pneumonia at the time, was transferred to the German Hospital.

As the Nazis prepared to unleash war on North Africa, conditions at the hospital deteriorated and members of staff were interned by the British protectorate government. Without proper medical care, young David lapsed into a coma. Lora wrapped him in a blanket and took him by taxi to the Church Mission to the Jews Hospital on the Street of the Prophets. Here the two doctors with Lora and her friends prayed fervently for his recovery. He remained in a coma for two weeks but by the grace of God recovered without deficit.

David clearly remembers his time of convalescence at the hospital. 'A man would come in on Sundays to show us glass lantern slides,' he said. 'One image was of Jesus with a lamb across His shoulders. I thought if Jesus cared that much about a lost lamb, He must care about me. So . . . I belong to Jesus.' He was 4-and-a-half years old.

When David was fully recovered, Lora decided to take care of him. But this was not an easy transition for either party. At 4 years of age he spoke only Arabic with the occasional Arabic swear word! His attitudes to women were those instilled in him by the other children. When Lora suggested that he should learn English, he responded that *she* should learn Arabic. She recalled that when she gave him an order he climbed up onto the table where they were sitting and slapped her squarely across the face. But it was through Lora that David developed a deep sense of trust in God's presence and provision that would stay with him through life. It was at this stage that he took the name of David, which seemed appropriate for one born in Bethlehem. He still had no family name.

Within twelve months Lora accepted an assignment in Ethiopia teaching English to the children of Emperor Haile Selassie, Amha and Princess Tenagnework.[3] She left David in Jerusalem in the care of the Christian doctor who had nursed him through the coma. The doctor was married with a daughter of David's age and for the first time he experienced family love.

David remained with the doctor and his family for two years. Just before his fifth birthday he was called into the doctor's study and presented with a watch.

'You must learn to tell the time, David, as you will soon be travelling to Eritrea to visit Aunt Lora.' But the ship was torpedoed in the Mediterranean and the trip never eventuated. A few months later it was decided to send him to England to stay with Lora's Aunt Agnes, but that ship was also torpedoed en route to Haifa. Later still, in 1943, arrangements were made to send him to England with the hospital matron. But plans were cancelled at the last minute as Matron was also to escort a young girl, Sally. The ship was torpedoed near the Straits of Gibraltar. Sally was drowned. Matron Hawkins was one of the few survivors.

During his time with the doctor and his family, David suffered what was believed to be sunstroke, again lapsing into a coma and this time taking three months to recover.

Eventually Lora returned from Eritrea and once again took over David's care.

'Most of the time we were desperately hungry,' he said, 'and there were times when we nearly starved, but God always provided. One day with no money to buy bread we went out to find food. "Lora," I said, "we have no money."

'"God will provide. Pray, David," she said. As we approached the market gate a raven overhead dropped a silver coin just in front of me. I dived on it. That coin paid for bread and eggs that morning.'

Lora was appointed warden of the Garden Tomb in Jerusalem where many believed Jesus had been buried.[4] One day, as they sat praying for food in the garden, David heard the postman.

"'Lora,' he said, 'there is something in the letterbox.'" It was a Palestinian £10 note in a letter from a Christian bank manager.

It was a strange life for a little boy. He would roam the streets in the early hours inspecting the bombed-out buildings, and during the day there was the constant quest for food. One day he found a building that had been totally destroyed except for the spiral staircase, which stood proud and erect from the rubble. He recalls this as prophetic of his survival in the context of abandonment and utter devastation. What was his purpose in life? What mysterious plan did God hold precious for a little boy with no name?

After the second battle of El Alamein[5] and Rommel's recall to Germany,[6] Lora decided it was high time to return home to Australia with her charge. The protectorate government advised that if she could make it to Cairo with David, then there may be room on a troop ship back to Australia. But David would need a passport and, indeed, a surname. On the advice of a British official she signed an affidavit stating that David was her nephew and he adopted her name of Claydon.

The railway line to Cairo was a single track over the mountains, with sidings to allow oncoming trains to pass. The train was segregated, with an animal carriage preceding the engine holding only Zionist passengers. Palestinians were housed in the carriages following. It was hoped that this arrangement might discourage terrorist attacks. This was a hazardous journey and not one to be undertaken lightly.

As it happened, the train was late and they finally boarded at 4 p.m. The train snaked its way south-west towards Cairo. As it approached a mountain pass it entered a siding to allow the passage of an oncoming freight train. David watched as the approaching train inched its way up the mountainside. But suddenly there was a flash and a deafening roar as the freight train was torn apart by a bomb. The carriages were incinerated, spilling flaming sheep down the mountainside in a fiery cascade.

At the military HQ in Cairo, David and Lora were assigned to a small ship which was to transport officers back to Australia. The battle against Japan was imminent and the government needed to repatriate these men from the Middle East without delay, for reassignment.

The captain took a zigzag course across the Indian Ocean towards Australia on constant watch for U-boats and enemy planes. After stopping briefly in Fremantle, they entered the Great Australian Bight heading east for Melbourne, only to learn that rogue U-boat 862[7] had sunk allied shipping in Port Phillip bay.

'That U-boat will pass you in the night on its return journey,' they were told, 'and will no doubt torpedo you.'

That night officers met in the saloon and prayed for protection. Depth charges and anti-aircraft guns were made ready, but no attack came. As they finally sailed into Port Phillip Bay, David saw the masts of the many sunken ships that had been torpedoed.

'As I stepped onto Australian soil,' he said, 'I recalled all the things that had happened to me and I thanked God that I was alive. I dedicated my life to God and told Him that I would serve Him. I was 8 years old.'

God's hand of protection was clearly upon David. He had saved him from crossfire, from starvation, illness, drowning at sea, aerial bombing and U-boat 862. He had rescued this small nameless boy without even a birth date from a coma, which I suspect may have been an expression of measles encephalitis, and brought him to the other side of the world to fulfil a purpose and a destiny that only He could have designed.

So, you might ask with expectation, what plan and purpose *did* God hold for this young man just 8 years of age?

Arriving in Australia, David and Lora first settled in Sydney where David attended Knox College using monies provided by the Palestinian government. But when funds were exhausted they moved to the Blue Mountains, west of Sydney, where he attended Katoomba High, taking on casual work after school to help pay for food and lodging. David later went on to study economics, education and theology and eventually became the National Director of Scripture Union

Australia, training youth workers throughout East Asia and establishing Scripture Union ministry in the South Pacific Islands. He served as Rector of St Matthew's Anglican Church, West Pennant Hills for six years and then headed up the Church Missionary Society of Australia, also serving as president of the United Mission to Nepal.[8]

But if you were to ask David what had been the most joyous and productive event of his life, he would no doubt refer to meeting and marrying Robyn.[9] Together they find identity and purpose in God's leading and provision.

You might also ask why God would allow a young boy that He loved so dearly to experience such torment and deprivation and to spend his early years completely without identity.

It was from that position of weakness that David found strength. It was in the context of those early childhood experiences that he found wisdom, insight and a simple trust in God. It has been said that when we have nothing left but God, we discover that God is enough. And it was in that very context that David found his prime identity and purpose for living. Even today the image of the lamb held lovingly on Jesus' shoulder is foremost in his mind.

There are times when God allows us to be caught up in the most difficult of circumstances. 'Father, why would you allow these things to happen?' we ask. Yet, if we persevere and trust in God, we will find that He gives us the strength to walk on. He will build in us an identity steeped in His provision and love to reach out to others in similar situations.[10]

Clearly David's heart remains in the Middle East. 'I often come across people who have come to Christ through a vision,' he said. 'Some of these visions are quite amazing, not at all straightforward. As an example, there was a Muslim man in Pakistan who was fishing and had a vision of Jesus walking to him across the water. Jesus showed him a picture of another man standing in front of a shop in Hyderabad. He recognized the street and the shop but not the man's face.

'"If this is for real," he thought, "and Jesus really wants me, I'd better go and see what this is all about."

'Catching the next bus to Hyderabad he walked down Jacob Road to the shop that he had seen in the vision. And there was that man standing outside. It was the Bishop of Hyderabad.

'"Jesus told me to come and see you."

'"Yes, I've been waiting for you," said the bishop, who took him to his home and later led him to the Lord.

'When the man's father heard that his son had converted, he sent *dacoits* to kill his son.[11] The man invited the *dacoits* into his home, sat them down, fed them and told them how Jesus had called him across the water and why he had become a Christian.

'The *dacoits* did not feel that they could kill this man and returned to the father who was furious and sent them back to complete their mission. But this time they could not find him and eventually gave up.

'Christian friends took the man into care for his own protection. He met a Christian girl and they were married. For safety, CMS sent them to Bible school in Singapore. Eventually they returned to Pakistan where the man became principal of a Bible college. He wrote later to say that he had had discussions with his father, who had also now converted.

'One of the big problems in the Arab world is honour killing,' said David. 'When there is a conversion there is honour killing, and it is difficult to get a flow on of conversions. These people need to be relocated.' David has arranged for many converts whose lives are at risk in the Middle East to come to Australia on humanitarian visas, and is currently bringing Christians from Syria and Iraq in association with the Minister for Immigration and the Barnabas Fund.

'So tell me about the Congolese soldiers,' I said.

'Well, I was in Africa with CMS at the time. With a MAF pilot[12] and a senior missionary, I had flown into a small dirt airstrip in Zaire to meet with the local bishop. But the bishop happened to be in another town and to our dismay the airstrip was bristling with Congolese soldiers. One approached our plane.

'"Give me your passport!"

'"But I'm in transit, I am not alighting from this plane."

'"Get out . . . now!"'

The Congolese soldier was armed and meant business.

Having no option, David climbed down from the plane to be led across the tarmac to a small tin shed where other soldiers sat laughing and carousing. Some lay sprawled on the ground, clearly inebriated. It was blisteringly hot and not a good scene.

David tried to explain his presence but within fifteen minutes his schoolboy French was exhausted and he had made no progress.

'You shouldn't be on this tarmac,' said the soldier, 'I'm going to lock you up until a senior officer comes from Kinshasa to interrogate you.'

David knew that such a man would be unlikely to travel nearly two thousand miles across the second largest country in Africa to interview him, and he began to fear for his life. The heat was oppressive. He moved to the door for a breath of fresh air.

And then he saw him. Across the tarmac walked a tall local man immaculately dressed in suit and tie, carrying a bundle of mail under his arm. The man approached the MAF plane, opened the door and placed the mail under David's seat.

'Can you help me?' David called. The man replied in fluent English. David explained his dilemma.

'Wait here,' said the man. 'I'll deal with it.'

He addressed the soldiers in perfect French, returning in minutes.

'All's well. You've done nothing wrong, but for his loss of face, apologize to the soldier and he'll give you back your passport.'

David apologized as instructed, then turned to find that the man in the suit was nowhere to be seen.

'Where's your man?' he quizzed the pilot, 'where's the other guy who helped me? He disappeared while I was apologizing. There are no cars. It's an open field. He couldn't just disappear.'

'I don't have a MAF representative here,' said the pilot.

'But you do. He put mail on the plane. I saw it.'

'But we don't take mail from here.'

There was *no* mail in the plane!

Back in Nairobi David wrote to the senior missionary who had been with them on the plane.

'Who *was* that guy? I want to thank him.'

Her reply: 'No such man exists.'

Canon Andrew White, 'The Vicar of Baghdad', heads up the Foundation for Relief and Reconciliation in the Middle East, a non-profit organization, which supports his work at St George's Church, Baghdad.[13] In his latest book he states that he had been sceptical of people claiming angelic encounters. 'But now I have seen angels for myself,' he says, 'and I accept that, in a church where the miraculous is the norm and incredible healings take place, the presence of the Almighty and His angelic hosts is tangible, and sometimes even visible.'[14]

David's life has been one of risk. Sometimes those risks have been thrust upon him and sometimes he has embarked upon them of his own accord. It has been through that risk-taking and by the grace of God that so much has been achieved.

Canon White visited Pope John Paul II in Rome during his time as chairman of the young leadership section of the International Council of Christians and Jews. The Pope's words to him at that time were: 'You are at the early stage of your ministry. You will go far if you take risks.' The canon now states: 'I know for a fact that whenever I have decided not to take a risk, I have limited the work of the Holy Spirit. So whenever the Lord has brought this to my attention, I've repented and next time been bolder in stepping out and trusting Him.'[15]

As we made our way back to the car the orchid, now shaded, continued to exhibit grace and beauty. I was tempted to ask for a bloom but thought better of it.

I recalled how David had received a silver coin from a raven when he was hungry and without money for food and was reminded of how the ravens had fed Elijah by the brook when he was near to starvation. And later, when the brook dried up altogether, a widow used the last of her flour and oil to bake bread for Elijah at great personal cost.[16] Each time the flour and oil were used they were replenished by God. And I saw that David and Robyn were that flour and oil. They will continue as such, until the rains come.

Author's note

1. Cecily Paterson has written a biography of David and his wife, Robyn, called *Never Alone: The remarkable story of David and Robyn Claydon* (SPCK Australia, 2006).

2. David Claydon's most recent book, *Who Do I Think I Am?* (Morling Press, 2013), explores personal identity and what it means to be 'in Christ'.

Preface to Chapter 7

Historic St Paul's Chapel was built in 1766. It is the oldest continuously used public building in New York City.

It was host to George Washington. It survived the Great Fire of 1776.

It is located 22 metres from Ground Zero.

Despite the total desolation of the 335-metre twin towers and adjacent buildings, it remained completely intact. Not a window was broken, the wooden steeple was undamaged.

It took thirty men three days to clear the rubble from the churchyard. It served continuously for twelve months as a base for volunteers, NYPD, NYFD and relatives seeking loved ones, providing refuge, first-aid, information, counselling and love.

It became known as: 'The Little Chapel That Stood.'

Ten thousand miles away, nestled on the northern shore of Sydney Harbour in the village of Kirribilli, stands the 'Church by the Bridge', formerly St John's Anglican Church. Its wooden spire rises proud of the surrounding restaurants and boutiques as a beacon to all who are lost, all who are lonely. It maintains vigilant watch at the on-ramp to the Sydney Harbour Bridge, northern gateway to the city of Sydney.

Eight years ago the church was dying, with a morning congregation of less than ten. It is now a vibrant community church of 700. A plaque inside the church declares this to be the Queen's church in Sydney. No monarch has set foot here for years. Yet there is an overwhelming presence of the King of kings.

The driving force behind this transformation is the pastor, Paul Dale. Paul is himself an enigma: a mathematician, an Oxford Don, ordained Anglican minister, ironman, servant to his people, husband, father.

This is his story . . .

7

Father to the Fatherless

*And the LORD called Samuel again the third time. So
he arose and went to Eli . . . Eli said to Samuel, 'Go, lie
down; and it shall be, if He calls you, that you must say,
"Speak, LORD, for Your servant hears."'*

(1 Sam. 3:8,9)

'Tea or coffee?'

'Whatever you're having.'

'I'm an Englishman,' he said. 'Tea every time.'

Paul sat poised and relaxed in jeans, loafers and finely checked shirt looking every inch the triathlete. His office – lined floor to ceiling with books and study guides – marked him as a man of learning and letters. An earring in his left ear made the bold statement that here was a man who would not conform lightly to worldly expectations.

'What's your identity, Paul?' I asked.

'I'm a follower of Jesus. I use the term rather than "Christian" as my security, my contentment, and my conscience are in Him. I live for Him. That's my identity, Ern, before pastor, mathematician, even husband or father.'

'And your relationship with God?'

'He's my heavenly Father who loves me deeply and knows me intimately. That was a hard transition for me to make, to understand the unconditional love of a father and to learn to approach Him as a child. As you know, I'd been the adult in my family, so to learn to be a child before God was difficult.'

'And your relationship with the Holy Spirit?'

'He's the one who illuminates wonderful truths to me. He's the one who convicts me of my sin but also of the joy of forgiveness. He's the one who empowers me day by day and who equips me to do whatever task lies before me. He gives me insight into life situations.'

Paul grew up in Coventry, England, the youngest of three children. His father was a maths teacher and his mother a full-time mum. 'It was a loving home,' he said, 'but we didn't go to church, except maybe Christmas and Easter.'

Although there was love, Paul's childhood was marked by sickness and sadness. His brother had kidney cancer, a Wilms tumour, and when Paul was 11 his father went into hospital for correction of a hole in the heart. Surgery should have been straightforward. But it wasn't. Tragically he developed multi-organ failure resulting in brain damage, and was on life support for two weeks.

'The doctor spoke to my mother and I. He said that *we* must choose whether to turn the machine off.'

'What a decision for an 11-year-old boy,' I thought, knowing full well that if his father did survive, his quality of life would be very poor.

Thankfully, Paul's father did come home, but he was bedbound and needed complete round-the-clock care. His brother and sister left home, leaving Paul and his mother to care for his father. For the next nine years he broached death at least once a year. Each time, the doctor would warn the family that Father's condition was critical and that he would be unlikely to survive for forty-eight hours.

Father's life became unbearable and when Paul was just 17 his father threw himself from the top floor window. It was Paul who found him. 'Miraculously he survived,' said Paul. 'But again and again I was faced with sickness, sadness and the prospect of death. "There must be more to life than this," I thought.'

But the Lord planted seeds in Paul's life, seeds of hope, causing him to ask himself, 'What happens when you die?' He had been given a New Testament with Psalms at school and he searched the scriptures looking for answers.

'My life was school, nursing Dad, homework and bed,' he said. 'That was it. As an escape, I threw myself into study and became an academic nerd. Then one day the teacher took me aside.

'"Paul, you have a gift for maths," he said. "You should think about applying to study at Oxford."' No one from Paul's family had ever been to university. He decided to apply and, aged 18, took up residency at Lincoln College, Oxford to study mathematics.

For the first time, Paul sensed freedom to lead a normal life style. Life at Oxford was exciting and he soon made new friends. David, a Buddhist, on hearing his story gave him literature and writings to help him.

'Academic nerd that I was,' said Paul, 'I decided that if I was going to look into Buddhism I should examine all world religions.'

At Blackwell's bookstore in Oxford, Paul bought five books. One was on Buddhism, one on Islam, another on Hinduism and one on atheism. The fifth was *The Lion Handbook to the Bible*. He spent his first term at Oxford studying maths and learning about world religions. 'As a scientific person,' he said, 'I soon realized that if I was going to seriously consider a world religion, it needed to have a historical basis. So Islam and Christianity were the two that grabbed hold of me.'

But it soon became clear to Paul that Islam and Christianity were incompatible. 'Either one was true, or neither. But both couldn't be true.' He developed a mathematical theorem to prove this for himself.

'I spent months talking to Muslims and then to Christians,' he said. 'My college chaplain was patient with me and answered lots of questions. I began to read the Scriptures and right there in the Gospel of Luke I came face to face with Jesus. I saw that He had power to heal the sick and this was very significant to me. I considered the paralytic and asked myself, what was this man's greatest need? Surely to walk. And my dad needed to be healed. But Jesus said what they really needed was forgiveness of sins.

'God opened my eyes to the fact that there was a bigger problem than human suffering. Almost overnight God helped me to park the problem of suffering, for a while at least. But I needed answers. Before I gave my life to Christ, I had to have some answers.'

At this point Paul came to the conclusion that if anything was going to be true it would be Christianity. Jesus intrigued him. He believed that He existed and he believed the works that He had done, but he wasn't ready to trust his life to Him. There were questions about suffering and about the Lordship of Christ.

'If God is God, how could He allow suffering when He had the power to heal? Why didn't He heal? Why did my brother get a tumour when he was 8 years old? Why did the operation go so horribly wrong for my dad when I was 11? Why were we forced to make a decision about turning off his life support? Why didn't God just take my dad out of it then and there and save us from nine years of misery? All that kind of stuff. And I knew how I was wired. If I became a Christian, Jesus would make demands on my life and I sure wasn't about to change.'

Then God threw another issue into Paul's life, the issue of hell. None of his family were believers. 'To someone with no church background, like me, it became very clear that if you believe in Jesus you go to heaven and if you don't then you go to hell. That was it. I was staring death in the face every day and my dad was not a believer. Could I trust a man called Jesus? If His words were true, my whole family was lost.

'Then God brought a man called Jean Vanier into my life, a student of Francis Schaeffer from *L'Abri* in Switzerland. He explained that the God of the Scriptures had experienced suffering also. Jesus Himself had suffered and He understood. So I began to ask myself, "Why not me, Lord?" Instead of asking, "Why did my brother suffer?" I asked, "Why wasn't that me?" Then reality hit me. Who was I to ask the God of the universe who should or shouldn't suffer?

'So at 20 years of age I had done with questions. I believed that Jesus was God. I believed that He died at Calvary for my sin. I was at the point of saying, "Lord Jesus, I trust you as Saviour." I believed in Him but I wasn't following him at all.'

At the end of term, Paul went home to find his dad in the best health he had known for nine years. 'We even went out for lunch as a family,' he said, 'but the next day Dad began to go downhill and four days later he quietly and peacefully passed away. I felt this complete cocktail of emotions: relief after nine years of nursing and caring, guilt that I should feel that way, and sadness that, from the age of 11, I hadn't really known my dad. I thought, "If what I know about Jesus is true and God is Sovereign, then as far as I know there is nothing to indicate that my dad trusted in Christ." That was the moment that I knew that I had to make a decision either to accept God at His word or just walk away. I chose God and accepted Jesus as my Saviour.'

At the funeral Paul read from 1 Corinthians 15 about resurrection bodies. He thought to himself, "This is actually true and has great significance for me right now. If *I* was in that coffin I would want a resurrection body."

'My testimony, Ern, is like the blind man who saw men as trees walking.[1] I knew that God still had work to do in me. Six weeks later, back at university, I told a friend that I had become a Christian. "Well, you're not living like one," he said. He had grown up in a Christian home but had walked away from Christ. He had the head knowledge but he didn't believe. I believed, but I had never been taught what it meant to live as a Christian. God actually used a non-believer to tell me to sit down and to find out what God demanded of my life.

'I went to the college chapel, which was Anglo-Catholic. The minister there loved Jesus and the Scriptures. Looking back, I can see that there were a lot of things that I would be uncomfortable with now, but as a new believer I was finding my way and learning the basics. I also went to the Christian Union at my college, where somebody asked me if I was a Christian and where I went to church. When I told him that I went to the college chapel, he said, "Well, then, you can't be a Christian." That really polarized me. I thought, "How dare you say that?" So I never went back.'

Paul spent eighteen months at the college chapel. As he said, 'I was swinging the incense and doing all that stuff. I read the Bible, met with the chaplain and asked lots of questions.'

Post-graduation, Paul stayed on to do a master's degree in applied mathematics. But the terms were longer and he was soon to discover that the college chapel closed down during undergrad vacations. He must find another church. One Sunday morning walking to Sainsbury's supermarket he walked past a church called St Ebbe's and heard singing and music very different to what he'd heard in the college chapel. 'It was lively and enthusiastic,' he said, 'There were drums and guitars. I was intrigued, so I went in. Revd Vaughan Roberts was preaching from Mark's Gospel. I sat there listening to Bible teaching as I'd never heard it before. He took it verse by verse. But it went on forever. I was used to an eight-minute homily and he preached for forty-five minutes! I thought, "Get on with it, man." But as I listened, the Word of God came alive. After the service, I met a student from Wycliffe who invited me to have tea with him that week. He explained to me the Navigator's wheel[2] and for the first time in my life I began to grasp the power of the Word of God and what it meant to be Christian.'

Paul commenced a PhD course in applied maths on models of wound healing and scar tissue formation. But he also spent a lot of time at St Ebbe's. 'My passion was kids' ministry and especially to the kids from the housing estate. We ran a boys' club for 7 to 9-year-olds. That's where God really gave me a heart for the marginalized. So here I was, living this life in tension where I was in an Oxford college with the elite and privileged, at the pinnacle of academic learning, but then a couple of days per week I was sharing a cup of tea in the housing commission with people who had absolutely nothing.'

Paul began to understand the power of grace. The people in the housing commission who accepted Christ, and the Oxford professor who had accepted Christ, were in God's eyes totally equal. 'Grace is a beautiful leveller,' he said. 'It just transforms your view of people. I stopped looking at people for their academic ability or material possessions. I just saw them as loved by God and in need of grace.'

On completing his PhD, Paul was awarded a junior research fellowship and then a lifetime fellowship. He was lecturing in applied maths, mathematical biology and mathematical medicine and researching cancer modelling and wound healing and loving every minute of it. It was at that stage that his pastor at St Ebbe's approached him.

'Paul,' he said, 'Have you ever thought about going into ministry?'
'No,' he said. 'I love teaching maths.'

Shortly after, whilst completing a postgraduate term in Christchurch, New Zealand, he was again prompted by his local pastor: 'Paul, I really think the Lord is calling you to ministry. I know you love maths and I know you're gifted at maths. But I think the Lord is leading you to ministry.'

'No,' he said. 'I want to keep doing maths.'

A third call to the ministry came from a most unexpected quarter. Back in the UK, Paul resumed his professorial position at Oxford. 'One evening at dinner,' he said, 'we were sitting at the high table in Lincoln College having processed in our academic gowns. It was like a scene from Harry Potter. We were served with a four-course meal with five types of wines. The man sitting next to me happened to be a visiting professor.'

'Paul, what are you doing for the weekend?' he asked.

'I'm running a youth camp for the kids of the housing estate in Oxford.'

'Why on earth would you do that?'

'Because I love them and because I enjoy telling them about Jesus.'

'Do you enjoy that more than mathematics?' he asked.

It was as though God put a flashing light before Paul's eyes and the answer was a resounding: 'Yes!'

'That was the night that the Lord said to me, "Paul, I'm calling you to ministry." I was still reluctant and hedged my bets for the rest of that year, taking on a full teaching load at Oxford and commencing part-time Bible college in London.'

But it became clear to Paul that he must make the full transition. So he left academia and enrolled at Oakhill Bible College, London, to the horror of his colleagues, who had never heard of anyone giving up an Oxford fellowship to enter the ministry.

In his third year at college, Paul began to apply for jobs. As he was sponsored by the Oxford Diocese, it was understood that he would return to that diocese after training. But the bishop had his own ideas.

'Paul, we think you are too narrow, theologically. You need to broaden out a bit so we are sending you to work in this particular church.'

Paul went along for an interview but soon realized that he could never work there.

'I had no problem with it being a high church, given my Anglo-Catholic background. But it was very liberal. They didn't believe or live according to the Bible. I thought, "I just can't work with integrity under that man."'

The bishop was unimpressed.

'If you don't go there, we won't ordain you,' he said.

'"Well," I thought, "what's more important, being ordained or working in a church where people teach the Bible and care for others?" But it was very humbling. I'd given up a professorial position at Oxford to go to Oak Hill College and I would be the only one in my year not to be ordained. I'd lost everything!'

But again God provided. A church nearby required an assistant minister so they employed Paul. 'I loved the work, just didn't have the title or the dog collar. I began to understand that I was not in ministry for a title, and to be quite honest I didn't care whether I was working in an Anglican, Baptist or Presbyterian Church as long as the people loved Jesus and the Scriptures. And then I got a phone call from Australia offering me a job at St Thomas', North Sydney.'

Paul wrote to his bishop to say, 'I'm going to Sydney.' The bishop wrote back:

'Dear Paul, wishing you well for your ministry in the colonies. We both know that your churchmanship is much more suited to the evangelical Sydney Diocese than it ever will be to the Diocese of Oxford. PS I am willing to offer you Letters Dimissory.'[3]

Paul came to Sydney in September 2002, where he was ordained on behalf of the Bishop of Oxford. He came expecting to be in Sydney for two years, and twelve years later he was still here.

Just as it had been with Samuel, God called Paul to ministry three times. On the first two occasions it was by the prophetic prompting of Christian men. The third time it was completely out of left field, by an academic non-believer.

The call had been to stand *down* from personal ambition and aspirations and from all the privileges afforded an Oxford Don. It was also a call to step *up* into a new life, one of ministry and care for others. Prayerfully and thoughtfully Paul had considered the options and had chosen to accept God's challenge. Yet, having abandoned one life aspiration, he was then to find that the other was not available to him, that of ministering as an ordained man. It was at that point that Paul abandoned himself to God's will. He walked away from all earthly pursuits and determined to release himself completely to God's will.

God gives to each of us unique abilities and talents. Paul was gifted in his understanding of mathematics, in logical thought process and in his ability to teach and impart knowledge. I was interested to know if he had walked away from these also.

'Not at all,' he said. 'God uses my abilities in an extraordinary way. When you're used to standing up in front of 500 people to lecture maths, you are comfortable speaking to large groups of people. In maths tutorials, you watch people's faces as they grapple with a concept. There are lots of concepts in maths. You walk them through the process of understanding until they get it. You can see it in their faces. So it is with teaching about God's love.'

'Did you have a problem reconciling science with faith?' I asked.

'Not at all. A lot of people thought I would, so they gave me books on science and Christianity. But I don't see any incompatibility. God created all things, including atoms.'

So Paul was ordained as an Anglican minister in Sydney with the blessing of his Oxford bishop, who had not the slightest idea how his interventions were to further the cause of evangelism in Sydney. Paul took up his position as assistant minister at St Thomas', North Sydney. Curiously, at about the same time, he developed an interest in long-distance running and spoke with a friend who had recently completed an Ironman triathlon.[4]

'I'd love to do that,' he said.

His friend laughed at him. 'Paul, you're too old and unfit.'

Never one to avoid a challenge, Paul took up the gauntlet. Six months later he completed a half-marathon and the next year, 2007, a full Ironman at Port Macquarie, repeating this in 2008 and 2010.

'Could you swim?' I asked.

'Of course not, I'm an Englishman. And I had to learn to ride a bike as well.'

It was while Paul was running across the Sydney Harbour Bridge that he first noticed the spire of St John's Anglican church rising from the centre of the village of Kirribilli and hemmed in on all sides by every manner of ethnic restaurant and boutique. On further investigation he found that here was a church with a morning congregation of less than ten English-speaking people. There was also a larger Cantonese-speaking congregation. Paul's heart since Oxford had been to bring Christianity into the community, and here was an opportunity. With the permission of his own rector and that of St John's, Paul established what was to become known as the Church by the Bridge, now a thriving community church.

'I realized,' he said, 'that there was a need to reach out to the 20 and 30-year-olds, especially the unmarried. Lots of churches do youth and family ministry well, but few reach out to these people, who often feel alienated.[5] If you're single in your thirties and early forties I understand the struggles of that,' he said, 'as well as the joys of being single.

'I'm an experiential, emotional kind of guy,' he said. 'So I thought, "Why not have a church where you teach the Scriptures, but people can also express their love for Jesus in worship by raising their hands, or by leaving them by their sides, and where no one is coerced to worship either way? Why not have a church where we are reformed charismatics, we are evangelicals but we believe in the work of the Spirit?"

'My vision is bigger than the church building. Our building only seats 120 people – but we get to do life together and know each other so well. We now have six congregations – more than six hundred people. That's amazing. Our vision is to be a light here in Kirribilli and beyond – into the lower north shore where there are lost tribes of people, especially in their twenties and thirties. Lots of hurting people, people searching for meaning and answers and hope.'

Paul met Rachel when he was 38. 'Would you like to meet this woman we know?' asked his friends. They were totally upfront: 'You need to know that she's a widow with a 3-year-old child.'

'I would normally have run a mile,' but 'yes,' he said. Rachel had been married to a man called Ben, an extraordinary man. He was a pastor and a high school teacher as well, and they had decided to train to be missionaries.

Rachel was six months pregnant when Ben began to feel unwell and tired all the time, so they went for lab tests. The doctor called them back in the next day.

'I've got some really bad news for you,' he said. Ben had myeloma[6] and needed a bone marrow transplant. Rachel went into labour that very day and Sam was born at thirty-seven weeks' gestation. While she was upstairs in the hospital giving birth, Ben was downstairs having tests.

For the first three months after Sam was born, Ben was in hospital. He had a bone marrow transplant and was looking good for the first ten days but then developed graft rejection. He passed away in the September after Sam was born in March. 'He was a most remarkable man,' said Paul. 'As he lay dying, he was texting Rachel verses such as "Fix your eyes on Jesus, the author of our faith"' (see Heb. 12:2).

The night Ben died, Rachel walked into the hospital room a 27-year-old widow with a 6-month-old child. She had a choice to make: 'I can either trust Jesus and lean on Him or walk away.' But as she later said, 'My identity was not as a widow and not as a single mum, but as a child of God. He will hold on to me.'

Paul met Rachel in October 2008 and they were married in April 2010.

'Ern,' he said, 'I've married a remarkable woman and God has blessed us with another son, Nathanael, born June 2011.

'God has taught me many things,' he said. 'I loved being single and the opportunities that brought to serve my Saviour. And I cherish the joys of being married and of being thrown into the deep end straight away with young Sam, who is now 9 years of age.'

Sam called his new father 'Paulie'. But then one Sunday morning after the 9:30 service as they were preparing to leave the church, Paul heard: 'Dad, Dad.' It didn't register at first. Paul just kept cleaning up and then Rachel tapped him on the shoulder.

'He's talking to you,' she said.

'And from that day on,' said Paul, 'he has called me Dad.'

I swallowed hard. We both paused. And then the thought occurred. What was God's response the first time He heard us call Him Father?

'You know, Ern,' he said, 'people ask me why God took me through those years with my dad. My answer is that God was growing in me compassion, a genuine love for people, selflessness for serving others. That's far more important than serving self. You can talk about God's sovereignty, but when you've actually been through tragic situations you ask yourself, "Do I really believe that God was in control? Do I believe He could have stopped that?" Yes, I do. So why didn't He? Because He chose not to. So that shaped my ministry as well. I developed empathy to sit with people who are grieving or who are suffering and to encourage and develop in them a deep trust in God's sovereignty.[7] People need to understand above all that their greatest need is for a Saviour and for a Father who will never let them go.'

And so a man who had lost his own father became a father to many, in the housing estates of Oxford, in the hallowed halls of Lincoln College and in his community. And finally to a small boy without a father whose name bore testimony to his faithful response to his own Father God.

Author's note

Nathanael (Nate) was born at thirty-two weeks' gestation and then, in January 2014, Elijah (Eli) was also born at thirty-two weeks. Paul and Rachel were reminded of their utter dependency on God's sovereignty and of the absolute joy of holding a 1.8 kg baby.

Preface to Chapter 8

In the feature movie *The Way*, Martin Sheen and his son Emilio Estevez play a father and son who just don't see eye to eye.[1] The father is a respected Southern Californian ophthalmologist; his son, Daniel, a Gen-X survivor who must explore his own potential and capabilities before settling down. Daniel decides to walk the 500-mile pilgrim trail from Saint-Jean-Pied-de-Port in France to Santiago de Compostela in the north-west of Spain in the Way of St James, also known as the Camino de Santiago. On the first day out, he is tragically killed in a snowstorm. His father, deeply shaken, flies from Southern California to France and after much soul-searching proceeds to carry his son's ashes the length of the trail. In so doing, he discovers his son perhaps for the first time, and also himself. Sadly, a 'cat's in the cradle' story.[2]

So often we spend our lives searching for purpose, a raison d'être or fulfilment, and all the time it may be staring us in the face: a meaningful relationship with our children. Those of us with children share prime responsibility and privilege to love and protect them, to stand by them, teach them where possible and prepare them for *the way*. Just as God loves us, so we should love those that He entrusts to us.

There are eight million orphans living in institutions across the world today, all needing the touch of a parent's hand, all needing love. How can we extend ourselves to help these children?

The following story of my friend Thomas tells of his journey of discovery to find just such purpose and fulfilment.

8

Thomas

For I will contend with him who contends with you,
And I will save your children.

(Isa. 49:25b)

He was 6 years of age but could have passed for a 4-year-old as he dashed past chasing the football, doggedly competing with boys twice his size. As a resident of this orphanage in Chiang Mai, Thailand, Noo Lek must fight for his place in more ways than one.

As Thomas looked on, he thought of his own precious son of 6 months. The thought occurred, 'This must be just as God sees us, fragile children in need of a father.'

Young, vital, with a casual demeanour and a penchant for English cricket and strong black coffee, there is something about Thomas that reminds me of Elijah Wood who played Frodo in the film *The Lord of the Rings*. Perhaps it relates to the epic journey on which he has embarked.

Born in Birmingham, England, Thomas was the first of three sons and one daughter born to parents who worked at the City Mission. 'We lived in the inner city,' he said, 'where most of our neighbours were Pakistani.' Young Thomas embraced his parents' faith and, as a boy lying in bed one night, remembers praying: 'God, I don't know what I'm going to be like when I'm older, but I'm worried I might not be a Christian any more. So I'm just telling you now, God, don't forget me. Have patience with me and I'm sure I'll come back.'

When Thomas was 11 his family moved to Pakistan, to a village called Khaplu in the northern Himalayas, 'as far north as foreigners can go,' he said, 'and just south of the Siachen Glacier.'[1] The invitation had come from missionary doctors who noticed that 50 per cent of the illnesses they were treating related to poor nutrition. His parents, trained in zoology and agriculture, were able to help improve local farming methods. They remained in Pakistan for thirteen years, initially in Khaplu but later in Abbottabad,[2] the home of Osama Bin Laden and where he was finally killed. 'My dad must have driven past him many times,' said Thomas.

Thomas attended the local high school and it was during that time that he confirmed his faith and entered into a deeper experience of God.

'Dad was driving me from Islamabad back to boarding school at Murree,' he said, 'and was answering some of my questions. Right there in the car this wonderful sense of joy and assurance came upon me. I didn't understand it at the time but guess it must have been the Holy Spirit.'

After high school, Thomas returned to London to study media arts and history at St Mary's University College, Twickenham. 'It's amazing how the study of history trains your mind to handle information and present it in a concise way,' he said. The skills learned have been immensely helpful to him in ongoing discussions with government and authorities about the future welfare of what might best be described as a global 'lost generation' of misplaced and unwanted children.

'I can see now that God was taking me on a journey,' he said. 'A wall poster at university challenged young graduates to teach English in China sponsored by the British Council.' Thomas met that challenge and, in 2002, went as a teacher to Shanghai. This was to be the beginning of his journey, testing and exploring God's will for his life.

In Shanghai he attended the International Christian Fellowship held in the local Three Self Church building.[3] 'You had to take your passport along to prove you were not Chinese,' he said. 'I should have thought that would have been obvious in my case.' He became one of the first to be baptized in that church for fifty years when the people discovered a baptistery under the floorboards, not used since before the Cultural Revolution.

One morning he introduced himself to the local congregation. 'My name is Thomas,' he said, 'I've been here for four weeks now and it's been great to get to know some of you.' As he was leaving the church, a woman approached him.

'It's wonderful to hear another English accent,' she said. 'You must come to dinner.' She introduced herself as Elizabeth Glover. Her husband, Robert, a UK social worker, had been invited by the Shanghai government to launch a pilot study to develop local family placement for orphans as an alternative to institutional care.

'Rob had a wonderful ability to communicate with the Chinese people,' said Thomas. But on Robert's return to the UK, he was summoned to the Foreign Office.

'I'm in big trouble now,' he thought. But such was not the case.

'What you've done is amazing,' they said. 'We want to make this a government-to-government issue and to fund it.' In 1998, Care for Children became the first joint venture social work project between the UK and the Chinese government.

Rachel Glover was at boarding school in the UK when Thomas first met the Glover family. She was one of six children, which he found amusing as her father was in China advising the government on child welfare, a country where a one-child family was the rule. Thomas first met Rachel when she came to Shanghai to spend Christmas with her family.

'She was an attractive 17-year-old,' he said, 'and I was 21. I tried to make conversation but it was tough going. Having arrived in the country that afternoon she was glazed-eyed and not giving me much back. But as she walked away I thought, "I could marry that girl one day." It seemed absurd. She was at school in England and I had finished university and was now living in China.'

The Glovers had moved to China in 1998 and Thomas in 2002. In 2003 he joined Care for Children just as the project was expanding from a pilot project in Shanghai to be rolled out nationally.

'I had been twelve months in the job,' he said, 'before I really began to understand what it was all about. We were being shown around an orphanage in central China by local authorities. I had seen many before. But this one was different, it was clean and warm. The staff were friendly and relaxed.'

Thomas approached a crib where a baby was lying, swaddled tightly in fresh linen. The room was remarkably peaceful. He placed his hand on the baby's chest, and instantly she became alert. 'Her eyes lit up,' he said, 'responding eagerly to my touch. If she could smile, I'm sure she would have done so! Then and there it dawned on me, these babies need to be touched all the time. If this one had a mum, she would be snuggled in her arms, enjoying the warmth of her body, and the sound of her coos, rather than lying motionless in a cot for most of the day. As well kept as an orphanage might be, nothing can replace a mother's embrace.'

It would be another eight years before Thomas would experience fatherhood for himself, but it was at that point that he began to understand the importance of touch and parental intimacy in a baby's life and development. The purpose of his journey was becoming clear. He began to learn how children's lives were changed as they were accepted into foster families as a result of Care for Children's work with the Chinese government.

He learned of Li Li, born with a hole in her heart. The condition made her so weak that she couldn't even sit up. She spent most of her time lying in her cot in an orphanage. It became clear that she urgently needed corrective surgery, but doctors feared that she would not survive the operation. It was decided to place her with a local family to see if her condition might improve.

Several months later, Li Li returned to the hospital for a check-up. The doctors were amazed to see a total transformation. She was radiant and animated. She wore a pretty dress and her hair, now grown long, had been beaded by her foster mum. Everyone was delighted, as it seemed as though she would be well enough for surgery. However, when the doctor returned from his room following her check-up, he was clearly moved with emotion.

'Li Li no longer needs surgery,' he said. 'Her heart has healed itself!' It was a story that caught the imagination of the press, the story of a mother's love that literally healed a little girl's broken heart.

Robert Glover OBE, Executive Director of Care for Children, believes this was a miracle and looks back on it as a significant moment in the success of the work in China. This was God at work in a new way.

As the work of Care for Children rolled out nationally in China, Thomas moved to Beijing. But Rachel was constantly on his mind. He knew that, if they were to have a future together, he would have to move back to Norwich in the UK where she studied midwifery at the University of East Anglia.

'I was confused and upset,' he said. 'I had come from Birmingham to Pakistan to London to Shanghai to Beijing and I was thinking, "What's next? Washington? Tokyo?" I honestly didn't know. But Norwich? What a comedown! As a young guy I had built up a bit of an identity as an international man of mystery, if you like.' Going back to a town like Norwich would be an assault on his identity.

'Then I made the great discovery,' he said, 'that my identity was in Jesus and not in the city, the country or the community in which I lived. Whatever He wanted, wherever He wanted me to go, that was fine by me.' The journey was now established and gained new momentum as Thomas began to understand his identity in God and the purpose to which he had been called.

So Thomas returned to the UK in 2007, five years after travelling to China, and ten months later he and Rachel were married. Rachel completed her degree in midwifery and found work straight away. They bought an apartment. 'It was exactly what we were looking for,' he said. 'There are times when it just seems likes God's joy to look after us. Eugene Peterson wrote that the kingdom of God is "relentlessly personal".[4] That's stuck with me over the years, that God is relentlessly personal, that He looks out for us even in small details.' That assurance buoyed Thomas and Rachel through their four years in Norwich and went as a beacon before them to Chiang Mai on 1 June 2012.

Moving to Thailand was something of a homecoming for Thomas, as his mother and father had lived there for nine years. They had left Abbottabad following a terrible massacre at the Murree Christian

School. This was the school that Thomas had attended and where his father had been chairman of the Parents' Association.

The attack on the school had been brutal and had occurred just after the 11 a.m. break on 6 August 2002. Four gunmen, cleanly shaven and in Western clothes, approached the school. One of them pulled a Kalashnikov assault rifle from a gym bag and shot the guard and a bystander. In pairs they searched the campus, killing at random. Firing indiscriminately, they shot the school cook and carpenter who were hiding in the trees. Six nationals in all were slaughtered. The school administrator heard them call 'God is great'.

Mercifully, they failed to break down the reinforced doors which had been locked to protect the 100 children and staff members. Thomas's brother, Bryn, had been hiding behind a couch in the staff room. 'As I did so,' he said, 'the events of my life flashed before my eyes.' David Wood, a teacher from Scotland, lay on the floor of his classroom with a student and prayed during the assault, which lasted ten to fifteen minutes. 'It was a miracle,' he said, 'that none of the children were killed.'[5]

As the situation continued to worsen in Pakistan, Thomas's parents moved to Thailand, where they continued their missionary work.

Now based in Chiang Mai, Thomas is the South East Asian Project manager for Care for Children.

'We only work with governments and when invited to do so,' he said. 'Recently we have completed a very successful pilot project in Chiang Mai where 60 children have been placed in families and a new agreement with the Department of Children and Youth will see the project rolled out nationally so that thousands currently living in institutions may experience the love of a mother or father for the first time. And as God opens doors for us to work with governments,' he said, 'so there is opportunity for the local church to respond with a clear mandate to care for orphans. The success of the Thailand project is leading to new opportunities in the ASEAN countries such as Vietnam, Myanmar, Cambodia and Malaysia.

'Care for Children has now helped to place 250,000 orphans in China into families,' he said. 'Goodness knows what would have happened to them if they'd grown up in institutions. We are seeing them placed into safe families where fathers can redeem them and mothers love them.

'Imagine, imagine, if you want to think of something extraordinary,' he said. 'What if the fathers of this world turned their hearts to their children? That would create something extraordinary. Something that seems so ordinary, so simple, almost too basic would produce the most extraordinary result.'

'What drives you, what keeps you going?' I asked.

'It's the idea that God created family to care for children. And by that I mean a man and a woman married and able to have children either biologically or by fostering and adoption. It's almost the cornerstone of life, as we know it. Apart from sin, if you boil down the world's problems to their essence, what is the problem with the world today? What's the problem? Men not being good husbands or fathers. I have this passion to see nations changed through that understanding. The very last verse of the Old Testament talks about turning the hearts of fathers to their children.[6] Then if you look at the opening chapter of the book of Luke, it speaks of John the Baptist coming in the spirit of Elijah to turn the hearts of fathers to their children.'[7]

'How do you think God has changed your life now, compared to where you might have been if you were not a Christian?' I asked.

'I have a passion for the simple things that God has designed and yet which are so profound,' he said, 'such as family. As a young Christian, I was quite liberal in my theology. But as I've gained a better knowledge of the Bible, I've developed a deeper understanding of the simple principles that God has established. Sometimes ordinary people doing extraordinary things are ordinary people trusting and following God in a very simple way. There's nothing complicated about it. It has nothing to do with ability but availability.

'That way of thinking has totally shaped my life as a husband and father,' he said. 'I can't be good as God intended at either unless I'm focused on Jesus. In the UK and here in Thailand I see communities devastated by sexual sin, poor fathers and poor husbands who don't understand what it is to be married and committed and to nurture children. I believe the Bible has the blueprint for family life as God intends it to be.

'I have no wish to trivialize faith,' he said. 'I know how complex and difficult faith can be at times. Yet working through and clinging to faith can be "the very stuff of life", to adapt a phrase from Jennifer Worth.[8] As I reflected on the theme of your book, *Nine Minutes Past Midnight*, about living extraordinary lives for God, it struck me how extraordinary it would be if, indeed, Thailand's fathers turned their hearts to their children. The nation would be transformed! And yet, how simple that is . . . surely one of the very core elements of life, as critical to our sustenance as food and water, to be cared for by loving mothers and fathers. I would say that it is in believing in God's created order, and trusting in His will, both collectively and individually, that creates extraordinary lives. We are the "ordinary", God is the "extra".'

Thomas shared with me some remarkable stories of children's lives that have been changed irrevocably:

Xiao Long is a 12-year-old boy who has now lived with his foster family for seven years. When first placed with his family, he couldn't walk or talk and was thought to have learning difficulties. Now he speaks well, attends the local school and has very few learning difficulties. Family life has brought out his passion for art.

Tian Tian was placed into a foster family when she was 4 months old. She'd had a traumatic start in life, born with congenital heart disease and bow legs. Her behaviour was often disturbing and irritating. She had sleep problems and cried a lot during the night, but her foster parents and grandparents remained remarkably patient and committed. She has now developed into a beautiful 4-year-old girl. Her heart has healed itself without medical treatment, and her bow legs were corrected. She is secure, confident, and well-liked. Whenever her little friends visit, she takes out all her toys and shares them with the other children.

When asked what the key was to making the miracle happen, Tian's foster father concluded: 'Having a loving and committed heart, accepting her unconditionally, making her feel loved, and trying our best to meet her physical and emotional needs whenever possible.'

Recently Rob Glover, Executive Director of Care for Children, went to visit a small boy and his foster family. The boy believed that Robert had come to take him back to the orphanage and was ready to fight to stay with his new parents.

In 2013 there were reckoned to be eight million children growing up in institutions around the world. There were seventy-one million orphans in Asian countries alone, more than the populations of Thailand, of the UK or of California and Texas combined.[9] These were only three of those children.

Thomas's 6-year-old friend Noo Lek remains in the orphanage, patiently waiting for an earthly father to accept him.

'That thought just about breaks my heart,' said Thomas. 'I can barely bring myself to imagine my own son having to fight through his early life without me. But there is hope. I pray that I, together with all fathers, will embrace compassion so strong, and respond to grace so audacious, that we reflect our heavenly Father's own heart, and open our eyes to see the orphans among us.'

Preface to Chapter 9

The path was narrow and often steep.
It took him to the high country through ravines
And across grassy plains.
Rocks and fallen trees blocked his way.
Some were monstrous,
Causing him to detour into unknown territory.

His shadow walked before him,
But sometimes it followed,
Trusting his resolve to find the way.
He saw dead men walk and good men fall,
He saw evil men prosper,
For a season.

Some gave him shelter
Others cast him out.
He was often thirsty and hungry
But there was always provision.
He found warmth in purpose.
And strength in abandonment.

Though often in peril,
He pressed on
To find the one for whom he searched.
But he was in error,
For that one walked beside him always.
He had only to take His hand.

E.F.C. 'Pilgrim', 2013

9

Twice Blessed

Yet, my brothers, I do not consider myself to have 'arrived', spiritually, nor do I consider myself already perfect. But I keep going on, grasping ever more firmly that purpose for which Christ grasped me. My brothers, I do not consider myself to have fully grasped it even now. But I do concentrate on this: I leave the past behind and with hands outstretched to whatever lies ahead I go straight for the goal – my reward the honour of being called by God in Christ.

(Phil. 3:12–14, PHILLIPS)

I have long regarded myself as a pilgrim walking the path that God has set before me. As a child I listened with awe as my teacher read from Bunyan's *Pilgrim's Progress*, but as much as I would have liked to travel one of the pilgrim ways such as the Camino de Santiago, this has not been my experience. Yet I find that life is a spiritual pilgrimage and now and again I meet other Pellegrinos on the way.[1] One such man is Gordon Stokes.

'I was just 6 or 7 when a kindly old man, a clergyman in Sunday school, told me about Jesus.

'"Gordon," he said, "I want you to know for the rest of your life that God really loves you and that He'll watch over you." I've invested so much of my time and energy into medicine, Ern, that other things have taken a bit of a back seat. But as I grow older, I long for a closer walk with God.'

Emeritus Professor Gordon Stokes reclined in what was clearly his favourite chair. He had just returned from a morning of golf and was relaxed and at ease. Silver hair brushed carefully back, checked shirt, casual trousers and loafers, he was a picture of casual elegance. We sat eye to eye in the privacy of his home on the Northern Beaches peninsula of Sydney, just a short stroll from beautiful Newport Beach. A world authority on the management of high blood pressure, Gordon reflected on a life of academic medicine, of serving others, and on the words of his Sunday school teacher so many years ago which had proven to be prophetic.

I had been aware that Gordon and his wife, Toni, had survived a near tragedy in the UK some years earlier in extraordinary circumstances, but little did I know that God had saved him twice from near-certain death.

'Toni and I were driving on the A1 from Sunderland to York,' he said. 'It was a busy road, a little wet and the traffic was moving at around 70 mph. We were in a small rental car, a Peugeot, beetling along and I was feeling quite uncomfortable. The flow of traffic was so fast that, as much as I tried, I found it impossible to move across to a slower lane.'

Then all of a sudden the traffic in front slowed rapidly. Gordon hit the brakes but there was no response. The car just kept going. 'I must be in a skid,' he thought, realizing that he had completely lost control. The car veered off to the left across a busy lane of heavy, lumbering trucks.

'Then just at that moment,' he said, 'I had the feeling that a pair of arms came down through the top of the car and took hold of the steering wheel. It all happened very quickly. I'd been trying to decelerate and I'd tried the brakes. It seemed to me that the car veered purposefully through two, maybe three lanes of busy traffic into the outer lane, still at speed. It rocketed for 70 metres along the barrier fence and was badly damaged. We were severely shaken. A road worker, who saw it all happen, scrambled down the bank to check that we were OK.'

The police arrived to find Gordon staring at the left front wheel, which was just a smouldering remnant. There had been a blowout. The hub was OK, but the tyre had disintegrated.

'Don't even try to explain,' said the police, 'we are happy just to see you both alive.' Gordon and Toni returned the car to the rental yard and watched the agent's face pale as he inspected the wreck.

'They gave us a much nicer car,' he said.

Under normal circumstances a left front tyre blowout would cause a car to swerve to the left. However, Gordon had braked hard and this would cause the car to swerve to the right and possibly cartwheel. The sensation of the controlling arms was itself remarkable. But even more so, the overwhelming sense of the presence of God and of His protection as the car passed safely across lanes of heavy traffic at speed.

'It was then,' said Gordon, 'that I began to understand that somebody up there really does care for me and mine. As the man had said so many years ago, "God loves you, Gordon, and He'll watch over you."'

But there was another occasion when God intervened to save Gordon's life. It occurred in 1980 in a remote refugee camp on the border of Laos and Thailand.

'There had been a call to Australian doctors,' he said, 'which came directly to me as chairman of the Christian Medical and Dental Fellowship.

'Laotian refugees pursued by communist troops had been flooding into refugee camps along the Mekong on the Thai Laotian border.' The total number of Hmong refugees in Thai camps by March 1980 was 48,937 with 998 new arrivals that month alone. The situation was dire. Doctors were desperately needed.[2]

'I was 45 at the time,' he said, 'and working as a specialist physician at Sydney hospital. Here was I, urging young doctors to go and assist in this desperate situation. It was painted more desperately than any other humanitarian crisis that I can remember before or since. "Maybe I should go myself," I thought.'

Gordon and Toni prayed for guidance and finally reached the conclusion that, indeed, he should go. 'When I arrived,' he said, 'I found the worst possible situation imaginable. Communist forces were chasing the hill tribes that had been infiltrated by the CIA and had taken arms against the lowland Laotians. They had pursued them right down to the border. But the Thais would not accept them. In one camp alone, Sob Twang, there were 10,000 refugees.'

The only medical services available were conducted from a small Christian clinic called Maejarim established by Dr Chris Maddox and his wife, Catherine. Chris and Catherine were the only doctors. A third was on leave to improve his language skills and Gordon's presence was much appreciated. 'I was working extremely hard but enjoying it,' he said. 'There were massive outpatient loads but I managed with the help of hill tribes people as interpreters.' Chris worked full-time in the detox unit. The only chance that these people had was for expatriation to France, the United States, or maybe Australia. But they had to be clean of drugs. 'This was right in the opium triangle,' he said, 'and it would only require a grandfather to test positive for the family to be denied refugee status. I looked after the village Thais and the camp with Catherine Maddox, a remarkably young 70-year-old.'

One morning, Gordon had a call from Catherine to come down to the outpatient clinic to see a patient urgently. He thought this unusual, as she was often there tending to patients well ahead of him. But to his dismay, he soon discovered that she was the patient.

'I think something's wrong with me,' she said, 'and I would like you to examine me!'

Gordon discovered a hard palpable abdominal mass. 'It felt malignant, possibly lymphoma,' he said, 'and I made urgent arrangements to send her for biopsy.'[3]

It was at that time that Gordon himself became ill. 'I developed a high temperature and was so weak that I was unable to work,' he said. I would retire to my cabin, douse myself with water and take lashings of paracetamol[4] to try to keep the fever down. Every day the outdoor temperature was 104 degrees Fahrenheit [40 degrees Centigrade] and that was my body temperature also. I was afraid that I would become delirious. I would lie there wondering what was wrong with me. It wasn't viral, I reasoned, and it wasn't the season for malaria. Then I noticed that I had a huge spleen. It had to be dengue or typhoid. Finally I determined that it wasn't dengue as there were no mosquitoes around. It must be typhoid. I had suspected the diagnosis in many of the people that I'd seen in the clinic who had subsequently died.'

Gordon consulted Chris. 'I think I've got typhoid,' he said.

'Yes, I agree,' said Chris. 'We should get you to medical care as soon as possible.' But there was a problem. That very night a major fire at Nan, the closest town, had destroyed all communications.

Chris got on the pedal radio and was able to contact an airline. They would divert a plane to Nan to transport Gordon to Bangkok. 'The plane will be here at 9 a.m.,' said Chris. In the interim the team gathered around Gordon to pray. There was a young engineer and his wife; a schoolteacher; and Chris. 'I was too weak to pray myself,' said Gordon.

At Bangkok the question arose as to whether Gordon should remain in Thailand for treatment or try to make it back to Sydney. 'I should really go home,' he decided.

'So they took me to the airport. I sat in the waiting room feeling terrible and all of a sudden the room went green and very, very foggy. "I don't think I'm too good," I said to those with me. "Maybe I should stay here in Bangkok." But an airport official had other ideas. "What are you doing?" he shouted. "Get on the plane . . . now!" I was half-standing and he bundled me into the stream of boarding passengers.'

Gordon staggered into the plane and slumped into his seat. Turning to the man next to him he apologized profusely.

'I'm sorry,' he said 'but I'm not well. I hope I'm not going to be a burden to you on the way home.'

'I travel this route all the time,' said the man. 'It would be unusual to have someone completely well sitting next to me.' The man had a great sense of humour and buoyed Gordon's spirits all the way back to Sydney.

At Sydney Airport there was an ambulance waiting. 'They took me straight to the Royal North Shore Hospital where the diagnosis of typhoid fever was confirmed. Even the students could see my rose spots,' he said.[5] Gordon had commenced a course of chloramphenicol before leaving Bangkok and the therapy was continued for another ten days. But it took six months for him to fully recover.

Normally a passenger as ill as Gordon would have been prevented from flying, but on this occasion the outspoken attendant, completely unknown to Gordon, had forcibly boarded him onto the plane. And the prayer of his friends had brought an assurance and a presence that only God could provide, which carried him safely all the way home to Sydney and waiting medical assistance.

Gordon's overriding memory of the whole experience was the time spent with the small faithful group gathered around him to pray at the border camp. 'During that time,' he said, 'I was aware of God's presence, of Him being right there with me. Not in a tangible way but I knew that He was there and that He cared. I had been thinking that I might even die there. But that time of prayer made a huge difference to my state of mind.'

As Gordon spoke I was reminded of an occasion in our Penrith rooms just twelve months earlier. I had been about to perform a cardiac stress test on a middle-aged man, a local pastor.

'You know I had a heart attack two weeks ago?' he said.

'Yes,' I replied, 'I'm aware of that.'

'I was in the emergency room at Nepean Hospital,' he continued. 'Jesus came to me and put His arms around me. You know, doctor,' he said, 'I now *know* Him in whom I once only believed. I said to the cardiologist in the ER, "I don't care, doctor, if I die tonight. Jesus is with me."'

My friend Paul, a family doctor, once said that it's not until we have nothing left but Christ that we realize that Christ is enough. When all our supports are stripped away, when we find ourselves in deep water, when oceans roar, it is then that we find that Christ and only Christ is sufficient for our needs. The night that my own father died, I sat and watched over him. He was deeply unconscious. The nurse came to wash him. 'Don't bother leaving,' she said, 'I'll only be a moment.' She undressed him and I was somewhat embarrassed to witness his nakedness. But I realized again that we enter this world with nothing and we leave with nothing. My father left that room the next morning at 7 a.m. with Jesus.

Gordon has also experienced God's intervention in his practice of medicine.

'I must tell you something remarkable,' he said. 'This concerns a patient whom I initially saw as a little girl of 11. She was a dear child. Kerry was her name. She had been admitted to the Children's Hospital with malignant hypertension in status epilepticus. Her blood pressure was 260/150.[6] I was just back from the UK having trained in all the new methods of treating and understanding blood pressure. The people at the Children's Hospital had asked me to see her as they thought that I might have some new ideas. I met with her mother who was a wonderful Christian lady, a devout Catholic. She had been told that Kerry would be unlikely to survive the week. I examined Kerry and agreed. There was no obvious underlying cause for her blood pressure but she had a terrible prognosis. I thought she would surely die.

'We started her on medication and at one stage had her on forty tablets per day. Somehow we got her to the end of the month. Gradually her blood pressure began to fall and she stopped having epileptic fits. Finally we got her to a stage where she was able to go home. Her blood pressure was down to 150/100, not ideal by a long shot, but much better.'

Gordon continued to see Kerry over the years and was able to start her on the new ACE inhibitor therapy.[7] 'Eventually she married,' said Gordon. 'I told her that she must not become pregnant under any circumstances, as this would be disastrous for her blood pressure. But she did. She had a horrendous pregnancy with pre-eclampsia.[8] Somehow both she and the baby survived. Then she became pregnant again and this time had a little girl with eventration of the diaphragm.[9] The baby was operated on postnatally and survived. Some years later that same little girl won the state junior sprint championship. I believe that her healing and the events that followed were as a result of the prayer of her godly mother.'

It was late in the afternoon and time to move on, but Gordon continued. 'I've had a conventional evangelical background,' he said. 'Can't tell you a time when I wasn't a believer.' 'Conventional maybe,' I thought, 'but you've experienced the presence of God in a remarkable way. On two occasions God has intervened to rescue you under extraordinary circumstances.'

Gordon shared his love for the Scriptures, of how they had been his guide and companion and how they had served as a benchmark for his journey over a lifetime. In particular he loved the Gospel of John, especially chapters 14 and 15 which express Christ's love for us as individuals. These were deeply meaningful to him.

I rose to go but there was a call on the kitchen phone. It was Gordon's son, Rob. I knew that Rob was a minister in the New South Wales State Government. I was also aware that he and his family were devout Christians. He had called to discuss a forthcoming pre-election event. It was clear from the very manner in which Gordon spoke that the love of Christ, with which he was so familiar, found expression in his love for family members.

As I drove home to the hills north-west of Sydney that afternoon, I recalled how Gordon had taken young Kerry's hand and led her from the tempest of malignant hypertension. So God had taken his hand and rescued him in perilous times. And his journey would continue. Each day there would be new discoveries, new challenges to consider, and new dimensions to explore. There would be bends in the road, highways and byways, but his destination was guaranteed.

For now we see in a mirror, dimly, but then face to face.

(1 Cor. 13:12a)

Authors' note

In the NSW state elections of March 2015, the Liberal government was returned under Premier Mike Baird. Rob Stokes was reappointed as Member for Pittwater and made Minister for Planning.

Part III

Stepping Out

Preface to Chapter 10

The sun was breaking over Smith's Lake as I paddled east towards
Sandbar Beach. There were no waves, not a ripple. And there was no
sound except for the soft stroke of the paddle and the muffled roar of
breakers ahead through the rising mist.

This was my quiet place,[1] somewhere to be alone, somewhere to
listen to God's voice. The tiny shell of the kayak suspended between
water and the heavens symbolized my utter dependence as I sat cradled at the interface.

We live at that interface. Doctors understand that wellbeing is a
narrow interface between health and disease. There are fine tolerances
of blood pressure, temperature, electrolyte levels and a host of other
factors that must be maintained. When mechanisms fail, illness occurs and a doctor must intervene. The interface is the tightrope of
safety that we walk between health and disease, life and death.

It is also a line drawn between the known and the unknown, light
and darkness, knowledge and ignorance, peace and fear, success and
failure.

But the interface is often a line of least resistance. It is a place where
men and women have no need to delve beyond themselves but to be
drawn along by the rhythm of life. There is room to move . . . but not
to grow. Not to explore new dimensions.

But there may come a time when we are required to step out into
unexplored territory. There may be risk. There may be danger. But if
we are prepared to accept God's invitation, to take His hand, to step
out in faith, the limits of what might be achieved are unbounded.

As Canon Andrew White, 'Vicar of Baghdad' walked the streets of
London with his great mentor, Donald, Lord Coggan, the Archbishop
gripped him by the arm.

'You're a young curate,' he said. 'I want to give you just two words . . .
Take risks.'[2]

10

Stepping Out – The Interface

When you're at the end of your rope, tie a knot and hold on.

Theodore Roosevelt

Sunday, 23 June 2013, Nik Wallenda stepped into history. In twenty-two minutes and fifty-four seconds he became the first man to walk across the Grand Canyon on a rope. And he did so without a safety harness. The event, which had been months in the planning, was broadcast live around the world on the Discovery Channel. People watched in awe as he braced himself against sudden gusts of wind of up to thirty-six miles per hour. His small form was almost visually lost, suspended 457 metres above the Little Colorado River.[1]

The event was visually stunning. But even more breathtaking was his dialogue with God as he walked.

'There's a view there, buddy. Praise God, this is awesome! Thank you, Jesus, for this beautiful view.' Just minutes prior to stepping onto the 5 centimetre cable he had prayed with his wife and family for God's protection.[2]

There are times when God calls us to step out. The view is stunning but the risk may be perilous. What if I fall? There is no safety net. Who will catch me? Will I plummet into oblivion or will I stand tall in the certainty that God has called me to something special that cannot fail?

***

For as long as he can remember, my friend Shane has had two ambitions in life, one to fly helicopters, the other to be a doctor. Now he has the best of both worlds. As a critical care specialist with training in emergency medicine and anaesthesiology, he spends much of his time as a member of a helicopter emergency medical crew.

Over a fourteen-year period he has attended more than one thousand helicopter retrievals bringing critically ill patients from disaster scenes back to the emergency rooms of major teaching hospitals. Many lives have been saved. When disaster strikes, Shane is the man that you want by your side.

I recently spoke with Shane in his home, north-west of Sydney. He sat back and relaxed, suitably attired in North Face fatigues, pointing out the features of a model helicopter that he had bought at auction.

'It's a Bell 412,' he said. 'The first helicopter that I rode in.'

It sat precariously balanced on top of his television set. 'Ironic,' I thought.

'Have there been many times when you've had to step out in faith?' I asked.

'That's part of my job,' he said. 'It's an everyday event with me now.'

He kicked off his shoes. 'There was a situation with a little girl called Abbey. Dad was at home, sick. Mum had put Abbey in the bath and left her alone for a few seconds while she attended to something boiling over on the kitchen stove. She returned to find that Abbey had slipped under the water and was not breathing. She lost the plot completely, grabbed the unconscious girl and ran screaming from the house. It was her worst nightmare come true.

'The next-door neighbour, hearing the commotion, ran to help. At the same time an ambulance just happened to be passing by with two level five paramedics on board.[3] They rushed the little girl into the back of the ambulance and commenced CPR.[4] We had received the code: 'Paediatric Drowning' and initiated emergency procedures. Flying to the scene we landed next to the ambulance and jumped into the back. Abbey was wet and slippery from the soap and bath water and quite blue by this stage with agonal respirations.[5] We couldn't get a vein so we tried bone injections into the tibia of each leg, but they didn't work. "God," I said, "I really want this child to live!"'

Eventually Shane managed to cannulate a vein and gave adrenaline. 'Abbey had one heartbeat per minute,' he said. 'She was essentially flat-line and had dilated pupils.

'We intubated her, kept the adrenaline running and went by road, lights and sirens to the Children's Hospital. She remained in the ICU for five days but made a remarkable complete recovery. Man, I recognized that as resurrection.'

A year later, on her second birthday, Abbey's mother brought her back to say thank you. She was completely normal. 'We put her photo on our Facebook and were amazed at the number of people that responded telling us how we had helped their children also.'

But not all accidents are as they seem. A few years back, Shane was summoned to a car accident south of Sydney. It was just before Christmas and a family sedan had rolled when the driver took a corner at excessive speed, throwing her from the car onto the road. She was a large woman weighing 24 stone (150 kg) and the force of the impact had broken the seat belt. The pilot managed to land the helicopter one block from the accident and Shane and the team were ferried by police to the scene of the tragedy. The police driver was pale and visibly distressed. He was shaking.

'Doc,' he said, 'I've never seen anything like it! Never seen such an accident. People are lying dead on the road and there are body parts everywhere.'

Arriving at the scene Shane quickly surveyed the situation. The driver was indeed unconscious on the road but she was OK with no critical injuries. As far as the body parts were concerned, the driver had been returning from her Christmas shopping. She had taken delivery of a 20 kg bag of meat off-cuts and bones for her dog. And there they were, littered as far as the eye could see.

But then there was the story of Danny, a 7-year-old boy. Danny was with friends at a school camp at a beach resort south of Sydney. He had been experiencing increasing symptoms of asthma during the morning. And then at lunchtime one of his mates gave him a peanut butter sandwich. 'Goodness knows why!' said Shane.

'Danny was highly allergic to peanuts and went straight into anaphylactic shock. He was unable to breathe and collapsed unconscious.

'The call came in to headquarters and we set out. The weather was dreadful. Heading south we had to skirt around a severe thunderstorm. The journey took fourteen minutes but seemed so much longer. During this time a road ambulance crew had been called down to the beach nearby on an emergency call that had proven to be a hoax.[6] They happened to be driving back past the camp when they also received the call and diverted. They found Danny blue and unconscious. His chest was frozen. He had no air intake at all. Five milligrams of intravenous adrenaline had no impact whatever.[7]

'We arrived to find Danny near death. We gave him more intravenous adrenaline and an adult dose of salbutamol. We anaesthetized him, put in an endotracheal tube and ran in our entire stock of adrenaline from the helicopter, 14 mg in all! I was shaking with the stress of it.

'We set out for hospital and arrived to find thirty-four doctors waiting in the ER. There were specialist paediatricians, anaesthesiologists, intensive care specialists and residency staff. But by this time Danny was responding. The adrenaline had done its work and he was getting good air entry.'

'What were you worried about?' asked one of the ER doctors with a wry smile.

'We took that as a compliment.'

Danny made a full recovery and was soon discharged from hospital. The media report made such an impact on the public that it was broadcast as a re-enactment on national television. At age 10, Danny was selected to attend a high school for gifted children. 'You know, said Shane, 'that really does excite me.'

A child of the 60s, Shane was born of teenage parents who moved house several times, making it difficult to engage with friends or settle into school. For a number of years his family lived in a caravan on the bushy outskirts of north-western Sydney, further isolating him from friends and social activities. He contented himself breeding ducks and geese and, in his spare time, worked in a nearby store raising money to pay for his first car. 'A 1976 HX Holden Kingwood, metallic gold,' he said with a faraway look in his eye.

Ill health plagued his childhood. At 9 years of age he had a major fall resulting in a chronic back injury, which excluded him from school sport. A bout of meningitis resulted in chronic headache and sleep disturbance.[8] He also suffered from food intolerance, which remained undiagnosed for years, expressing itself daily as abdominal pain and other unpleasant symptoms. Migraine was also a problem. But looking back on that time allows him to identify with people in need in his present occupation.

'My own struggles have given me enormous empathy for the patients that I see.'

A bright boy, Shane topped his first year at high school. From that point on he set his mind towards university. By year twelve he had it all worked out. Plan A was to be a doctor and plan B a helicopter pilot with the Australian Defence Force. He knew that he would need a mark of 430 plus in the final exams to qualify for medicine at the Sydney universities. This he would likely achieve but it was not guaranteed. The new medical school at Newcastle accepted students after successful interviews and a satisfactory guestimate of their final year mark. Shane applied. He interviewed well but an invitation was not forthcoming. The mark submitted by his acting headmaster was for the wrong student and was too low. Invitations had already been issued to successful candidates. He would not be accepted.

Shane's world fell apart. He was unwell, he was isolated from friends and his plans to study medicine at Newcastle had foundered on a clerical error. The future looked bleak. There seemed little to live or hope for. In the bush land near his home he sat on a rock contemplating his future.

The next afternoon on his way home from school he stood on the kerb watching the cars speed by, considering the finality of his next move. His headmaster had failed him. His parents and friends had let him down. Even God had failed him. But just then God intervened in a most unusual and unexpected way.

A firm hand seized him by the arm and an unfamiliar voice rang out: 'Don't worry, son, you're going to be a doctor one day.' Shane spun around to find himself transfixed by the stare of a man whose eyes were on fire. He had observed this man each day on his way home from school. He generally had a bottle in a brown paper bag and Shane recognized him as a local alcoholic. Having spoken, the man released his grip, turned and shuffled off down the street.

'Ern, that really shook me up,' he said. 'It was bizarre.'

Shane returned to his rock in the bush, this time with his school Bible. Opening it at random he looked for something, anything that might help to lift his spirits. It fell open to the first chapter of Ecclesiastes.

'Meaningless! Meaningless!' says the Teacher.

(NIVUK)[9]

'That was it. That was the turning point,' he said. 'God was trying very hard to get my attention and this time it worked.'

'You found *those words* encouraging?'

'Yes, here was I completely miserable and without hope and all those years ago someone else who was a king, no less, and who had everything, had gone through the very experience that I had. I was hooked and I read the whole thing.'

And in the final chapter he read:

Remember him [your Creator] – before the silver cord is severed,
    and the golden bowl is broken;
before the pitcher is shattered at the spring,
    and the wheel is broken at the well,
and the dust returns to the ground it came from,
    and the spirit returns to God who gave it.

(Eccl. 12:6,7, NIVUK)

'There must be *so* much more to this life,' he thought.

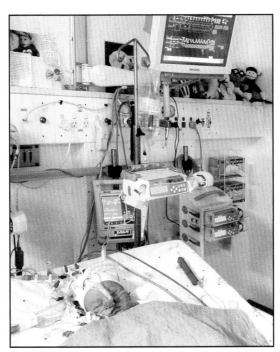

Elliott in the Neonatal Intensive Care Unit, 2014.
See chapter 1.

Elliott 'The Brave', August 2016.

Dr Grace Warren and Dr Jo Anne Ader.
See chapter 3.

Revd Paul Dale receiving his doctorate at Oxford.
See chapter 7.

Thomas with a foster family in Northern Thailand.
See chapter 8.
© Care for Children. Used with permission.

Clinical Professor Emeritus Gordon Stokes.
See chapter 9.

Lieutenant General Ajai Masih (Retd).
See chapter 12.

Gospel Chapel, Mymensingh.
See chapter 13.

Gladys Staines with the author, 2012.
See chapter 14.

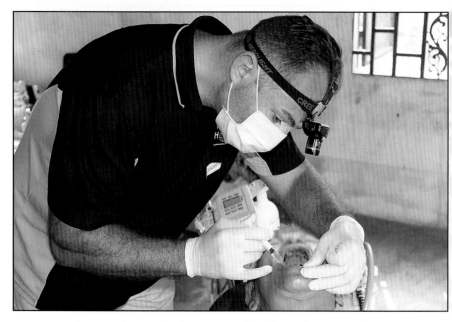

Jason treating a patient in a remote village in North West Cambodia.
See chapter 15.

Borin interpreting for the author in Phnom Penh.
See chapter 16.

The author with his son Sam in Phnom Penh.
See chapter 17.

An exhibit in the War Remnants Museum,
Ho Chi Minh City, 2014.

Pastor Vijay in Cambodia.
See chapter 18.

Pastors Miranda Riddington and Andrew Chan in the chapel,
Kerobokan Gaol, Bali. 'When Iron Gates Yield.'
See chapter 21.

It would not be until sometime later that Shane accepted Jesus as his Saviour. But from that point on he found hope and direction in the presence of a loving God who had a plan and purpose for his life.

'A lot of doctors rubbish Christianity as complete fantasy,' he said. 'But I know that in my faith I find peace and calmness of mind in the most torrid situations. That is my life, Ern. That is what I do. I've looked at doing other things but I know that this is what He's called me to. And I can see now how He's allowing me to achieve His purpose.

'Ecclesiastes confirms to me that it's still the same way now that it was 2,500 years ago. It's the same humanity, the same struggle, the same God. My own difficulties have allowed me to find strength and peace in God and given me enormous empathy for my patients.

'When you take that call,' he said, 'you never quite know what challenge lies before you. There are hoax calls, of course, but most are legitimate. I have seen experienced doctors and paramedics freeze when a call comes in for a child drowning or major car accident. You never know how each scenario will impact on you personally. That drowning child may remind you of one of your own kids or that of a friend.'

'So how do *you* deal with that?' I said. 'How do you prepare yourself?'

'I feel God's presence as a calmness that comes upon me in the most extreme situations,' he said, 'when I know that my intervention is critical. One morning I came across a major car accident on the M7 on the way to work. I called in a helicopter and was able to treat the woman who had been thrown from the car, rescue the two kids who were trapped upside down in the vehicle and to calm everyone down at the scene. I felt God's presence in that situation. I've also found when I'm pushed to extremes God prompts me on what to do and what not to do.'

Shane's role is critical to the survival of hundreds of people. In the book of Ecclesiastes he finds that he is not alone in going through deep waters. Others have been there before him. His faith allows him to respond in the sure knowledge that God will provide all the resources and support that he needs to achieve his task.

He is also well aware of the delayed impact of stress on himself and his fellow workers.

Dr Bill Nash was a US Marine Corps psychiatrist during the battle against insurgents in Fallujah in Iraq in 2004. He is now retired from the army but remains one of the leading researchers on the effects of trauma on medics in the military. He was recently interviewed by Sally Sara on the ABC's *Foreign Correspondent* programme.

'I found that the medics,' he said, 'were more likely to be treated for post-traumatic stress disorder than the marines who were the trigger pullers and I realized, in treating some of them, that their trauma was in failing to save lives . . . What bothered them,' he said, 'was when they failed to do something that they counted on themselves to do, when they failed to protect their buddy, failed to keep someone alive. The medical people were hugely vulnerable to this.'[10]

'That's right,' said Shane, 'we don't always win. We were called out in the helicopter to a 2-year-old who had been run over by a 60-ton excavator. There was absolutely nothing we could do to save that child. We comforted and counselled the family as best we could.

'There is a belief among people in my line of work,' he said, 'that when your time's up, your time's up, and to some extent that thought absolves us from the guilt of not being able to help. But I have found that I can always bring something positive to a situation like that. I can bring love and I can bring acceptance to the families and friends involved.'

Shane has found that in times of stress the empowering presence of God's Holy Spirit and His enduring grace buoy him up and provide him with all the resources, physical, mental and spiritual, that he needs. He has learned the truth of the verse:

Walk with me and work with me – watch how I do it. Learn the unforced rhythms of grace.

(Matt. 11:28,29, *The Message*)

Few of us will be called to step out into such challenging situations as Shane faces daily. Yet there will be times in our lives when we will be challenged to step out. There will be family, business and personal circumstances where we need to intervene, and this may require a mighty step of faith.

Stepping out in faith does not mean exposing ourselves to some unnecessary task with its associated risk, but responding to the call of God and knowing that He will lead us through. When Peter stepped out of the boat in the storm the other disciples remained within the safety of the boat. He alone sought permission from Jesus to step out and he alone received that permission.

On troubled waters Shane, like Peter, has learned to keep his eyes fixed on Jesus. In so doing, he will never be overwhelmed. His journey will lead him into the embrace and nurture of a loving God who will never fail him.

I sat editing this chapter in the lobby of the Hotel La Palma overlooking Lago Maggiore in Stresa, Italy. Shane's words from Ecclesiastes were loud in my spirit. Around me were all the elements of a beautiful and gracious lifestyle. People planned the day's activities, attendants in green vests delivered steaming espresso and aperitifs as the mist rising from the lake cradled the snow of the distant Alps. 'Vanity?' I thought. Maybe . . . but I have learned to value such experiences as I know that tomorrow life will return to what I would normally regard as routine. God gives us such moments, transient as they might be, as an insight into the richness that he is able to instil in our lives. What is essential is that we recognize them as such and not as an end in themselves.

One day the silver cord will be severed, the golden bowl broken. But before that time we have the standing invitation to embrace God and the unique plan that He has for our lives. That plan will challenge us every step of the way. It will lead us along paths of discovery that are extraordinary and wonderful. If we keep our eyes fixed on Him, we cannot fail.

Are you ready to step out of the boat and take His hand?

To him who is able to keep you from stumbling and to present you before his glorious presence without fault and with great joy – to the only God our Saviour be glory, majesty, power and authority, through Jesus Christ our Lord, before all ages, now and for evermore! Amen.

(Jude 1:24,25, NIVUK)

Preface to Chapter 11

> *At that time I will deal with all who oppressed you.*
> *I will rescue the lame; I will gather the exiles. I will*
> *give them praise and honour in every land where they*
> *have suffered shame.*
>
> *(Zephaniah 3:19, NIVUK)*

11

God's Liberator

When you make it across the river, look for a cross. The people there will take care of you and hide you from the secret police.

It was hard to imagine that the young man sitting opposite had already crossed the notorious Tumen River from North Korea into China three times, once in the bitter cold of winter. He was no more than 26 years old with a clear and open face, searching dark eyes and a maturity far beyond his years.

We sat drinking the local coffee in the shade of a giant banyan tree at the YWAM[1] base in Kailua Kona on the 'big island' of Hawaii. It was winter, but the warm Pacific breeze, and the friendly banter of students socializing as only students do, rendered the story that he was about to tell almost unimaginable.

'As a young man growing up in North Korea,' said Ha-neul,[2] 'I had never heard of Jesus, God or even organized religion. Kim Jong-il was god incarnate and to publicly hold him in lesser esteem meant arrest and possible execution by firing squad. My uncle had been executed for possessing a South Korean flag.[3]

'The conditions in North Korea were dreadful,' he continued. 'Between 1992 and 1994, 3.2 million died of starvation.

'I left school at 17 and was immediately pressed into military service. Normally this is for a period of ten years. But I was discharged unwell after three and a half years. The government then sent me to work in a factory, which manufactured electronic parts.

'My younger brother, totally disillusioned by the corrupt political system, did as many before him had done and escaped into China across the Tumen River seeking a better life. Escape was dangerous but doable.'

At that time the 'iron fence'[4] was not yet complete 'but there was always the risk of a bullet in the back,' he said. The BBC covered several instances of people dying as they fled.[5] The dangers were legion. Some crossed with illicit drugs. Others sold their bodies, anything to buy safe passage. But the reception on the far bank was always uncertain: sometimes, Chinese border guards disguised as civilians, other times criminals and sometimes, Korean secret police. People crossed through the icy waters naked, in the dark of night, clothes held above their heads. Bullet-ridden bodies were discovered encased in the ice of the frozen river only to wash away when the waters thawed.

'It was in the winter of 1998 that my brother escaped across the river into Mainland China,' he said. 'Ethnic Korean Christians occupied the first house that he approached. They also were refugees and had established an underground church. It was in this house that my brother received the gospel and became a Christian.' Here was spiritual freedom and the hope that his brother had never known. And in the summer, he returned home to bring the gospel to his family.

'The Korean secret police visited our home many times to discover where my brother had been but he told them that he had been visiting his grandmother who was not well. He told me about Jesus. But I didn't believe a word of it. After all, God didn't exist, right? I thought if there really was a god then Kim Jong-il would not be able to behave (do politics) as he did. To my brother's dismay, our entire family rejected the gospel.

'You have to understand,' said Ha-neul, pausing for a moment, 'that to become a Christian in North Korea is a crime against the government. It's a dangerous business. You will be arrested and imprisoned. The charge against you will be changed to murder, theft or conspiracy, and the penalty is death. Three people will each fire three bullets into you, two in the legs, one in the back, three in the heart and then three in the head. Executions are performed publicly as a warning to others.' He searched my face. Did I really understand what he was saying?

But Ha-neul had noticed that his brother had returned from China a different man. 'He would pray and sing songs and he cried a great deal. Finally, when he believed that he could do no more, he told our family that he was going back to China to study theology. My mother was greatly saddened, but she pleaded with me to go with him for my own safety.

'"There is freedom there," she said. At that time all of her younger brothers were political prisoners and one had been executed.'

So, in obedience to his mother, Ha-neul agreed to return to China with his younger brother. It was February and the days were freezing cold. They travelled first by train and then walked for two hours in the darkness to reach the river. It was midnight when they arrived. The river was frozen over and it was bitterly cold.

'There were soldiers patrolling with their guns,' he said, 'and I was so afraid.

'There was nothing we could do but pray to God. We prayed and we prayed. All we could do was to pray. Slowly, step by step we began our crossing, praying that the soldiers would not see us. God covered their eyes and we reached the other side safely. Praise God!'

Once across the river, Ha-neul and his brother found shelter with a family of Korean refugees. They were Christians and in that one-room house they cared for seven young North Koreans, all in their teens, who had also sought refuge there.

'We were to learn that the house functioned as an underground church,' said Ha-neul.

'But the Chinese police came to the house suspecting that we were illegal immigrants. They hammered on the door and shouted at us. I thought they would surely break it down. They would have sent us back to North Korea where we would have been arrested and likely faced a death sentence. I was terrified, and even though I was not a Christian at the time I prayed with my brother and the others that God would save us. I had no one else to lean on, and even though

I didn't believe in God I just prayed. Eventually, to my amazement and to the delight of us all, they went away and left us alone.'

Ha-neul began to read the Bible. He read John 18 about how Jesus had been arrested and beaten and how Peter had denied him three times. He remembered that when he was a boy in grade ten, his own father had abandoned him. 'Yet Jesus loved me so much,' he said, 'that He gave His life for me. When I realized that, I cried for three days. I repented and accepted Jesus into my heart and after a few more days the Holy Spirit came upon me and I began to speak in tongues, a totally new experience.'

For the next six months Ha-neul lived in that one-room house where he cooked for the orphans and read his Bible daily. But life was to change and as he read the Bible God gave him a scripture that would determine the future direction of his life.

As he approached Jerusalem and saw the city, he wept over it and said, 'If you, even you, had only known on this day what would bring you peace – but now it is hidden from your eyes. The days will come upon you when your enemies will build an embankment against you and encircle you and hem you in on every side. They will dash you to the ground, you and the children within your walls. They will not leave one stone on another, because you did not recognise the time of God's coming to you.'

(Luke 19:41–44, NIVUK)

'Jesus was crying over Jerusalem,' he said. 'And I was crying over North Korea. God showed me that North Korea is the Jerusalem of the Far East. I was crying over the Jerusalem of the Far East. It was then that I knew that I must go back.'

So in 2002, eight months after becoming a Christian, Ha-neul crossed back over the Tumen into North Korea. His family, thinking never to see him again gave him a wondrous welcome. But the police were suspicious. They visited the family home many times. Where had he been? What had he been doing? Why . . . visiting his sick grandmother, of course.

Ha-neul told his mother, his uncle and his older brother about Jesus, about how God had saved him from the Chinese police and how the Holy Spirit had fallen upon him and given him a peace such as he had never known. But they were frightened. Such talk was dangerous. His family would not accept the gospel and so, reluctantly, after eight months, he made his farewells and returned to China, once again crossing the Tumen River by night.

Back in China he reunited with his brother and together they studied theology in an underground seminary. During that time Ha-neul trained young Korean refugees who had become Christians. There were thirty-seven in all. All were determined to return to North Korea to share the gospel. They were prepared to die for their belief and, as he said, 'They actually expected to die.' Two of these people were arrested in North Korea and sent to the notorious Number 22 political criminal prison where they were executed.

Ha-neul met with Korean Christians in an underground church in the borderland of North Korea close to the Tumen River. Between them they possessed one Bible, which they kept in a plastic bag buried in the yard. The house was searched frequently. It was simply too dangerous to keep a Bible in the house. In the evening they would retrieve the Bible and read it with curtains drawn. They ate, worshipped and prayed quietly. They praised God silently, mouthing words of praise.

Ha-neul eventually made his way to South Korea and currently works as a youth pastor in a church in Seoul. Here he met his wife-to-be. They married and have two young girls.

I asked Ha-neul what God meant to him.

'He is my "love dad",' he said. 'He has changed my identity, my thinking, my perspective and my vision.'

'And so what is your identity now?' I asked.

'I am now God's son,' he said without hesitation. 'Before that I didn't know who I was.'

'And what is your vision?' I asked.

'To bring the gospel to North Korea,' he said. 'There are tens of thousands of North Korean refugees in China and 80 per cent of them are Christian.'[6]

'Why such a high percentage?'

'Because they are told that as soon as they reach China they must find a building with a cross. The people there will look after them. There are Chinese Christians and missionaries from many countries including Australia and the United States, all willing to help. My vision is to train these people as leaders and to send them back to spread the gospel. Most of them want to go back as they have family there.'

My heart went out to Ha-neul, his wife and his young children. I decided that I would pray for them daily. Shortly after returning to Australia, I received an email from him. His church had now offered him a full-time position as youth pastor. This would mean safety and security for his young family. But he had turned them down. 'I must follow the Lord's instruction,' he said. 'He will lead me and He will guide me. He has given me a strategy to spread the gospel in North Korea and this is where my heart is.'

As I prayed for Ha-neul, God gave me a scripture for him. It was the same as the one that He had given me before my journey to Cambodia with World Hope Network. I relayed it on without hesitation.

Do not fear, for I have redeemed you;
    I have summoned you by name; you are mine.
When you pass through the waters,
    I will be with you;
And when you pass through the rivers,
    they will not sweep over you.
When you walk through the fire,
    you will not be burned;
    the flames will not set you ablaze.
For I am the LORD your God,
    the Holy One of Israel, your Saviour; . . .
Do not be afraid, for I am with you;
    I will bring your children from the east
    and gather you from the west.
I will say to the north, 'Give them up!'
    and to the south, 'Do not hold them back.'

Bring my sons from afar
  and my daughters from the ends of the earth . . .

(Isa. 43:1b–3,5,6, NIVUK)

Author's note

In March 2015, Ha-neul planted a church in Seoul where people from North Korea and South Korea could worship freely together. He has plans for seven more such churches.

Preface to Chapter 12

Shadrach, Meshach, and Abed-Nego answered and said to the king, 'O Nebuchadnezzar . . . our God whom we serve is able to deliver us from the burning fiery furnace, and He will deliver us from your hand, O king. But if not, let it be known to you, O king, that we do not serve your gods, nor will we worship the gold image which you have set up.'

Then Nebuchadnezzar was full of fury . . . He spoke and commanded that they heat the furnace seven times more than it was usually heated. And he commanded certain mighty men of valor who were in his army to bind Shadrach, Meshach, and Abed-Nego, and cast them into the burning fiery furnace. Then these men were bound in their coats, their trousers, their turbans, and their other garments, and were cast into the midst of the burning fiery furnace. Therefore, because the king's command was urgent, and the furnace exceedingly hot, the flame of the fire killed those men who took up Shadrach, Meshach, and Abed-Nego. And these three men, Shadrach, Meshach, and Abed-Nego, fell down bound into the midst of the burning fiery furnace.

Then King Nebuchadnezzar was astonished; and he rose in haste and spoke, saying to his counselors, 'Did we not cast three men bound into the midst of the fire?'

They answered and said to the king, 'True, O king.'

'Look!' he answered, 'I see four men loose, walking in the midst of the fire; and they are not hurt, and the form of the fourth is like the Son of God.'

(Dan. 3:16–25)

12

The General

Don't let the world around you squeeze you into its own mould, but let God re-mould your minds from within . . .

(Rom. 12:2, PHILLIPS)

Slender of build, slightly balding, sporting tee shirt and casual trousers, I would never have known that this was the man who led 120,000 Indian troops against the Pakistanis, in the highest battle ever fought, on the Siachen Glacier between India and Pakistan 6,000 metres above sea level . . . until he spoke. The tone of his voice and the tenor of his speech badged him as one who might well lead men into battle, as one who men might even be prepared to die for.

Born in Delhi, the son of a Methodist minister and grandson of a pastor doctor, Ajai Masih was destined for the clergy, medicine, or possibly both, if Grandmother had her way. But in 1958 his father fell ill and, as the oldest of three sons, he felt duty bound to help support his family.

'I needed to get on my feet fast,' he said. 'No more studies.'

An ad in the local newspaper called for trainee assistants at the local cigarette factory. His mother wept. 'No son,' she said, 'not a cigarette factory.'

But the political tide was changing in India and the Chinese were building for war.

'The five "sister" states of northern India stuck out like a chicken's neck,' he said, 'and the Chinese wanted to chop them off.' Another newspaper ad called for able-bodied men to train as commissioned officers at the Dehradun Military Academy in northern India.[1]

'Why don't you apply?' said his uncle.

Three hundred and fifty young men applied. Two were accepted, one was a Hindu and one a Christian. That man was Ajai.

'I was 19 when I went to the academy,' he said, 'and 20 when I received my commission. I was assigned ten men at graduation and within fifteen days was on the Chinese border straight into battle, a raw man. I was second lieutenant. That was 1962.'

'As a Christian, how did you survive as part of a small minority in a Hindu country, especially in the armed forces?' I asked.

'That was my biggest challenge,' he said. 'From day one I had my Bible with me starting at the academy. It was my rock. I had a five-minute devotion every morning. Academy life is different, you see. You get seven to eight minutes to finish breakfast, maybe fifteen for lunch. So it was often just a quick word of prayer while I was getting on my bike.

'But the real challenge came when I joined my battalion. The structure of the Indian army is something like this. Of the 1.8 million-strong armed forces, 4 per cent are Christian, 16 per cent are Muslim and 80 per cent, Hindu. So in a battalion of 1,000 men you would be lucky to meet one other Christian. Of the 780 battalions there were only three with more than 100 Christians. These were from the north-east of India where the Baptist missionaries had been.

'The constitution laid down that any unit with more than 100 people belonging to a particular caste or sub-caste must have a religious teacher meeting their needs. And so every battalion had the equivalent of a chaplain. In Hindu parlance this was a *pundit*. Every battalion had a pundit.

'Commanding officers, no matter what their faith, were expected to follow the traditions of the majority of their men, which in most situations was Hindu. Until I made colonel, I had no choice but to obey the rules. Every Sunday morning there was a *mandir* parade[2] instead of church parade. It was a regimented affair. The whole battalion sat squatting in the *mandir*. Five minutes before it started the officers would take their seats. And just before it began the commanding officer would enter with his entourage.

'First of all the pundit would approach the commanding officer and with his thumb mark his forehead with a *tikka*. This is a black spot, which represents the third eye of the Hindu god and is supposed to keep evil at bay. The understanding was that you are under the protection of the gods. Then he would do the same to the officers, then the junior commissioned officers and finally the enlisted men. This might take up to two hours.

'By the time I became a major I was in real spiritual turmoil. The Bible says not to bow down to graven images, yet here was I paying homage to the Hindu gods. As the adjutant, the commanding officer's confidante, I was supposed to be a strong man. So I bit the bullet and I went to him.

'"Sir, I am a Christian. I'm sorry, sir, but I am not going to attend any more of these *mandir* parades."

'The CO was scathing: "The British commanding officer used to attend," he barked. "Are you a better man than he? Obey the constitution or you are out."'

Ajai believed that God had put him in that battalion for a purpose so he obeyed orders but continued to watch and pray.

Eventually a Christian commanding officer was posted to the battalion. As expected, Ajai would accompany him to *mandir* parade, inspect the men while the CO remained outside, then bring his report: 'Sir, present for parade: six officers, fifty junior commissioned officers and 783 ranks.' But he was soon to discover that the CO was going through the same spiritual turmoil. So he approached him.

'Sir must we attend this parade?'

'Yes, I'm commanding officer, I must obey protocol.'

'If that is the case, sir, must we sit there for the whole two hours?'

'What are you suggesting?'

'Sir, because of the constitution we have to attend the parade. But why don't we walk in, stay for thirty seconds and then get out of there?'

'Very well,' said the CO, 'you will accompany me to parade. I will stand outside and have a puff of my cigarette. You will bring me the report and then we'll go in together. After thirty seconds I'll give you the nod and we'll say to the pundit, "Thank you, man, we're off."'

And that's exactly what they did. They satisfied the protocol yet maintained their Christian stand.

'We "rendered unto Caesar",' he said. 'I was strongly criticized and called the equivalent of a dog. They sniggered and referred to me as "*Chura*", a Punjabi word meaning "sweeper", which inferred that I was untouchable. Yet I had broken the spiritual bond. I was a major at the time. Eleven years later I was promoted to colonel and, once that happened, I determined never again to attend *mandir* parade. That was my decision as commanding officer and could be challenged by no man.'

But it was important as a motivating factor that Ajai identify with his men.

'If you take men into battle,' he said, 'and expect them to follow you, they must see you as a leader, a father figure. So, occasionally, I would step into the parade – maybe once every few months – to keep faith with the men. I would bring them my blessing using the Hindi generic word for God instead of using the names of the Hindu gods. By the time I made brigadier, at 45 years of age, the whole issue became irrelevant. I could be challenged by no man and I never attended parade again.'

For a brief period, Ajai was posted to the UK where he worked with the diplomatic corps. On his return in 1980 he was promptly promoted to colonel. Almost immediately he was posted to a battalion of 1,000 men on the Pakistani front line.

'My machine-gun bunker was no more than 20 metres from the Kashmiri bunker,' he said. 'That's eyeball to eyeball.'

In the Indian Army, officers served upfront with the enlisted men and were under their direct scrutiny. But in the eyes of his men, Ajai was untested and he knew that he must prove himself to gain their respect.

'A man's reputation is made or broken by his action under fire,' he said. 'Whatever he does will be amplified with the passing of time. It will resonate through his years of service and never be forgotten.

I needed to expose myself to the enemy, risk my own life, but with the knowledge that, should something go dreadfully wrong, the boys would stand by me. What I did was, in retrospect, foolish in the extreme, but I needed to prove to the men that if you can expose yourselves to the enemy, so can I.'

So Colonel Ajai Masih stepped out of the bunker in full view of the enemy and shouted to the Pakistani commander: 'You let off one burst of machine-gun fire and I will let off ten bursts. Go ahead, if you have the guts.'

'That's the kind of thing you might do once,' he said. 'That one incident will remain etched in the hearts and minds of your men with the thought that this commanding officer is worth dying for. I had stepped onto the battlefield and I had to make a statement. I would show these Pakistanis who was boss.'

Immediately there was a loud metallic click from the enemy bunker.

'When you hear that click,' he said, 'you know that the machine-gunner has charged his magazine. An ammunition belt has thirty-five rounds and as soon as the trigger is pulled once only, all of these bullets will be fired within a matter of seconds. And that is the size of the bullet,' he said, holding up his index finger.

'Something else which was stupid,' he said, 'was that I never wore a helmet, always my red beret which indicated special forces, and that made me a prime target. It marked me as a very senior man but a very foolish and a stupid man at that.'

'Duck! Hit the ground,' shouted my machine-gunner in Hindi. He didn't care whether I was Christian or Hindu. I was his commanding officer. As soon as we heard that click the men didn't wait for what was to follow. My machine-gunners opened fire all along the line. On the battlefield you are not holding on to a post, but defending a front which may be 5 to 7 km long.'

'You must have been fearful,' I said.

'Yes, but let me tell you something about fear on the battlefield. Fear under fire vanishes with the first bullet whizzing past your head. If you have survived that, then that is the end of fear. The first sense of battle occurs when that shell explodes near you and you get up and discover that you are still alive. After that there is no room for fear. It's called battle inoculation.'

In 1999 Brigadier Ajai Masih was posted to the Siachen Glacier between India and Pakistan, the highest theatre of war in the history of the world.[3] Here at 6,000 metres, with temperatures falling to minus 55 degrees centigrade, he commanded 120,000 men.

The glacier was a desert of ice shrouded in snowdrifts up to 6 metres deep.

'Our posts were 5–7 km apart,' he said, 'and the only means of transport was snowmobile.' But any movement on the ice was fraught with danger. The Pakistanis would fire at any black dot they saw moving across the ice. They knew it was the enemy and would fire off five or six belts of machine-gun fire. Anything that moved must be shot at. The bullets were effective up to 1,800 metres and travelled at 760 metres per second.

'On a glacier there is an echo effect,' said Ajai, 'so for one salvo of artillery of, say, ten rounds, the impact is like 100 rounds. For a newcomer with no battle inoculation, this is deafening and the heart seems to stop beating.'

It was in that context that Ajai received a new third officer. He was overweight and not battle-hardened. 'Lose 15 kg or you're a dead man,' he was told.

One of the duties of a new man was to visit the outposts by snowmobile, encourage the men, bring gifts of fresh food or maybe a bottle of scotch and return to headquarters with news. The weight limit on a snowmobile was the equivalent of one man with a heavy pack or two men with a small pack, otherwise the vehicle would stall after 50 or 100 metres.

'I'll take you,' said Ajai. 'Sit behind me and hold on tight. I'll look ahead, you watch for the flash of machine-gun fire.[4] If you see a flash, abort, fall off and I will put my foot down.' What happened next was entirely unexpected. There was no machine-gun fire. Instead, a salvo of artillery, 45 kg shells, six flashes in all. The third officer shouted and threw himself from the snowmobile. Ajai sped away. Shells rained all around. A half-mile on, Ajai looked back but could see no sign of the officer.

Retracing his path, he found him on the hard ice, his spine fractured. Fortunately, he recovered completely and lost some weight in the process.

'Why do you think God protected you over and over again?' I asked.

'I don't know. I have asked myself the same question many times and the answer I will give you straight. I had defied Him and I had violated Him. But I have a gut feeling that He must have seen inside me a man struggling, a man in need, but a man who loved Him desperately. The reason that I'm standing here before you now is perhaps 99.9 per cent that the Lord was with me and 0.1 per cent bad marksmanship on the part of the Pakistani soldiers.'

'You seem to be more committed in your faith now, Ajai, than when you were serving in the army,' I ventured.

'In retrospect,' he said, 'if I had been a solid Christian in the real sense of the word then, I would have either quit or evangelized my entire battalion, my brigade and my division. Either way, I would have been out on my ear. But God allowed me to progress as a Christian commanding officer. My first command was ten men but at the time I retired there were 122,000 men under me.

'The Bible that I carry today is the Bible that I received on the day of my commission. It has been through six bloody wars starting from 1962 with China, 1965 with Pakistan, 1973 with Pakistan, 1975 with Pakistan, 1989 with Sri Lanka and in 1998 against Musharraf in Pakistan.

'My Bible was with me in my trench, my Bible was in my bunker; I used to read it by candlelight. My Bible was with me at 50 degrees C in the desert. My Bible was with me at -55 degrees C on the Siachen Glacier.'

'What is your identity Ajai? Who are you?' I asked. There was a pause and the general's eyes filled with tears.

'I'm a servant of Jesus, in every sense. Today if I had to give up everything I would not hesitate to do so. The only thing I want is to live for Him. I have no desire for money, I don't even have a roof over my head. Now my wife, Tahira, and I are working here in Australia with refugees and our greatest desire is to do whatever we can do for them.

'This is my prayer, every morning: Lord, give me that life that you have for me but it must be to live for You. I am a cancer patient now, Ern. I have prostate cancer and every day is a bonus. If He wants me to live, I will.'

There are powerful lessons to be learned from Ajai's story. His grandmother was a godly woman and it was her fondest desire that Ajai follow a career path as a doctor/pastor. Yet God had other plans. And those plans realized his potential for leadership to the point where as Lieutenant General he became a leader and father-figure to 122,000 troops in times of crisis.

As a parent I'm aware that our desire is often for our children to conform to the plans that we have for them. We may wish to see them channelled into a family business or a profession because it seems right or perhaps it fulfils an unmet need in our own lives. But God may well have other plans. And if those plans are implemented, then the life of that child is enriched and fulfilled and, like Ajai, they are able to trace the finger of God through their lives.

Another lesson addresses one of the greatest challenges facing us today, the pressure to conform to the will of the world when we know this to be wrong. This may take the form of peer pressure, unreasonable or unethical demands in the workplace, the corrupt demands of an administrator or ruler or even, as in Ajai's situation, the pressure to pay homage to a foreign god.

We can bend to that pressure or we can take a stand for what we believe. If we bend, we are compromised and diminished. If we take that stand, there is one who stands with us.

Nebuchadnezzar cast Shadrach, Meshach and Abed-Nego into the fiery furnace for refusing to bow down to a golden image. The fire was so hot that even the men who threw them in were destroyed. But when Nebuchadnezzar looked, he saw four men walking in the flames free and unbound 'and the . . . fourth [was] like the Son of God.' Who is that man? It is Jesus, the son of the living God. He was the fourth man in the fire.[5]

That man walks with us today as surely as He did then. Have you met Him yet?

Preface to Chapter 13

'What's the value of your life . . .? The cost of a bullet. That's it. Unless you tell me what I want to know.'

'But I've told you everything. Anything else would be a lie to save my skin.'

It was a claustrophobic little room with a small wooden table and two chairs.

Zahir sat eye to eye with the Pakistani Intelligence Officer.

It was May 1971 and it was hot, very hot.

13

God's Freedom Fighter

A bullet traded for a pearl of greatest price.

In September 1965, Zahir woke to the sound of sirens and martial music. India and Pakistan were at war again, this time over the disputed territory of Kashmir. There were thousands of casualties on both sides, but no victor.

As a boy growing up in the town of Mymensingh, eighty miles north-west of Dhaka in East Pakistan, Zahir observed the soldiers returning from war. He listened to their embellished stories and watched in awe as they were lauded as local heroes. He too would serve his country one day, at the cost of his life if necessary. He would become a commissioned officer. But first, he must study and learn English.

Near the railway station of his town, the Australian Baptist missionaries conducted regular church services in English. 'What an opportunity to learn English,' he thought. His father, who was the local police inspector and a Sunni Muslim, was delighted at the prospect and gave him time off from duties to attend.

'I went along to learn English,' said Zahir, 'but they taught me about Jesus. I came to admire these people but they were just too good to be true. I searched their homes looking for signs of Western decadence but I found none.

'One night,' he said, 'I dreamt that I was already a commissioned officer and that I had been told to bring in a man dead or alive. In my dream, the window opened and there was a brilliant burst of light.

Then a voice challenged me: "Who are you to destroy my creation?" I woke up and realized from that point on that I had no right to destroy life.'

East and West Pakistan coexisted in a balanced democracy.[1] Both were founded on Islam. But there were problems. West Pakistan dominated the civil service and the armed forces. East Pakistan generated the finances but more was spent on the West. Language, food, culture and traditions were totally different. And so it was that the people of East Pakistan began the move towards independence.

In mid-1970 at age 17, Zahir was accepted into the army as a cadet in training. But by that time the country was at boiling point. The people of East Pakistan demanded provincial autonomy.

In Dhaka, Mujibar Rahman, leader of the East Pakistani Awami League, was jailed.

There were protests and strikes. Lawlessness reigned and the country became ungovernable.

Under immense pressure, President Ayoub Kahn released Rahman. But pressure continued on the president who finally resigned surrendering his responsibilities to General Yahya Khan, who promptly suspended parliament, declared martial law and scheduled a general election. The East Pakistan Awami League won easily and Rahman should have been the new prime minister but the National Assembly was deferred indefinitely.

East Pakistan erupted. People demanded that their elected leader should govern. In Dhaka the flag of independent Bangladesh was raised and the Declaration of Independence read. Rahman declared:

> Our struggle is for liberation, for independence. Blood we have given, blood we shall give. God willing this time we shall be independent.

The new President Yahya Khan and opposition leader Ali Bhutto arrived in Dhaka for meetings with Rahman. But while this was occurring, the Pakistani army took steps to secure East Pakistan. Covertly they shuttled Bengali troops out of Dhaka by commercial flight, replacing them with their own men.

Then, on 25 March 1971, West Pakistani troops launched a campaign of terror. Rahman was arrested yet again and taken to Karachi in the West.

The commanding officer of the few Bengali troops remaining in Dhaka, in East Pakistan, proclaimed the independence of Bangladesh from in hiding. The war for liberation had begun.

The Pakistani army mobilized, moving out of Dhaka in all directions to occupy East Pakistan and to annihilate freedom fighters. Each organization was faced with the decision whether to support Pakistan or join the Bengali liberation movement. In Zahir's town of Mymensingh the police and paramilitary joined forces to defend the town against the advancing army. Criminals were released from prison. The police armoury was looted and people armed themselves in preparation. West Pakistani men serving in the East Pakistan Rifles were beheaded and their bodies paraded around town on the bonnets of 4WDs.

People fled the advancing army and Mymensingh became a ghost town. In fear of his life, Zahir set out on his bicycle for the Joyramkura Christian Hospital, thirty miles to the north and not far from the Indian border. But the hospital staff were reluctant to take him in. He was a freedom fighter and his very presence would put their lives at risk. As a compromise they hid him in the women's quarters by day. He was free to come out at night.

The Pakistani army advanced rapidly on Mymensingh. There were skirmishes and bridges were destroyed to halt the advance. But eventually the army took the town and then moved northwards searching for freedom fighters.

Thousands of people passed the hospital each day, fleeing north to the Indian border. High-ranking officials and even the hospital's doctor fled. Though secured by high fences and a flooded creek to the south, the hospital was totally exposed to the east and west. Armed criminals and opportunists moved in, surrounding the hospital.

'We feared for our lives,' said Zahir. 'We knew that we would soon be invaded by these desperate and ruthless people.'

Patients were discharged and there was a growing concern for the welfare of the three Australian missionary ladies on staff. 'The army was

approaching rapidly,' said Zahir. 'I could hear the heavy artillery and machine-gun fire. So we decided to relocate to the Panihati mission compound, a further ten miles to the north-west and very close to the Indian
border. Trainee nurses were escorted and our valuables were transferred
in metal trunks and 44-gallon drums. Finally, together with the Australian ladies, I left the hospital and we drove along the border road to the
Panihati Mission. It was almost dark and very hot and humid.'

But the nursing sisters at the mission would not accept Zahir as a Bengali. 'He's a spy,' they said, 'a Pakistani spy who has learned the language.'

'I had to wait in the 4WD while they decided what to do with me,'
said Zahir. 'It was hot, dark and very noisy. There were freedom fighters all around staging night attacks on the army. Finally we moved on,
crossed the Pakistani border then forded a creek to the Indian side of
the no-man's land which separated India and Pakistan. Overnight we
remained in our vehicle. As the sun rose we watched as thousands of
people fleeing East Pakistan crossed the border into India.'

Later that day, the local commander of Indian Border Security
came out to meet them. He was concerned for the safety of the three
Australian women.

'If they are harmed,' he said, 'it will create an international incident.'

'He requisitioned a hut for us near the creek just five minutes from
the Indian border,' said Zahir. 'It was a straw hut with an earthen
floor but it was set back from the main road and gave us some security. We transferred our goods and settled in for the night.

'The next morning, we watched again as thousands of refugees surged
towards the Indian border. I could hear machine-gun and artillery fire
and I was terrified, but the three Australian ladies remained completely
calm. They prepared meals and went about business as usual.

'"We are not worried," they said. "We're in God's hands." But I
was in a constant state of fear. I shook my head in disbelief. "There's
something wrong with you people," I said.

'I was feeling pretty bad about life at that time, especially the property that I had destroyed. In the army they say: "the more blood you
see the more you like it". I felt just the opposite. What did these
women have that I needed so badly?'

Finally, after some weeks spent in the hut, and when hostilities had settled somewhat, arrangements were made for Zahir and the Australian ladies to return to East Pakistan. Mission officials in Dhaka negotiated with the Pakistani army for a male missionary to collect them and their supplies and return them safely to their homes. But as Zahir was a known freedom fighter, his association with the missionaries may well have put their lives at risk. So it was decided to smuggle him back across the border in a 44-gallon drum in the back of the Land Rover. A side vent would provide ventilation. The journey would take four to six hours. It would be hard going as the roads were rough and heavily potholed. Each day they rehearsed this for half an hour.

'They would seal me in the drum and roll me around,' he said.

On the appointed day, locals moved their goods back to the creek to be picked up by the missionary in his truck. Zahir was sealed in the drum with water, a towel, some cashew nuts and a block of Kraft cheese. But suddenly there was a change of plan. They rolled him out of the drum, held him down and to his horror slashed his big toe with a razor. It seems that the garrison leader back in East Pakistan had approved his return, but as their wounded patient.

The missionary was to meet them at the creek, but there were more problems. On reaching the creek he was held up at gunpoint by freedom fighters who insisted that his driver was an army spy. The missionary protested that he couldn't drive a truck and needed his driver. He was stranded in the jungle beside the creek.

'Later that afternoon,' said Zahir, 'we took the Land Rover across the no-man's land to the creek where the truck was stranded. Freedom fighters appeared from the jungle and held us at gunpoint. They ordered me out of the vehicle. Their commander had demanded to see me, they said, before I returned to East Pakistan.

'"If I'm not back by 8 p.m.," said Zahir, "leave without me and go back to Mymensingh."'

For thirty minutes they led Zahir along a jungle path. On reaching a clearing they seized him, tied his hands, blindfolded him and ordered him to sit down. It was an hour before sunset.

'It soon became clear that I was to face a firing squad,' he said. 'I later learned that my grave was already prepared. Freedom fighters were eliminating their leaders so that there would be fewer to share the spoils of war.

'"You are a spy!" they said, and prepared me for execution. But just as they were about to fire, a senior officer arrived, claiming to be my friend, and demanding my release. They removed my blindfold.

'"Do you know this man?" they asked.

'"No," I said, "I do not." There was an argument. The officer said that if they executed me they would have to kill him also. Finally, they released me into his charge.'

The senior officer claimed to know Zahir because of his military training. He wanted his support to fight the Pakistani army and together *they* would share the spoils of war.

'I was invited to visit his camp later that evening for wild deer curry,' said Zahir. 'And I was to let him know my decision: Would I support him or not? His guards would escort me.'

It was a warm and humid evening as Zahir was escorted by open-top Jeep to the camp of the senior officer. 'As I sat there in the darkness,' he said, 'Jesus, in an extraordinary encounter, appeared to me and spoke audibly: "All the earthly things that you've ever wanted, power, position, rank, property, wealth, are here for the taking; but they won't last. On the other hand, I want to give you all that will last, for eternity – you are in the last moments of your life – choose now." I knew it was Jesus and I said, "I give you my life."'

After the meal Zahir confessed to the officer that he had no heart to fight. The man was angry, but ordered his men to return Zahir to the stranded truck where his friends would still be waiting.

It was midnight when they arrived. In Zahir's absence, the freedom fighters had driven the truck into the creek. One of the Australian ladies had jump-started it and driven it out. But the freedom fighters drove the truck back into the creek, where it became hopelessly bogged down. They were completely stranded.

Two hours later the officer who had saved Zahir from the firing squad arrived. He was livid. 'Why are you still here?' he demanded. 'Load your essentials into the Land Rover and get out of here, now!'

As they made their way back along narrow jungle tracks towards the East Pakistani border, they were fearful. Their pass had been approved for travel on that road between 4 and 6 p.m. the previous day. It was now in the early hours of the next morning. The Pakistani army was on high alert. They would shoot first and ask questions later.

Matron made a white flag from her petticoat. As they approached the border post, the male missionary walked ahead of them bathed in the glow of the headlights and waving the flag as they sounded the horn. There were voices from the check post, but permission was given to proceed, and they headed south-east back towards the Joyramkura hospital.

It was approaching 4 a.m. when they arrived. By vehicle lights they could see the devastation and it was heartbreaking. Anything not bolted down had been stolen. Larger equipment such as X-ray machines had been destroyed with axes and machetes. It was like a war zone. After breakfast they left for Haluaghat to report as requested to the captain of the army garrison who had sanctioned their return.

'He checked my wound,' said Zahir, 'believed our story and allowed us to return to our homes in Mymensingh. We arrived safely at the Baptist Mission compound late that afternoon with much rejoicing.'

The commanding officer of the town sent word that he wished to thank Zahir personally for looking after the Australian ladies. 'I was escorted to headquarters,' he said, 'and ordered to wait as he was delayed. As I did so, a man in street clothes entered. He told me that the brigadier was delayed indefinitely and that I should accompany him. He led me to a building signed as an army dormitory and into a small room with a table and two chairs, then ordered me to sit down.'

The man identified himself as an intelligence officer, a major in the Pakistani army. He showed Zahir photographs of freedom fighters in training. 'Do you know any of these men?' he asked. At that stage he made it very clear that 'the value of Zahir's life was the price of a bullet'. He should tell him everything he knew.

'I've already told you everything I know,' said Zahir, 'anything else would be a lie to save my skin.' Eventually the intelligence officer accepted Zahir's word and drove him home, much to his annoyance as he did not want the officer to know where he lived.

It was dangerous for Zahir as a young Bengali to remain in East Pakistan. Each night men were taken from their homes by the military and murdered. Families were ordered to retrieve their bodies from the river next morning. To survive, he knew that he must leave the country as soon as possible. In Dhaka he applied for a travel visa. Any travel without an ID and permit was highly dangerous. On one occasion whilst travelling from Dhaka to Mymensingh by train, a soldier with a machine-gun had demanded to see his ID. As he did not have one the soldier made him stand by the door.

'I decided to jump him and throw him off the train,' said Zahir, 'but I knew that if I failed he would shoot me and all twenty-five passengers. Fortunately, he found another man without an ID. We were searched for weapons, warned and finally released.

'Strangely enough,' said Zahir, 'the intelligence officer became my friend. I guess he thought that he might learn more that way. I asked if I could travel with him by car to Dhaka. He said no, he didn't want my blood on his hands as freedom fighters were setting road mines. I found this difficult to accept, as I knew he had authorized the deaths of hundreds of young Bengali men. Why would he care about me? He visited my home frequently, each time intending to imprison and interrogate me. But as he later confessed something would always prevent him from doing so. He had no idea why that should be.'

As time passed, the Pakistani army was losing its grip. Freedom fighters were gaining territory. India blockaded the Bay of Bengal and controlled air space, cutting off supply. There were now more than half a million freedom fighters, greatly outnumbering the 90,000 Pakistani army troops. The army began a systematic withdrawal. As they did so, soldiers raped and looted and killed the academics and intellectuals, prompting India to declare open war against Pakistan. They dropped 226 kg bombs and flyers ordering them to lay down their arms.

The Commander-in-Chief of the Indian forces ordered the Pakistani army to surrender to avoid further bloodshed. Terms were negotiated and surrender was formalized. The new flag of Bangladesh was raised in Dhaka.

Over a nine-month period, one million Bangladeshis had been killed, ten million had fled to India and 250,000 had been raped. Several mass graves were discovered. Justice Choudhury was sworn in as the first president of the People's Republic of Bangladesh. Rahman returned from captivity and was finally sworn in as prime minister.

After the war, the man who had saved Zahir from the firing squad returned to Mymensingh. Over a meal, he told Zahir just how close to death he had been.

'Your grave had already been dug,' he said. 'Oh, and something else you didn't know, the commander of the Indian border forces had been authorized to shoot the Australians and the civilians. The Indian press would say, "Australians trying to return to their bases were murdered by the Pakistanis." There would be no civilians left to tell the truth. World opinion would be swayed or, at least, Aussie opinion would go against Pakistan.'

Bangladeshi troops returning from Pakistan were accommodated in the regular army. The government also set up a paramilitary force, *Jatiyo Rakhi Bahini* to accommodate freedom fighters. But it became a shadowy and corrupt 'Gestapo-type' organization. Ex freedom fighters declared themselves national heroes. They had power, land, money and women for the asking.

'I had none of this,' said Zahir. 'It bothered me big time. Why shouldn't I have the same? I began to doubt my Christian belief. I was a better person than these guys. Had I made a big mistake?'

Prime Minister Rahman was immensely popular but not a strong man. He struggled to address the challenges of poverty, unemployment and corruption. His response was to limit judicial powers, ban all but government newspapers and all political parties but his own.

Early in 1975, Rahman declared a state of emergency, assumed the presidency and amalgamated his political supporters into one party, the Bangladesh *Krishak Sramik Awami* League. The paramilitary had been responsible for the torture and killing of up to 40,000 people. But he granted them immunity and freedom from prosecution.

By doing so he was seen to betray the causes of democracy and civil rights.

There was rising friction between the army and the paramilitary. Finally a plot was hatched. In August a military coup staged by middle-ranked officers stormed the presidential residency killing Rahman, family members and supporters. The coup had been spearheaded by disgruntled members of his own staff.

The army disbanded the paramilitary. Corrupt members who had become rich and powerful were charged, taken before a military tribunal and executed within days. Others fled to India.

'It was only then that I realized,' said Zahir, 'if I had continued as a freedom fighter I would have met the same fate. For the first time I began to understand the gravity of my decision to give my life to Jesus and accept Him as Lord and Saviour. Because of that decision I had not followed in the footsteps of my friends who were now dead. They had returned as "national heroes". I had envied their power, and possessions. Now I realized, as God had said to me that night in the back of the Jeep, that it was all worthless. It had cost them their very lives.

'God had saved me from Pakistani army atrocities, from the firing squad and also from death at the hand of the military tribunal. I began to understand that He *is* Sovereign and that He could use anyone, even me, to fulfil His plans and purpose. I began to thank Him for saving my life and at that stage surrendered myself to Him completely.'

Eventually Zahir was baptized. This placed his father under a great deal of pressure from the local mosque for not being able to rein in his son. Zahir wanted to travel abroad to study engineering. His father, who now owned a trucking company, agreed to fund him if he renounced Christianity, but he refused. The relationship with his father deteriorated and he was fired from the family business and asked to leave home.

In late 1976 a scholarship became available for travel abroad to study commerce, medicine, theology or engineering. Zahir did not understand why this had taken so long to eventuate.

'Have you ever asked God why this was so?' asked his missionary friend. 'Have you ever asked Him what He wants?'

So for the first time Zahir began to seek God's will for his life, eventually deciding to study theology. In Dhaka he completed the necessary paperwork at the Australian High Commission and applied for a visa. But his records were lost and he was told that he must resit the medical and English exams. Eventually a visa was issued.

Within eighteen hours Zahir was at Dhaka airport to catch his plane. His uncle, who was Civil Aviation Director at the time, walked him through the departure lounge and onto the tarmac. He was on his way.

Zahir was welcomed and cared for by his new Australian friends. All of his needs were met. He enrolled as a student at the Morling Baptist Theological College in Epping, north of Sydney. Years later, one of the missionary ladies from Mymensingh with whom he had fallen in love returned to Australia and they were married.

His student visa was renewed each year. But in the third year there was a delay. At the immigration office in downtown Sydney, he was told that he had been issued the wrong visa. 'I was on a pearl diver's visa,' he said, 'normally reserved for Japanese pearl divers.'

The clerk assured him that all was well and that the correct visa would be issued. 'You know,' he replied, 'it *was* the right visa; I have been diving into the Word of God for the last three years to gather gems and jewels. She thought that I was some kind of religious nut and told me to sit down.'

Zahir graduated from Morling College to became assistant pastor at a nearby Baptist church. I met him during his chaplaincy training at Westmead Hospital where I was a director at the time. We became lifelong friends and have since shared our faith and experiences over many fine curries. He is a wonderful cook.

Today Zahir is senior pastor of a multicultural Sydney church. He is a leader of men and has a gifted ministry to the many fine Australians who have come from troubled spots of the world.

In his old life he had been offered power and riches to sell his soul just as Christ had been tempted on the mountain. But instead he chose the 'pearl of greatest price' and inherited the riches of God's kingdom.[2]

'I want to bear witness,' he proclaims, 'to the grace and mercy of our Lord and Saviour Jesus Christ that has continued in my life as I serve Him. I want to bring His message of salvation to all who will hear.'

The pearl diver's visa was not a mistake. It was prophetic!

Preface to Chapter 14

Many patients who come to me are fearful. They have received bad news or they are anticipating bad news. One man had been told that very morning that he had lung cancer. He had come straight from his doctor's surgery for a bone scan and a CT.

'I haven't even told my wife or kids yet,' he said, staring at the floor, fighting back tears. The fear in his voice was tangible.

My advice to such patients is, 'When God is in the room there is no room for fear!' We know that God is love and that perfect love casts out fear. We are never alone. Jesus said: 'If anyone loves Me, he will keep My word; and My Father will love him, and We will come to him and make Our home with him' (John 14: 23) and 'If you love Me, keep My commandments. And I will pray the Father, and He will give you another Helper, that He may abide with you forever – the Spirit of truth' (John 14:15,16).

No matter how alone we may feel, no matter how isolated we may consider ourselves, God is always there. All we have to do is call on Him. He is less than a heartbeat away. Not only does He remain with us, He prepares us for the way, He leads us through the deep waters and prepares the path ahead of us.

As I have listened to stories from friends, I have marvelled at the way in which God has led and supported them through the most difficult of circumstances. But none more than that of Gladys Staines and her daughter, Esther. Here is their story.

NB. This will be a difficult story for some and may need parental guidance. It continues to speak of the supernatural nature of forgiveness and the veracity of the angel's words regarding the risen Christ:

He is going ahead of you into Galilee. There you will see him, just as he told you.

(Mark 16:7b, NIVUK)

Reality check: Galilee – a real place, a real time,
God leading the way then, so now.

14

Never Alone

Be strong and courageous.
Do not be afraid or terrified because of them,
for the LORD your God goes with you;
he will never leave you nor forsake you.

(Deut. 31:6)

The drums were beating as a group of young Santals[1] joined in a traditional Dangri dance. It was just past midnight, 23 January 1999, in the town of Monohorpur in the north-east Indian state of Orissa.[2]

Graham Staines and his two boys, Timothy aged 6, and Philip, 10, had dined with friends that night. For fourteen consecutive years Graham had returned to this tiny village in the foothills of Keonjahar to run a Christian camp in the jungle. To do so he had travelled 120 km north-west from the mission home in Baripada across ravines and the most inhospitable countryside. He was a familiar face to the 150 Santal families in the area. It was a happy time and spirits were high following on from his birthday celebrations with family just four days prior.

At 9:45 p.m. he and the boys made their way to their friend Willy's station wagon where they were to spend the night. Graham opened the wagon, pulled out blankets and pillows and prepared a bed for the boys. They huddled together and prayed for those back home and for the people in the leprosy mission, as was their custom.

At 12:20 a.m. a mob, armed with clubs and tridents came screaming from the fields. They surrounded the vehicle.

'*Maro, maro . . .*' they called. 'Dara Singh, *Zindabad.*' (beat, beat, Dara Singh, victory)

Their leader, Dara Singh, a radical well known to police, slashed the tyres while others smashed the windows. Graham and his sons were beaten mercilessly and stabbed with tridents. Then Singh, in an unspeakable act, doused the vehicle with petrol and torched it. The killers stood back and watched as the young family was promoted to Glory in the inferno, locked in each other's arms in a final embrace. Local villagers attempted to control the flames but it was too late, they were threatened by the mob and warned to stay back.[3]

It was next morning before Gladys and her daughter, Esther back at the mission were to learn what had really happened. Friends shielded them from the truth.

'The boys are missing,' they said. 'The station wagons have been burned.' Then the truth: Graham and the two boys had been brutally murdered. Even then, Hindu friends sent to advise Gladys of the facts said, 'We are not sure if this actually happened.' This apparently is a very Indian characteristic, to shield people from harsh reality.' It was 9:30 a.m. before Gladys was sure of the facts.

'God gave me this amazing strength as He always does,' said Gladys. 'People came to comfort me but I found myself comforting them. The media came right into my home and challenged me. "Aren't you angry?" they said. I kept thinking that Graham and the boys had died in the name of Jesus. I knew that. I thought, "Even if I'm not allowed to stay here, I'm going to use this opportunity to talk about Jesus." So every time a mike was put before me, I did so.

'This was not something that I had anticipated,' she reminisced. 'But when I heard that my husband and the boys were dead, I said to Esther: "We're alone now, Esther . . . But we'll forgive those who killed them, won't we?"

'"Yes, Mummy," she said, "we will."'

The president of India, Mr K.R. Narayanan described the killing as belonging to the 'world's inventory of black deeds'. He said, 'That someone who spent years caring for patients of leprosy, instead of being thanked and appreciated as a role model should be done to death in this manner is a monumental aberration from the traditions of tolerance and humanity for which India is known.'[4] This statement was acknowledged and welcomed by the British Minister of State, Foreign and Commonwealth Office, Mr Tony Lloyd.[5]

At the funeral, Gladys and Esther were a tower of strength.

'I am proud that my father was considered worthy to die for God,' said Esther, aged 13, and she and her mother sang, 'Because He lives, I can face tomorrow'.[6]

Shortly after, Gladys was at Esther's boarding school in South India when one of the mothers approached.

'I don't know how you can forgive those people,' she said. 'I could never forgive them if they killed my kids.'

Esther turned to Gladys.

'Mummy,' she said, 'why don't they understand how we can forgive them?'[7]

'When I heard that,' said Gladys, 'I knew that God was working through her too.'

Dara Singh was arrested and brought to trial in 2003. Local Christians maintained a vigil outside the courthouse with a life-sized image of Graham and the boys which was inscribed: 'Lord, You died for us. We died for India.'[8,9]

Graham was born in 1941, the second child of William and Elizabeth in Palmwoods, Queensland on the beautiful Sunshine Coast north of Brisbane. He became a Christian, aged 10, at Nambour Presbyterian church, little knowing that he would develop a heart for India and that he would be called to serve the poor lepers in Mayurbhanj.

As a boy of 15 he became pen pals with Santanu Satpathy, an Indian boy whose address had been forwarded by a family friend who worked in Rairangpur. For years they exchanged photos and dreams. In those letters Graham expressed his love for God and over a period his heart and mind were drawn irrevocably to India.

As a young man, Graham studied accountancy. He was offered a managerial position in his Uncle Ben's timber yard in Brisbane. It would have meant security and prosperity. But he knew that God had called him to India and turned the offer down. 'You're foolish,' said his uncle and accused him of throwing his life away. But Graham's words were these: 'The child of the King will do the King's work.'

In 1965 he joined the Evangelical Missionary Society in Mayurbhanj, which ran a leprosy home affiliated with The Leprosy Mission. The journey, which would define his life and destiny, had begun.

For thirty-four years, dressed in casuals, sporting his trademark hat and wheeling a bicycle, which he meticulously maintained, '*Saibo*', as he was affectionately known, was a fixture in that town, tending and nursing leprosy patients in a specialty home on the town's outskirts. These were the untouchables, shunned by society and even by family members. But he was their friend. He was the one who cared. It was here at the leprosy mission that he met Gladys in 1981 during her tour of duty with Operation Mobilisation.[10]

Gladys was born into a family of dairy farmers near Ipswich, Queensland in 1951. As a girl of 13 she committed her life to Christ at the Flinders Congregational church and from that time on decided that as long as she lived it would be for Christ alone. She studied nursing, completing general studies at Ipswich general hospital and later midwifery at Queen Victoria Hospital, Launceston, Tasmania. At age 18 she felt called to mission work and joined Operation Mobilisation, going on to serve in Singapore, Malaysia, Europe and India.

During her time of service in India, she had several narrow escapes. One night she and her friends were stranded in the Punjab, hundreds of miles from anywhere, when their truck broke down. Many Christians had been murdered in the Punjab and they were acutely aware of God's protection that night.[11]

Although Gladys and Graham had lived only 30 km apart in southern Queensland, they had never met until the day that she visited the mission home in Baripada in 1981.

They were married in Ipswich in 1983, returning to India the following year. Together they worked at the leprosy hospital and in the rehabilitation home 10 km out of town.

'Graham was often in dire need,' said Gladys, 'but never complained. He would simply say. "I am a child of the King of kings, why should I ask for human help?"'

It was late on a Tuesday evening in October 2014. I listened carefully as Gladys spoke, scarcely knowing how to question this remarkable woman. I had read the accounts, I had seen the dreadful photographs, and I was in awe of the presence of God's love expressed by her life. I knew that God would speak to me through her words and experience. My role was to listen, to discern and to record what He would say through her.

'Many have come to Christ right across India in the wake of what happed to Graham and the boys,' she said. 'Sometimes from families that had rejected the gospel for years. People said, "Why did we, who have had Christianity all this time, have to have a foreign missionary come to tell us about Jesus? What are *we* doing about it ourselves?" Young Indian men and women have taken up the challenge to be missionaries across India. Yet they know that what happened to Graham could happen to them also. Police leaders have told them that perhaps they shouldn't wander from village to village. "No," they say. "God has given us a job to do. If we die, then we die."

'People were saying to me, and this is a very Indian thing,' she said, 'that it was God's will that Graham and the boys had died. But let me tell you: God does not plan bad things to happen, but sometimes He allows them for His greater glory. That realization to me was a great comfort. I have only one message for the people of India. I am not bitter, neither am I angry. But I have one desire that each citizen of that country should establish a personal relationship with Jesus. He gave His life for their sins.'

'Gladys, did you sense God's presence through these events?' I asked.

'Looking back,' she said, 'I believe that He prepared me for the trial I was to go through. On the morning of 7 January, just sixteen days before the event, I was reading my devotional notes for the day. The story ran something like this: There was a 12-year-old girl in hospital, losing her sight. Her pastor came to visit her and she said to him, "Pastor, God is taking away my sight." For a long time the pastor kept silent and then he said, "Jessie, don't let Him." The girl was puzzled, then the wise pastor said, "Give it to Him."'[12]

Gladys was able to provide me with the original text and the accompanying note, which read:

If we know that a loved one will probably die, or if we are told that we may be permanently disabled, let us give that to God as a love offering. As Abraham surrendered his precious son Isaac on Mount Moriah (Gen. 22:1–14), so let us pray, 'Father, I am not clinging fiercely to this cherished person or this rich blessing that has temporarily been mine. I am grateful to You for lending me this life-enriching good, but now I freely give it to You.'

'Jesus has since been my tower of strength,' she said, 'and the light in my darkest hour. My life today belongs to Him, the Good Shepherd, and there is nothing that I want. "Even though I may walk through the valley of the shadow of death I fear nothing, for God is with me"' (see Ps. 23:4).

It's been my own continuing experience that God equips and prepares us for events that we must face. I have observed this in the lives of my friends. Ken Clezy was the surgeon on call at the Baptist Hospital, Jibla, Yemen on 30 December 2002. This was the day that a radical Islamist entered the hospital with a Kalashnikov cradled in a baby's blanket and shot dead Dr Martha Myers, administrator Bill Koehn and purchasing officer Don Caswell. Ken was having breakfast with his wife, Gwen, at the time when the call came through, 'Yemenis . . . Mr Bill.' He ran to the scene of the shooting and was able to save the life of the pharmacist who had been shot in the abdomen. Those murdered were mourned in Yemen and around the world. Thousands lined the streets next day to honour Martha Myers, who was buried in the hospital precinct. Her makeshift tombstone simply said in broken English: 'She love God.' A *Lancet* obituary praised her life and work.[13]

Earlier that day, Ken had spoken at morning devotions. The hospital was to have been closed the very next day due to lack of funding and he chose his words carefully. His text was from the book of Hebrews, 'He though dead yet speaketh.'[14] The words refer to Abel who had offered to God a more excellent sacrifice than his brother, Cain, and was murdered in a fit of jealousy for doing so.

The words were, of course, prophetic. The hospital was closed the day following the massacre but then reopened by presidential decree. It now receives government funding and is a fully functioning multicultural institution. The lives of those martyred have inspired and strengthened the hearts of many. Their love for the Yemeni people is enshrined in those who now serve in that hospital.[15] Those who were present on that day are able to trace the hand of God as He led them through.[16]

But not only does God prepare us, He also takes us by the hand and leads us through the shadows of our lives. Gladys was very much aware of this in the days following the attack. I have also been aware of God's presence in the dark times of my life.[17] There have been times when, not knowing how to proceed, I have sat on my bed and simply prayed, 'Please help.' And He has done so. He has never failed me. *Paracletos* is a Greek word often associated with the Holy Spirit. It means to come alongside and support. And God's Spirit does so as counsellor, comforter, strengthener and guide, leading us through the most difficult circumstances.

At the recent Summer Celebration of 2014 in Plymouth, England, Canon Andrew White, 'The Vicar of Baghdad', told of news that he had received on the BBC that morning: the people of his congregation at St George's, Baghdad were to be put to death by the ISIS insurgents. He called Marian, one of his older parishioners.

'Marian,' he said, 'Are you all right? Will we be able to get you out quickly?' And she said, 'Am I all right? ... Last night when I was asleep Jesus came to me. And Jesus took my hand and He said, "I'm not leaving you, I'm going with you."'[18] For some years now the people in Canon White's church have known dreadful persecution, but they have been constantly aware of God's presence with them.

Some months ago I received a call from a doctor friend who was to face a medical tribunal the next day. One of his patients had died and the family had lodged a formal complaint. He was distraught. 'This may be the end of my medical career,' he said.

He was a good man and a caring doctor. I agreed to meet with him and his wife early next morning to pray with them. Before doing so I asked God what I could say to bring comfort and support. The words came clearly: 'Read him Isaiah 12:2.'

I checked it out on my iPhone.

Behold, God is my salvation, I will trust and not be afraid; 'For YAH, the LORD, is my strength and song; He also has become my salvation.'

(Isa. 12:2)

We sat and prayed and I shared the verse. Tears were shed and he held his wife's hand tightly.

'Write the verse on a piece of paper,' I said, 'so that you can read it through the day when things get tough, and remember: keep your eyes fixed on Jesus, just as Peter did when he walked on the water.'

The day *was* a tough one. He was grilled for several hours.

He called that afternoon but this time his tone was entirely different. All had gone well, and with some provisions he would continue to practise.

'Oh, and I must tell you,' he said. 'During the day my daughter-in-law called. "I have a verse for you," she said . . . "Isaiah 12:2."' This confirmed to us both God's presence with him that day.

There are also times when God places his imprimatur, His sovereign seal, on those periods of our lives when we may have felt very much alone. This may occur years after the event, long after we have ceased to ask 'Why?' and when we have regained some spiritual perspective. By doing so he confirms that He was not oblivious to the turn of events at the time, that He was there and that He was in control.

In *Nine Minutes Past Midnight* I told of my friend Graeme, now a senior obstetrician/gynaecologist practising in Sydney. As a young doctor he worked at the Royal Hospital for Women in Paddington. Though a Christian, he had yet to experience God's power to heal.

Early one Sunday morning he was out jogging when he received an urgent call to attend his teaching hospital for an emergency Caesarean section on one of his patients.

'Ern,' he said 'it all seemed to be fine, until about halfway through when everything went terribly wrong.' The patient, it seemed, had placenta accreta, a condition occurring in one in 2,500 pregnancies where the placental tissue invades the muscle layers of the uterus, making it difficult, sometimes impossible, to remove. She developed DIC, a condition where essential blood clotting agents are consumed by the body and bleeding is unable to be controlled, and began to haemorrhage torrentially. Graeme and the surgical team worked frantically to stop the bleeding. Finally a hysterectomy was performed but bleeding persisted. It began to dawn on him that he just might lose this young woman. In desperation he quietly prayed and, immediately, the bleeding came under control!

I have recently spoken with Graeme again years after the event, which had clearly made a permanent impact on his life.

'The situation was dire,' he said. 'I had closed the patient after surgery, but I knew all was not well.

'I called my wife, Bron, at home and asked her to pray while I struggled to restore the patient's blood volume. By this stage I had given her sixteen pints of blood. Bron went down to our church, St Bede's Anglican at Drummoyne, for the evening service. The whole congregation prayed and within half an hour the news came through that the bleeding had stopped.'

Only recently Graeme spoke to a man who had been at the service that evening so many years ago and who clearly remembered the events.

'And can you guess what the Gospel reading set down for that service was?' said Graeme. 'It was about the woman with the "issue of blood", the woman with uncontrolled gynaecological bleeding who had touched Jesus' robe and been instantly healed when doctors had given up.

'You know, I still see the patient from time to time,' said Graeme, 'and I have made her aware of the miracle of her healing. I also see her baby, now as a patient.'

The attack upon Graham Staines and his two boys was not an isolated event.

The cover story from *India Today*, 9 February 1999 stated the following:

> Last year witnessed at least 30 Hindu-Christian clashes in 10 of the state's 30 districts. . . . There were at least 60 attacks on churches in Orissa between 1986 and 1998, 'the highest number in any state'.

In 2014 the attacks on Christians continue around the world. Even this month ISIS insurgents have persecuted Christians in Iraq and Syria. Thousands have escaped across borders but many who have remained have been brutally murdered, some beheaded, some crucified. Two of my friends in Cairo have told me how careful they must be when walking in public. This is as the world has always been and it is not about to change. Jesus knew that, hence His words:

'I have told you all this so that you may find your peace in me. You will find trouble in the world – but, never lose heart, I have conquered the world!' (John 16:33, PHILLIPS).

Few of us will face such persecution. Few of us will have to stand strong in circumstances such as Gladys and Esther found themselves. Yet each of us will find ourselves from time to time in deep and turbulent waters. No matter how deep the water ahead may seem, no matter how difficult the journey, God prepares us and equips us for 'The Way'. His Spirit as comforter, guide and counsellor leads us through and, when the time has passed, He meets with us in a safe haven just as He promised to meet His disciples.[19] It may not be until that point in time that we fully understand . . . that we were never alone.

Following the Welsh revival of the late nineteenth century, missionaries travelled the world bringing the good news of Jesus Christ. Some travelled to Assam in north-east India, a primitive region at the time inhabited by many aggressive tribes. Young men practised head hunting. The number of heads severed and displayed on the walls of their lodges badged their strength and virility.

One of the missionaries was successful in converting a local young man, much to the fury of the chief, who summoned the people of the village, and then the young man and his family.

'Renounce your faith,' he said, 'or face public execution.'

The young man responded with the words, 'I have decided to follow Jesus. There is no turning back.' At that, the young man's two children were shot through with arrows. As they lay dying on the ground, the chief, enraged by the response, spoke again.

'Renounce,' he said, 'or your wife will die also.'

His response, 'Though no one joins me, still I will follow,' and then, 'No turning back, no turning back.' Immediately the archers also murdered his wife. Then a final ultimatum:

'Renounce, or you too will die.'

His response, 'The cross before me, the world behind me,' and then, 'No turning back, no turning back.'

The young man was also struck down by the archers. And then, something remarkable happened. The chief was deeply moved by the faith of this young man. 'Why would he die for another who lived 2,000 years ago and in a country far from here? There must be a supernatural power behind this family . . . I want it also.

'I too shall belong to Jesus Christ,' he said. When the crowd heard his confession, the whole village converted and accepted Christ as Saviour.

When the missionary returned to the village he found that revival had broken out. He passed reports of these events to the Indian evangelist Sadhu Singh who took the martyrs last words and put them to a traditional Indian tune. The hymn is still sung today to that same tune, Assam. It concludes with these challenging words, which are as valid and confronting now as on that fateful day.

Will you decide now to follow Jesus?
Will you decide now to follow Jesus?
Will you decide now to follow Jesus?
No turning back, no turning back.

Part IV

Cambodia

Preface to Chapter 15

I have been a physician in Nuclear Medicine for most of my working life. Computers, gamma cameras and radiopharmaceuticals are my stock in trade.

Sure, I can deal with everyday medical issues and I'm familiar with the emerging range of cholesterol lowering drugs and other medications. But family medicine is in my past and I no longer regard myself as at the cutting edge of general practice. Yet, in late 2012, I received an unexpected invitation from my surgical friend Malcolm to travel to Cambodia with a World Hope Network[1] medical team to provide basic health care to people in remote villages north of Phnom Penh. Malcolm was insistent. 'We need you, mate. You'll be fine.'

My immediate reaction was no, this is not my scene. But as days passed I began to understand that God was calling me to a new challenge. He had opened a door into the spiritual vacuum of Cambodia, a door that no man could close, and He was challenging me, along with others, to step out, take a risk and walk through that door. He would provide the means and He would lead, every step of the way. This was unknown territory to me and it challenged my certainties.

> We do not go to that far-distant field to speak of doctrine or theory, but of a living, bright, present, reigning Saviour.[2]

15

Cambodia

After prayerful consideration I accepted Malcolm's invitation to join the Cambodia team and invited my son Sam to come along also. He accepted eagerly. As a professional photographer, his skills would be invaluable. But we shared an ulterior motive. We would watch each other's backs in case things went pear-shaped in some of the more remote areas that I knew we would visit.

Thoughts of the 'killing fields' daunted me. Up to three million people had been brutally murdered by the Khmer Rouge in the three-year period from 17 April 1975. Anyone with an education, with smooth hands, who wore spectacles or whose skin was light in colour was targeted. I began to realize that not one person in Cambodia today would be unscarred by the legacy of that dreadful ordeal. I was also aware that Cambodia was a spiritual stronghold, a Buddhist enclave and that radical Islam was gaining a strong foothold. Only recently an al-Qaeda cell had been intercepted in a mosque just north of Phnom Penh.

As the day of departure drew near, I became uneasy. Did I have the necessary skills for what I was about to attempt? And what about the safety factor?

'Do you really want us to go, Lord?' I prayed. 'If not, please make it clear now.'

But His quiet inner voice was unmistakable. 'I want you to read Isaiah 43 and I want you to read through it every day for a week.' The words were not audible. They were completely out of left field and I knew from past experience that they were of God.[1]

Fear not . . .
I have called you by your name;
You are Mine.
When you pass through the waters, I will be with you;
And through the rivers, they shall not overflow you.
When you walk through the fire, you shall not be burned . . .
For I am the LORD your God . . .
You are My witnesses . . .

                                        (Isa. 43:1–3,10)

There it was again: 'my witness', 'my witness'. I had read these words many times before and they came alive on the page. I knew by now that one of my purposes in life was to be a witness to the intervention of God in the lives of men and women. And here was another opportunity.

It has been said that when fear is upon us, everything rustles. Well, a quiet peace settled upon me and with new confidence I claimed the verses as my own and began to look forward with anticipation to the time ahead.

On the day of departure, the team assembled at the Gold Coast airport near Brisbane. There was Daniel, our intrepid leader, and his wife, Jeanice, who were busy distributing tee shirts with the words 'World Hope Network' emblazoned upon them. Malcolm, my surgical friend, and his wife were there. Also a young accountant from Sydney, a family from Queensland and, of course, Sam. All had taken leave, some without pay, to participate in this venture of love. The tour started badly. Air tickets to Phnom Penh had not yet materialized and the travel insurance had not been processed. 'Great start to a trip to a third world country,' I thought! Had I misinterpreted what God was saying? No . . . His words were clear. I began to realize that something wonderful was about to unfold and that I would be a party to it all.

The overnight Air Asia link to KL was at best cattle, or perhaps water buffalo class. I wedged my 6-foot frame into the window seat for the eight-hour flight with little chance of stretching my legs as a Malaysian gentleman in the aisle seat popped some sedatives and descended into a deep sleep. The monotony was broken only by a flight attendant serving green curry four hours out of Brisbane.[2]

In Phnom Penh we cleared immigration and were joined by Jason, a dentist from Sydney who had come via Angkor Wat. I didn't know Jason, but sensed an immediate affinity. We were brothers called to the same purpose. Local members of Campus Crusade for Christ made us welcome. They would be our eyes and ears in Cambodia. I recognized the love of God in their faces as we greeted in traditional manner, hands together in an attitude of prayer. The troops were assembling.

Later that morning, after formalities, we visited the Tuol Sleng Genocide museum in downtown Phnom Penh. Originally a school covering twenty-four hectares, this complex had been commandeered by Pol Pot on 17 April 1975. Designated 'S-21', this prison had been set aside for the detention, interrogation, torture and slaughter of detainees after forced confessions, sometimes from their own children. Twenty thousand Cambodians had been 'processed' in this prison alone over a three-year period. Detainees were housed in cells measuring 0.9 by 2 metres. Iron bed frames in larger rooms were littered with instruments of torture and on the walls were life-sized photographs of bodies sprawled on those very beds. 'Do not touch!' said the signs. A rough wooden gallows, originally a child's plaything, dominated the courtyard. Here people had been hung upside down. Monuments marked the graves of bodies retrieved in the final days of the regime. There were endless galleries of photos of those who had perished. Their tortured faces would haunt me in the days to follow and I would recognize those very same expressions in so many of my patients.

As we stood at the main gate of the jail waiting to board the minibus back to headquarters, a young Cambodian man approached.

'Are you Dr Crocker?'

'Yes,' I responded, feeling quite apprehensive.

'Is this your passport?'

The man had found my passport somewhere in the expansive complex of cells and torture chambers and had traced me from my photograph. God, my silent partner, was on my case and I wondered if I would be equally proactive in helping the people represented by the photos that I had witnessed.

Later that day, as shadows lengthened, we headed north-east in our Toyota 4WD across the Mekong and on towards Kampong Cham. Our driver, Borin, had insisted that we wear neck braces. I soon understood why as the divided freeways gave way to miles of roadworks. Red dust limited vision to 9 metres at times. Tuk-tuks careered perilously close to trucks carrying impossible loads and motorcycles weaved in and out, sometimes carrying whole families precariously balanced. Other loads included pigs, racks of live chickens tied at the feet, sacks of rice and gas cylinders, even a refrigerator. Massive multi-headed cobras guarded the gates of the Buddhist temples that we passed. And there to the left, nestled behind walls away from prying eyes, was the mosque where the al-Qaeda cell had been apprehended.

'Do you eat spiders?' asked Borin.

'Well, no,' I said, hoping to change the subject.

'There are shops ahead in Skuon that specialize in them.'

Within minutes we pulled into a servo to be inundated by women and children thrusting plastic bags of sliced pineapple and red dragon fruit bristling with tiny black seeds through the windows of our 4WD. On a red plastic chair under canvas sat an elderly, diminutive woman in Khmer garb. The lines of time drew her face into an expressionless mask. In one hand she clasped a Gucci bag and in the other a ceramic bowl containing about 3 kilos of black furry tarantulas swirling in a sea of yellow marinade.

'Crunchy with soft centres,' someone ventured. I was not tempted. They do taste like chicken with a hint of tuna, I was told.

At dusk we pulled into a hotel in Kampong Cham and were delighted to find Western toilets, bottled water and best of all, air-conditioning and comfortable beds. But we were to spend the first hour finding rooms with taps that worked and toilets that flushed and were finally advised that a long-handled plunger was kept in the lobby next to the drinks machine for the ready convenience of guests. After a meal and several hours of sorting through pharmaceuticals in preparation for the next day, we fell into bed, exhausted.

Breakfast next morning was barbecued pork, the ubiquitous green curry and Chinese tea. The curry was great but somewhat curious as even casual inspection revealed an anatomical assortment of easily recognisable animal products unlikely to pass muster in a respectable stir-fry.

Clinic that morning was to be at the local army base of Kg Cham. This was a special privilege made possible by military brass, some of whom were Christians. A tree-lined avenue marked by metre-high posts fashioned as ordinance, and painted accordingly, led the way to a parade ground. Here sat 200 people, army personnel and family members waiting patiently on red plastic chairs in the morning sun. Officers barked orders and children ran to and fro revelling in the excitement.

After meeting with the commanding officers and exchanging greetings in traditional manner, followed by firm handshakes all round and the obligatory photographs, we launched into the clinic. Word filtered down that we were most welcome but that we would be required to stay until the last patient was seen. 'Well, this *was* the army after all,' I thought, and took some comfort in being welcomed and accepted by the powers that be.

That day we treated patients with severe undiagnosed hypertension, there was one case of malaria and many complained of stomach and joint pains. We despaired at the number of people with advanced cataracts and pterygia[3] rendering them virtually blind but were able to provide *prêt-à-porter* budget spectacles. I was amazed how such a simple inexpensive gift brought joy to so many.

The surgeon removed shrapnel from soldiers' legs and treated advanced haemorrhoids.

'You need an injection and surgery,' he told one man, gesturing with his hands as to what must occur.

'Don't you have any pills that I could take?' the horrified man retorted, backing hastily out of the clinic.

Dental hygiene was poor and, as I peered into mouths and inspected rotting teeth blackened by years of chewing betel nut, it became clear that many would require extractions. Jason was right on my case.

'Ern, you need a crash course in dentistry,' he said. And so that day he taught me to do mandibular blocks. The next day I would be extracting teeth.[4]

'You can't do any damage,' he said. 'Whack the needle in there. Give two cartridges of local, the first one slowly. Imagine it's your maiden aunt.' I suspect that my maiden aunt would not have been impressed.

We worked till sunset. Each patient was examined, treated and then counselled by members of local house churches. Ninety-five people were honoured and respected and had their medical needs met.

Dinner that evening was at the home of James, a young Asian aerospace graduate of the University of Florida. He was vital, intelligent and animated. He had built a four-storey building in the backyard of a rented house on a quarter-acre block not far from the centre of town. The building was to provide support and housing for local people in need, and for itinerant travellers. The remaining space had been converted into an aquaculture system where he bred fish to feed local house-church people. The effluent was filtered and recycled to irrigate a market garden, and waste from the garden fed to an impressive collection of turkeys, ducks and chickens. He had achieved all this with the help of young people rescued from the slums of Ho Chi Minh City. One was a converted prostitute, others were street kids and many were ex-addicts. But their faces told of transition from destitution to a future and a hope.

James was our go-to man for the week. He was able to procure at a moment's notice anything required from a flash card to a bottle of Coke. From my understanding he had a difficult past and was not in himself physically well, but his passion for people and his love of God transformed him into a veritable powerhouse.

Dinner was whole fish baked in spicy herbs, steamed and served with a curious canned drink called *grass jelly*, which was not even remotely similar to anything that I had ever tasted before. We quickly decided that Coke was a better option.

But the news of the night was from Dr Wong, one of our GPs. She had treated a patient that day with severe uterine prolapse. There was little that she could offer in terms of conventional medical help, and surgical correction was not an option. But she offered what she did have at her disposal . . . prayer. And to her absolute delight the woman was totally healed. She said that she had treated this condition many times in Singapore by conventional means but had never experienced such a wonderful result.

In days to follow we visited remote areas close to the Vietnamese border. This was a strategic region, in the sense that it had been Pol Pot's point of entry into Cambodia and that it offered ease of access to any future invading force. It was strategic also in a spiritual sense as Christianity was essentially unknown here. Most of the party travelled by motorcycle along pitted, dusty roads through heavy jungle and past ancient Khmer ruins. My son, Sam, forged ahead with Jason on a bike which we were later to discover had no functioning brakes. And later that night on the return journey they would find that the headlight dimmed whenever they accelerated. Sam admitted to falling off only once.

We set up clinic in a grove of coconut trees in the village of Prey Vang to the amusement of local children and under the watchful eye of two water buffalos grazing nearby. Dogs and chickens patrolled the waiting area and at one stage there was a dogfight under the dental chair. Many patients were seen that day and many became Christians. One lady was carried in unconscious from a nearby village. With rehydration and a healthy dose of glucose we were able to revive her before sending her off to hospital.

Many required urgent dental attention, some requiring five or six extractions. I was asked to provide the mandibular blocks; Jason and his students would handle the extractions. I prepared twenty syringes and was in the process of injecting a young woman when it all went horribly wrong. I managed to stick myself with one of the used needles even though I had taken every precaution. I knew of the high incidence of HIV/AIDS and of hepatitis B and C in the Cambodian people.[5] I was also aware that despite repeat vaccinations I was not immune to hepatitis B. How could God have allowed this to happen?

The remainder of the afternoon was something of a blur to me. We had been making great headway in helping so many, but the risk of contracting HIV/AIDS or chronic hepatitis weighed heavily on me. Sam was upset, as were team members.

Whenever we are about God's business we may expect spiritual oppression. As my friend Jamal in Bali says, 'The Jesus business is risky business.' Many people today believe in God but they are reluctant to believe in satanic opposition. 'Surely in this day of enlightenment,' they say, 'we can put aside such out-dated and archaic ideas.' But today, perhaps more than ever before, we are able to observe for ourselves the abject evil present in the world as exhibited by death cults such as ISIS and Boko Haram. No, spiritual opposition is very real. I have seen it in drug dens in Hong Kong, in death camps in Germany and Cambodia and have witnessed it in young lives here in Sydney. To deny its existence is to place ourselves at great risk, somewhat analogous to the soldier on the battlefield who is unaware of his enemy.

Two days later we returned to Phnom Penh. I was scheduled to speak at the annual Professional's Dinner at La Paranda Hotel and Restaurant that evening. Sixty people had accepted invitations, including top military brass, bankers, lawyers, businessmen and doctors. That afternoon I sat on my bed in the Chea Ly Hotel asking God what I should say to the people that night. The room was windowless and in the semidarkness I sensed the presence of God as I scribbled cryptic notes on the back of a business card. I knew that I must remain sensitive throughout to what must be said.

The dinner proceeded as planned and I was seated next to an army general. The food was wonderful but my mind was on what was to follow. I found myself pacing the corridor outside, searching God's mind, until finally it was time to speak. It was then that I understood why God had brought me to Cambodia.

I told them that God was my silent partner and that He had never once let me down. That He was with me twenty-four hours per day as a doctor, father, businessman and husband. I told them how He had demonstrated His healing power by raising to life a lady who had died following a cardiac arrest during a home visit. I told them also of my friend Zahir who had been a freedom fighter for Bangladesh during the Pakistani civil war. He had been arrested and placed before a firing squad. Moments before he was to be executed, God sent a man to rescue him from what would have been certain death. I told them of Dr Ken Clezy, a farmer's son from Victoria, who had been mightily used of God at a massacre at the Baptist hospital at Jibla in Yemen when an al-Qaeda insurgent murdered several of his staff. I told them also of a doctor friend who had been on duty at the embassy in Djakarta when the bomb had gone off and who had been instrumental in saving so many lives. All were Christians. All had their lives changed from the mundane to the extraordinary.

As the conclusion of the dinner, fourteen attendees accepted Christ into their hearts and a further sixteen requested more information.

On the final day we visited one of the many 'killing fields', located in an ancient orchard on the outskirts of Phnom Penh. I believed that my medical training would insulate me from what I would observe. But this was not so. An audio tour led us in the footsteps of those who had perished, to the spot where the buses had brought blindfolded prisoners, and then 50 metres along a gravel path to a series of mass graves where they had been summarily clubbed to death. Electricity had been provided for lighting so that executions could proceed through the night. A tree stood nearby from which a loudspeaker played martial music to hide the screams and moans of the dying. The catchcry had been: 'To kill you is no gain. To lose you is no loss.' I immediately drew a comparison with words from Jeremiah 29:11:

> For I know the thoughts that I think toward you . . . thoughts of peace
> and not of evil, to give you a future and a hope.

I gazed into a mass grave from which the skeletal remains of 450 people had been retrieved. It was no larger than a domestic swimming pool. 'Lord,' I said, 'what do you have to say about this?' The words came so clearly, 'From this valley of dry bones I will raise a mighty army.' The killing fields were to become harvest fields.

During that week I met a man 50 years of age. In white shirt, matching baseball cap, blue parka and horn-rimmed glasses, he was quite a cool dude. He had been a playboy in previous years but had accepted Christ and his life had now changed. He had become an evangelist to the people of north-eastern Cambodia, quite close to the Vietnamese border. I heard him preach in a remote village and was overwhelmed by the rigour and conviction of his testimony and the raw spiritual energy of a man clearly empowered by the Spirit of God.

I also met a Cambodian army general who was an inspiration and helpmeet to local Christians and a man who had survived the regime of terror, spending his childhood in a detention camp after his parents were murdered, and who now spent his days bringing others to the Lord.

There were also university students abandoned by Buddhist families when they converted to Christianity who worked tirelessly amongst the local Christians and with students at the university.

We had come to love and to honour the Cambodian people. Theirs was a life of sharing and caring. They were descended from a rich heritage but the events of the years had robbed them of peace. Wars, rumours of wars and genocide had ravaged their wellbeing and stripped them of peace of mind and often their trust in others. Though younger adults spoke freely of the impact of Pol Pot, older people were more guarded and reluctant to speak openly.

I returned home marvelling at what had been achieved in just one short week. Our patients had been honoured, given new hope and, where possible, their health restored. Three hundred and twenty-four people had become Christians and would be instrumental in bringing others to Christ in months to come. But why had it been so tough? Why had it been a battle every step of the way? Certainly there had been spiritual oppression, this was to be expected, but could not God have made for an easier passage?

The answer came two weeks later on the other side of the Pacific in Kona on the big island of Hawaii. Lynne and I were attending a medical gathering at the Youth With A Mission base. The speaker was a Canadian cardiologist, Dr David Demian. He quoted Christ's words to Simon Peter from the book of Luke.

> Simon, Simon! Indeed, Satan has asked for you, that he may sift you as wheat.
>
> (Luke 22:31)

God has the option to stop this from happening. But I now realized that sometimes He allows it to proceed. *He* wants to sift us too. But the difference is this, when Satan sifts us he removes the grain leaving the chaff. When God sifts us, the chaff is removed leaving the grains of wheat which, when planted, bring forth new life. The killing fields were in transition. They were becoming the harvest fields and I had been privileged to see this with my own eyes, to sow some seeds and to tend them for a while.

In the following chapter, I tell of my friend Borin who was my interpreter at the businessmen's dinner. Having suffered as a child under Pol Pot, he rebelled as a young man against society, finally fleeing Cambodia but returning triumphant as God's revolutionary.

Author's note

After the needle stick injury, on returning to Sydney I submitted myself to serial blood tests over several months. All results were negative.

16

God's Revolutionary

. . . they dragged Jason and some brethren to the rulers
of the city, crying out,
'These who have turned the world upside down have
come here too.'

(Acts 17:6)

I knew little of our driver, Borin. Others had embraced him lovingly
when we met at the airport earlier that day and there was clearly something special about him, something that set him apart. I observed him
closely in the days that followed. He had a heart for the Cambodian
people like no other that I had met, and clearly a gift for evangelism.
When I had spoken at the businessmen's dinner, at the conclusion
of our tour, he was my interpreter. With conviction he broadcast my
words into the hearts of all those listening. Army brass, bankers, lawyers and prominent businessmen became Christians that night, with
others expressing an interest for 'further information, please'.

Here was a man who clearly had the call of God on his life, a native
Cambodian who had lived through the horrors of Pol Pot. How had
this come to pass? How had he evolved from a small boy growing up
in a Buddhist family of seven children to become what I now recognized as God's revolutionary?

Borin was a teenage boy when Pol Pot seized power on 17 April
1975. The city of Phnom Penh became a ghost town within three
days. Borin was sent to work in the rice paddies 400 km from Phnom
Penh. He was made to carry 100-litre containers of water balanced on

a bamboo pole up a steep hill from the stream and to clear with his bare hands 10 metres of jungle per day for farming. Failure to achieve this resulted in severe criticism and punishment. His father was deployed elsewhere as a farm labourer.

Then in 1979 the Vietnamese communists stormed across the north-east Cambodian border, crushing the Khmer Rouge and bringing to an end four years of indescribable brutality.

People returned home, seeking their families. But one in four Cambodians had been murdered and reunions were often heartbreaking. Travelling on foot back to Phnom Penh, Borin located his father. He was critically ill and after a short period, he died. Broken-hearted, and with the help of friends, Borin cremated his father and buried his bones in a shallow grave before continuing his journey back to Phnom Penh.[1]

Reunited with family and as the oldest of the siblings, he assumed the role of provider for his mother and sisters. Searching the countryside, he found old car and motorcycle engines which he sold for profit. With that money he was able to feed his family and send his younger brothers to school.

But these were wild and unlawful times in Phnom Penh and Borin soon fell into bad company. He embraced a life of heavy drinking, gambling and immorality.

'I owed people money,' he said, 'and brought much heartache and disappointment to my mother.'

In 1984 the Cambodian government began to conscript young men to the army. By that stage Borin owed money big time and was being pursued by creditors and the local authorities alike. He decided to flee from the army and made his way on foot to a refugee camp on the Thai-Cambodian border. His intention was to join a guerrilla force in Thailand. The journey took three days.

Life in the camp was tough. The United Nations Border Relief provided for women and children only, and Borin suffered greatly.

'One day,' he said, 'I was very low and at the point of begging for food. I heard a man call me by name and turned to find that I knew him. He was an old schoolmate and in a similar plight to me. He encouraged me to attend an English class run by missionaries in the camp and gave me two books and a pencil. Well, what did I have to lose? On the first day we were asked to stand up, to close our eyes and pray! I can tell you, that was a brand new experience for me, doctor.'

Borin was intrigued by the stories told by the old pastor about Moses, Joshua and David.

'I was fascinated to hear how God had guided and protected them. The stories gave me hope. I wanted the same protection that God gave to these men. Maybe He could do the same for me.' Borin approached the pastor and asked to be accepted. From that point on he was able to stay at the church and was given food and shelter.

On Christmas Day 1985, the camp came under attack by the Cambodian-Vietnamese communist army. Fearing for their lives, people fled across the border into Thailand. Away from his new Christian friends, Borin soon resumed his old ways of drinking and gambling. Eventually he found work with the army interviewing conscripts regarding their political, business and military affiliations.

But in 1989 he was invited by a friend to attend a seminar conducted by a Singaporean Christian who was looking for workers to assist him. Borin needed the money, that was for sure, so he signed up for a three-day programme.

'One of the messages spoke to my heart,' he said. 'I began to understand that God had a plan for my life, yes me, Borin. He began to reveal to me who He really was and why Jesus had come to die for me. I gave my life to God that day, doctor. But then, in the final message people were called to be revolutionaries. I hated that word "revolution". It had claimed my father's life, cost me an education and was responsible for where I was, away from family and without hope. I stormed out of the meeting.'

But as Borin left the meeting, a friend took him by the arm and invited him home. On the table in that house was a small red book. No, not Mao's little red book but another of similar size called *Come Help Change the World* by Bill Bright.[2]

Borin was fascinated by the book and asked to borrow it.

'I couldn't wait to read it,' he said. As he paged through it later that night, there again was that word, *revolution, revolution, revolution*. But this time it was a different kind of revolution. It was spiritual revolution.

'God spoke to me that night, doctor,' he said. 'I kneeled down and asked Him to accept me as his "Spiritual Revolutionary". He confirmed that to me in John 14:12.'

> Most assuredly, I say to you, he who believes in Me, the works that I do he will do also; and greater works than these he will do, because I go to My Father.

Borin was repatriated to Cambodia, where he was assigned to work with students at Campus Crusade for Christ. By the power of the Holy Spirit, he has led many students to Christ and discipled them. Some have become prominent members of society: pastors, leaders of large organizations, doctors and businessmen.

'I believe that as long as I stay willing and humble,' he said, 'God will use me. I am honoured and privileged to be a servant of God, here in Cambodia, bringing good news and hope to my people.'

I Skyped Borin last week. It was miserable reception. He was driving back to Phnom Penh from a mobile medical clinic somewhere in the north-east.

'Something I need to ask you,' I said. 'What does it mean to you to be God's revolutionary?'

'It's all about change, doctor,' he said. 'I wanted to see lives changed. I wanted to see people set free from the bondage of Satan. I wanted to be a revolutionary like Jesus. He came to serve and to save and to change lives. He came to bring freedom and I wanted to be part of that, and to see that in my people.

'I have now seen that happen, Ern,' he said. 'One man couldn't read or write. He was a gangster and unfaithful to his wife. Yet God changed his life. Another was a playboy, a useless character, yet God changed him too and now he serves the people. He has become an evangelist and has brought a thousand people to the Lord in the last twelve months.[3] God is opening doors here, doctor, and I want to be part of it.'

'Have you seen healing miracles?' I asked.

'Yeah, yeah,' he said. 'One boy couldn't walk, and the doctors couldn't help him. Our people prayed and he was healed. I saw it with my own eyes, doctor. When I visited his home church. I asked him to walk and he walked normally.'

We don't like the word 'revolutionary'. It conjures up visions of men in far-off places in black balaclavas with semiautomatic rifles and weighed down by swathes of machine-gun bullets. In Borin's mind it had stood for all things evil, everything that had taken away his freedom, his family, his right to an education, even his hope.

Yet God called him to be a spiritual revolutionary, one who would change the world. And he is doing just that, right now.

Come, help change the world!

17

Good Morning Vietnam

Now abide faith, hope, love, these three; but the greatest of these is love.

(1 Cor. 13:13)

In January 2014 Sam and I once again found ourselves in Cambodia with the team. This time we travelled north-west to the Thai-Cambodian border visiting Kampong Cham, Siem Reap (gateway to the Angkor region),[1] Sisophon and finally Battambang, close to the Thai border. Here we were warned not to stray from the paths, as many landmines remained undetected.

Our team included family doctors, Jason, my dental friend, Malcolm and, of course, our intrepid leader, Daniel. There were also medical and dental students from Phnom Penh, a social worker from Sydney and other willing helpers from home and abroad.

These were turbulent times for Cambodia. Clothing workers for corporates such as Gap, Nike and Wal-Mart rebelled against low salaries and several had been shot dead in bloody street demonstrations.[2] The American Embassy had issued a warning to US citizens to avoid travel to Cambodia and we were specifically advised to avoid 'hotspots', especially the airport region of Phnom Penh on certain days. We watched as convoys of heavily armed police and security forces patrolled the city. But we were undeterred. We knew that God had opened a door of opportunity that no man could close.

Our programme was similar to that of the previous year. We conducted clinics in villages under canvas and coconut trees, in a church hall and in a school classroom surrounded by acres of rice drying on tarpaulins. Chickens pecked at the dentist's feet as he extracted teeth well beyond their use-by date and, as previously, there was a dogfight under the dental chair. Farm animals were tethered nearby and hordes of children looked on. It was the best show in town. On the day of the first clinic, a snake was discovered under the pharmacy table as the surgeon, just a few metres away, excised a mass the size of a baseball from the back of a local man. Hundreds attended the clinics each day and we did our best to accommodate each one.

Clinical decision-making was often difficult. Whether or not to treat a child with an ear or throat infection was a no-brainer. But we were acutely aware that there would be little, if any, medical follow-up for many of our patients. Some presented with life-threatening hypertension or symptoms of coronary artery disease. There were others with chronic pain and one with florid thyrotoxicosis.[3] Management decisions were made on a case-by-case basis. Often we would issue medications with the instructions, 'If these pills help, find a doctor and have him prescribe some more. Otherwise, you may be able to buy more at the pharmacy.'[4]

Minor surgery was performed under local anaesthesia. But this again posed problems, as follow-up was difficult even in close liaison with family members and local medicos. One man, against advice, travelled home five miles on his motorcycle post hernia surgery, returning later having lost several sutures.

Young women presented with rotting and broken teeth. They had never before had access to dental care. Jason was able to fill and cap their teeth. He gave them back their smile and with that smile, confidence and hope.

During that week I met people whose life experience would expand my vision and build my faith. One was a Malaysian woman who had been freed from Hindu curses placed on her by her grandfather and saved from certain death. Her story follows this chapter. Another was a young man who had suffered dreadfully under the Pol Pot regime:

'The Khmer Rouge killed my father,' he said. 'They came to our house and took him away. "We'll take you to another town to work," they said, but they were lying. He was taken to a killing field just kilometres from our home in Sisaphon and brutally murdered. There were more than 10,000 killed there. You can still visit the area and see human bones lying on the ground. He was a good man,' he said, 'but paler skinned than I, and that made him a target.'

Pastor Chea leaned forward, and studied my gaze. Had I really understood the significance of what he'd said?

I had met him over a meal with the team at Kampong Cham and he had agreed to meet with me early the next morning to tell his story. We sat face to face in the hotel lobby, two guys from entirely different backgrounds, but sons of the same God.

'They took me from my mother,' he shared, 'and with 200 other children I was assigned to work duties on a farm. We cut wood, worked the land, made chicken houses and dug pools for water. We lived in a dorm in the care of a Khmer Rouge woman who fed us rice and water, nothing more. I was only 5 when they first came for me.'

Then in 1979, when Chea was 11, the Vietnamese army swept down from Ho Chi Minh City and destroyed Pol Pot. 'I was released,' he said. 'I had no idea where my mother was, or even if she was still alive, so I ran from place to place searching for her, calling, "Mummy, Mummy." Finally I found her. She was well and still living at home.

'After Pol Pot was deposed,' he said, 'there was widespread civil war. Bombings were frequent. I joined the Cambodian army and fought against the Khmer Rouge.

'There was open combat, and many of us were killed by landmines. I became part of a spy team providing intelligence for government forces.'

When Chea was 18 he began to hear about Jesus. 'I had two or three idols to protect me,' he said, 'but my army friend said, "They can't help you; they can't see. They can't hear or touch." He was not a Christian but he knew about Christianity from a relative in the United States who had sent him a Bible. From my discussions with him I began to understand that I was a sinner, and because of that I believed that when I died I would go to hell.

'Books are my friends, Ern,' said Chea. 'Because of Pol Pot I had no education. So I read everything that I could get my hands on. My army friend was not a believer. But when I went to his home, I saw that he had a Bible.

'"Can you lend me this book to read?" I asked.

'"I'll give you a New Testament," he said. "When you read that I'll give you the whole book."

'I read it in three months. I read in John 1 about God creating the world. "Interesting!" I thought. Dear Jesus! During this time I continued as a member of an undercover spy team for the government. We wore plain clothes and just watched things for the government.'

It took Chea a year to read the whole Bible. 'Oh, it was wonderful!' he said. 'I read in Genesis about God creating the world. But who is this God? And who is this Jesus? Is Jesus God? Would Jesus protect me? And then I began to see miracles. There was much shooting. People around me were being killed but I was still alive. Sometimes we walked through minefields. One day I was walking along a path and my friend was following me. All of a sudden there was an explosion.' Chea looked back to see his friend lying on the ground, his legs blown off. 'Yet I was safe,' he said. 'I was alive and I had walked in exactly the same spot only seconds before.'

Chea began to understand that God was taking special care of him.

'One day we were ambushed,' he said. 'My backpack was hit and blown apart. It contained books, clothes, a Bible and some ammunition. I was thrown to the ground but I was not hurt.

'"Chea is dead, Chea is dead," they cried. But I was OK. "Chea, Chea what happened?" they asked. I said, "I don't know, but I'm OK." Some people became fearful of me because I seemed to have special protection over me. Other soldiers around me were being shot dead but I was OK. I became frightened as I could easily have been killed myself, and from what I had read from the Bible I would have gone straight to hell. It was then that I decided to become a Christian.'

Chea began to learn more about Jesus and from that time on walked with Him daily.

'God would often warn me in my spirit of what lay ahead,' he said. 'One night, I was asleep in my house. God woke me up and said "Get up, there are thieves in your house." There were indeed thieves. I got up and chased them away. So I learned to pray and to trust God daily.

'It was a Buddhist culture in our home,' he said. 'Before becoming a Christian I had been preparing to become a monk, much to my mother's delight. She would have been so proud of me and have been greatly respected. But I said, "No, I won't become a monk because now I know Jesus and who He is." I stood up to my family and told them about Jesus. That was very difficult and created big problems for me.'

Then in 1999 Chea's mother became extremely unwell with gross swelling in one of her legs. 'Pray to the Jesus, Mummy,' said Chea. 'He can heal you.'

'She did pray,' he said, 'and it was wonderful. God healed her over the next week. No medicine was given. She also became a Christian. "Jesus healed me," she said. "He is the real God."'

At this time Chea felt called to become a preacher. 'It was a difficult time,' he said, 'because Cambodia had closed the door to outside Christians. But there were some home churches. I joined one and the pastor taught me more about Christ and encouraged me to become a pastor. After that I attended a seminary in Phnom Penh over a three-year period.'

Chea has now been a pastor for twenty years. And during that time he has seen God's hand move in mysterious ways. 'One day a man had a fever. I went with my young people to his home.

'"What's wrong with you?" I asked.

'"I'm hot," he replied.

'I said, "I want to pray for you." His father was a shaman but he could not help his son. I reached out and touched the man's head. He cried out, "Oh, the pain, who put a needle into my head?" I placed my hand on his forehead and said, "In Jesus' name, fever be gone." I knew that he had an evil spirit and I said, "What is your name?" But he would not tell me so I commanded him to go out from this man.

'A young man with me said, "Pastor Chea, stop, because he is dead already." He was lying quite still with no movement. But in a few moments he woke up and said, "What happened?" His body was wet, but the fever had gone. I said, "Jesus has healed you and He loves you." He accepted Christ.'

It was time to move on but I had two final questions:

'Pastor Chea, why did God choose you when you were in the army?'

'Because He loved me and called me to glorify His name.'

'This time a tough one,' I said. 'Why did God allow Pol Pot to come and to create such havoc?'

'Because my people had rejected God, but now, praise God, that's all changing.'

At the conclusion of the Cambodian tour, several of us travelled on to Ho Chi Minh City in Vietnam. We were to establish a mobile medical clinic in the basement of a church hall not far from Long Tan, Phuoc Tuy Province. As an Australian, Long Tan was of particular interest to me as it was here on a rubber plantation on 18 August 1966 that 108 men from D Company, Sixth Battalion fought a fierce battle against more than 2,000 Viet Cong from 275 Regiment. Eighteen Aussies were killed, as were 245 Viet Cong and many others were wounded. Etched indelibly in my mind was an entry from a report of those who retrieved the Australian bodies. 'Every man,' they said, 'had died facing the enemy.' Though hopelessly outnumbered, every man had stood his ground. The new enemy now was poverty and spiritual oppression. We too would stand our ground.

Leaving Phnom Penh posed its own problems. Our coach reservations were not confirmed and before equipment could be loaded it became apparent that money must change hands. More violent clashes with clothing workers had been predicted for that day and we observed the heavy military presence as we left Phnom Penh. We crossed the Mekong and after several hours of swatting mosquitoes, a quick meal and rest stop at the border, we arrived in Ho Chi Minh City.[5] Scooters, motorbikes, taxis, tuk-tuks and trucks surged along city roads in an unrelenting torrent. Yet there was an order, a cleanliness and sense of social progression that I had not been aware of in Cambodia. Friends escorted us through the tumult to our hotel.

We were tired and some of us, myself included, were unwell and recovering from gastrointestinal upset. One member of the team clutched a roll of toilet paper in one hand as if his life depended upon it as he sat in the lobby waiting for room allocation. But as my friend Thomas says, 'God is relentlessly personal and it just seems like His joy to look after us.' Daniel had managed to book us into a wonderful little hotel not far from the palace and war museum. The food was excellent and the beds were comfortable. There was plenty of hot water and the Western toilets actually worked.

Later that afternoon, once unpacked and settled in, we set out to explore Ho Chi Minh City. I stood with Sam at the palace gates recalling footage of the fall of Saigon as tanks stormed those gates in April 1975. The gates were now fully restored but those same tanks sat nearby on the palace lawns, a menacing reminder of that day. And at the war museum, I saw the photo of a young boy maybe 10 years of age in US military uniform armed with an automatic rifle sitting pensively, head bowed among graves of fallen soldiers. The words inscribed at the foot of the photo in English and Vietnamese were familiar:

> When I was a child, I spoke as a child, I understood as a child, I thought as a child; but when I became a man, I put away childish things.
>
> (1 Cor. 13:11)

I pondered this photo and these words for the remainder of my time in Vietnam. It was clear from other exhibits in the museum that feelings ran deep even so many years after the war. Perhaps this photo had been discovered following the fall of Saigon. Perhaps it was a more recent expression by the Vietnamese people, a statement to would-be aggressors. I hoped the latter as to me this would indicate a measure of healing of memories with the passage of time and new hope for the future.

But now it was next morning. I was the one remaining doctor on this tour of duty and together with Jason, had agreed to one final clinic before heading back to Sydney.

'We'll keep it small,' they said, knowing the rigours of our previous week in Cambodia. 'Twenty-five patients, max.'

In the basement of a church we set up shop, Jason on one side with his portable dental clinic searching as usual for a power adaptor, myself on the other with my interpreter, a pretty local girl who I had been told was a photographic model. Her English was reasonable. My Vietnamese was non-existent. But somehow we managed. Amy, a social worker from Sydney, was my pharmacist for the day and Sam helped with logistics.

By 9 a.m. the clinic was well under way. There were patients recovering from malaria, dengue fever and hepatitis. There were amputees from farm and war injuries and others suffering from all manner of aches and pains. Low back pain from heavy farm labour featured prominently with both men and women.

'Work faster,' they said. 'You must work faster!'

It was then that I realized that there were already seventy-five patients waiting and others still arriving.

We were making good time until I looked up to see a tall slender man with a shock of black hair sitting before me, hands tightly clasped. Deng was a good-looking young guy of maybe 26 with a boyish face, who no doubt would have turned the heads of many a young lady in his village. But today he sat unable to meet my gaze. His face was stained by tears, his voice faltered, his feet shuffled restlessly.

'How can I help you?' I asked.

There was a pause as he glanced around aware that others would hear his every word.

'I'm going to kill myself,' he said.

Can you possibly imagine my thoughts at that time? What could I do to help this man in the limited time that I had? Patients queued behind him and others pressed in, hoping to hear details of his story. Deng had previously attempted suicide by swallowing pesticide at the family farm. Somehow he had survived. He desperately wanted to live but in his particular circumstance could see no other option but to take his own life.

I took him aside and, with the help of an interpreter, counselled him as best I could. We prayed and then I entrusted him to the elders and the senior pastor. It would be a long road back for Deng, and under close supervision. However, that day he met Jesus, the only one who could meet his needs, the only one who could restore meaning to his life and give him hope. I knew that God had a plan for this young man's life and the words from the book of Jeremiah once again resounded loudly in my spirit.

> For I know the thoughts that I think toward you, says the LORD, thoughts of peace and not of evil, to give you a future and a hope.
>
> (Jer. 29:11)

Later that afternoon, the experience with Deng still fresh in my mind, I travelled with others by motorcycle to the homes of two single ladies. Both had been homeless until the previous year when a World Hope Network team had visited their village and built them small houses. Two hours on the back of a motorcycle on bush tracks played havoc with my back. And when we crossed a fenceless bridge not more than 4-foot wide over a river, I seriously thought that my time had come, especially when I realized that the traffic was two-way.

The newly painted dwellings stood resplendent in the afternoon sun as the occupants greeted us warmly with a hug and hot tea. Scriptures on the walls told of their newfound faith and assurance.

That evening church members met in the hall for a service of thanksgiving. They sang and prayed and the senior pastor spoke. I didn't understand a word that he said, and with severe back pain stood to one side trying to find a comfortable position. At the conclusion of the service everyone stood. And then one by one they approached and hugged each of us in turn. There were tears; there were smiles and an overwhelming sense of the presence of God in that room. I gazed at the men embracing me. Many were in their sixties. I knew that they had experienced the horrors of war and that some may well have been Viet Cong. But memories and my back pain were healed that night by prevailing love.

Later we slept soundly on camp beds in the church basement. It was still dark, 5:30 a.m. according to my iPhone, when I woke to the strains of music emanating from a room at the end of the hallway. Investigating, I found some of those same people singing quietly in Vietnamese to the strum of an old acoustic guitar, badly in need of tuning. Jason had also heard the music. I joined him in the back row so as not to disturb the sense of God's presence. We were overwhelmed by the heartfelt devotion and love expressed by the words they sang:

> Alas and did my Saviour bleed
> And did my Sovereign die?
> Would He devote that sacred head
> For sinners such as I?
>
> At the cross, at the cross where I first saw the light
> And the burden of my heart rolled away
> It was there by faith I received my sight
> And now I am happy all the day.[6]

Then quietly, and with few words, they dispersed into the dark.

The sun would soon rise. It was a new day.

This morning as I write, my assigned reading for the day is from 1 Corinthians 13:

> And though I have the gift of prophecy, and understand all mysteries and all knowledge, and though I have all faith, so that I could remove mountains, but have not love, I am nothing.
>
> (1 Cor. 13:2)

A few verses below this are written the words from the photo in the war museum. I had discovered again that God *is* love and that love alone conquers all. His blessings are new every morning. They are new every day.

18

Vijay

'I became a Christian,' she said, 'because He saved me from certain death.'

Vijay, Phnom Penh, 12 January 2014

I have never heard anyone pray like Vijay.

'Send down the fire, Lord!' she said. 'Man,' I thought, 'when you get prayed for by Vijay you stay prayed for.' Diminutive, with a smile a metre wide, she clearly has the call of God on her life.

It was with these thoughts that I shared a jasmine tea with her in the lobby of the Chea Ly Hotel in Phnom Penh. We had just returned from a medical mission outreach to Battambong in North West Cambodia, where she had been a tower of strength. It was a remote town close to the Thai border and no stranger to recent violence. It was also a heavily mined area and we had been advised to stay on established paths. Several of us, including myself, had been quite ill. Yet Vijay was always there praying, encouraging, helping wherever possible. We talked, and we talked . . .

Vijay was born in Kulim, on the western border of Penang, on 8 March 1961. Her parents had been separated, making it difficult for her mother to cope. But just before Vijay was born, Grandfather managed to reconcile her parents, and father returned to the family home. But, he had ideas of his own:

'Come away with me to Seremban,' he said to Vijay's mother. 'I will look after you there.' Seremban was a long way from home on the far south-west coast of Malaysia. And so, a month before the birth, they moved to Seremban. When Vijay's mother went into labour, her father would have no part of it. It was the local women who escorted her to the district hospital. After the delivery he visited the new baby, assigned her a Hindu name then left, never to return.

Vijay's mother was abandoned in her hospital bed with no support and a new baby girl.

'The hospital administrators threatened to keep me as payment unless the bill was paid,' said Vijay. 'Finally, Grandfather came from Kulim and paid the bill in full, but he was furious. He took us back to his home but told my mother, "We must not keep this child, she is a curse on our family."'

Four generations of Hindu curses were passed on to Vijay by her grandfather. From that time on she became ill with recurrent fevers and chest infections.

'Whenever I got sick, grandfather became angry and threatened to stamp on me to kill me,' she said. 'But something always prevented him from doing so. He insisted that I have the cheapest food available and even as a baby I was fed rice water instead of milk. Grandfather had three wives and when other grandchildren were born they were kept separate and cared for normally. My three grandmothers looked after me but Grandfather hated me with a passion.'

Schooldays were a nightmare for Vijay. She was constantly ill and fell far behind in her studies. Other children shunned her and as a result she spent much of her time alone and in tears.

Then, at 11 years of age she volunteered for the school walkathon. Here was something that even she could do for her school. It was a five-mile walk. She started well but, as the miles passed, became progressively short of breath, finally collapsing at the finish line. At the local hospital, doctors examined her and told her that she had a 'weak heart'. But in the teaching hospital an echocardiogram revealed a hole in her heart with a shunt of blood from one chamber to another. The cardiologist said that surgery was not an option. 'We will just let her slowly die,' he said.

Vijay's condition deteriorated. As time passed she became progressively weak and short of breath. Her grandfather prayed for her at the idols of the Hindu and Chinese temples but to no avail. By the time that she had reached 20 years of age she was breathless to the point where it was difficult for her even to speak audibly. Her body swelled with retained fluid and frequently she noticed that she would become quite blue, especially around the lips.[1] Even her vision began to fail. Finally she was admitted to hospital under the care of the cardiologist who had been treating her for several years.

'There is nothing we can do,' he said. Rather, he told Grandfather that she would die within the week. He should take her home, build a coffin, and prepare for the funeral.

Vijay was about to turn 21. Her family had been preparing for a coming of age party. This was expected of them and to fail to provide this would be to invoke considerable loss of face. Yet here she was, dying, and instead of a celebration with gifts and best wishes, Grandfather made arrangements for her funeral and built her a wooden coffin, an easy task for him as he was a builder. 'It was a good coffin,' she said, 'but it was to be my last birthday present.'

And then . . . an unexpected guest arrived. A young Indian girl from the local school came to visit.

'I know you can't see me, Vijay,' she said, 'but I want to tell you that you are not going to die. You are going to live. If you will call upon the name of Jesus, you will be healed.' The girl was three years younger than Vijay and had apparently accepted Jesus recently at school.

Grandfather was scathing. 'All these years we have been praying with no result, and now you want to try? Go right ahead, young lady.'

So with the help of her new friend, Vijay began to ask for healing in the name of Jesus. She was not a Christian and had little understanding of what it meant to be a Christian. But each day she became stronger. Over a two-week period, her breathlessness eased and the cyanosis disappeared. She grew in strength and the swelling resolved. Best of all, for the first time that she could remember, she was filled with joy and laughter. This was indeed a miracle, which no one, least of all Vijay, had expected.

She read notes given to her by her young friend on how to become a Christian and soon gave her life to the Lord.

'I became a Christian,' she said, 'because the Lord saved me from certain death. I didn't know how to pray at that stage but I said, "Jesus, I will worship You and no other god." I just knew that I could worship no other god.'

When Vijay told her grandfather what she had done, he was furious.

'Tomorrow you leave this house,' he said. 'We do not practise Christianity in this house. If you are a Christian, then you must leave. If you deny Christianity, you can stay and I will take care of you. That is my condition.'

'But I was healed. I could see the difference,' she said. 'The blueness went and I was breathing normally. Best of all, I was happy for the first time in years. My grandfather chased me out of the house and then went looking for the father of the girl who had led me to the Lord.

'My mother was in tears.

'"Where will you go?" she asked. I had no idea.

'"Why don't you stay with my sister?" she said. "She is a Christian and will look after you."' So Vijay took a bus to her aunt's house where she stayed for three months.

The girl who had prayed for Vijay was also thrown out of her home by her parents after the visit from Grandfather. She came looking for Vijay. Together they decided to find a small house and take care of one another. They found a church and went there to worship. 'Sometimes there was some swelling in my legs,' said Vijay, 'but each time I would pray and it would go away.'

Three months after the healing, she returned to her cardiologist.

'This time when he performed echocardiography he found no hole in my heart,' she said. 'Usually an echo took ten to fifteen minutes but this time they spent forty-five minutes searching for the hole. No hole was found. The doctor was shocked.

'"Never in my life have I seen such a thing," he said. "You are extraordinary." After the scan, he brought other doctors to check his findings.

'The cardiologist had been my doctor for five years,' she said. 'He told my grandfather that my blood pressure was fine and that my heart was now completely normal. Much to the annoyance of Grandfather, he stopped all my medicines. He was not a Christian man but he told me to "continue to find this God", despite my grandfather berating him. He said that he didn't want to see me again unless I had problems.'

Shortly after the healing, Vijay applied to study nursing in Penang.

'I had a routine medical,' she said, 'which included echocardiography. The doctor performing the study said, "Are you a heart patient? I can see a line on the inner wall of your heart."'

Vijay could only assume that this was where the hole had been. He commented that he suspected that she had suffered from heart disease at some time in the past but now agreed that she was completely well.

The doctor who interviewed her when she applied to do nursing asked if she had academic qualifications.

'Yes,' she said. 'I have a BA.'

'Bachelor of Arts?'

'No,' she said. 'I am Born Again.'

The doctor accepted Vijay into the training programme and encouraged her to pray with patients. It was a Christian hospital. She worked a fifteen-hour day and continued in nursing there for twenty years.

At 23 years of age she was baptized in her local church. The pastor prayed over her regarding the four generations of curses that her grandfather had placed upon her. She said, 'I fell to the ground, but on standing again I realized that I had been completely released from years of demonic oppression.' Eventually she and the pastor were married.

When Vijay's grandfather died, she paid a visit to her family home and brought her mother back to live with her.

'I am able to support you now, Mother,' she said. '*I* will care for *you*.' Her mother began to attend the same church where she too became a Christian. Her life was changed. She became very much involved in social work and prayed for many people, especially Hindus suffering under the curses laid upon them by family members. She died several years ago but in her final years she was known by all those who loved her as their own 'Mother Teresa'.

Today Vijay has her own ministry in Malaysia. 'I hear from the Holy Spirit very clearly,' she said. 'He told me to go to a certain place to meet a widow, just like Elijah. This widow was a Catholic with no husband, but two children to support. I was able to pray for her for strength, freedom and provision. Through meeting that woman I now look after 150 needy people.'

Recently Vijay wrote to me from Malaysia. She had visited her local hospital to pray for the sick. There she found a women crying openly and greatly distressed.

'What is the matter?' she had asked.

'My son is dying,' replied the woman. It appears that two days earlier, while eating his breakfast, her son, Maran, had lost consciousness and could not be roused. 'I didn't know what to do,' she said. 'His pulse was very slow. Neighbours called for an ambulance and we brought him here. They put in a drip, took him for an ECG and X-rays but couldn't find anything specifically wrong with him.' By the third day he was conscious but remained extremely weak and was short of breath. Still there was no definitive diagnosis. This was a government hospital, she said, and the test results were slow in coming.

Finally a doctor approached Mary, his mother. 'We've done all the tests,' he said. 'They show that his kidneys are not functioning and he's not responding to treatment.' Mary was devastated, as she was given to understand that her son would be unlikely to survive.

'Mary,' said Vijay, 'our creator is looking for His creation but creation is looking in all the wrong places and seeking wrong advice from the wrong people in all the wrong ways. If you and I believe in this one man, Jesus, who has taken our sins, pains, curses and all of our difficulties upon Himself, He will help us.'

'I gave up talking to God a long time ago,' said Mary, 'when my husband was killed in an accident. There is no God.'

'I am the living testimony,' said Vijay. 'And I'm giving you this promise, if Jesus can heal me, He can heal your son. I stand before you as a living miracle. Of all these gods that you are praying to, have any of them given their life for you? Well, Jesus did. You don't have to pay a price. Jesus has already paid for you and your son.'

As Vijay spoke, Mary, who was a Hindu, looked up at her. 'I'm confused,' she said. 'I don't know what to do. This is my son.'

Vijay continued. 'Jesus is waiting for you. If you will open your heart to Him and believe, Maran will be healed or something good will take place.'

'I only want my son to live,' Mary pleaded.

'If you call upon that mighty name, you will save your son and the Hindu curse upon your family will be broken. Jesus will set you free.'

Mary pulled Vijay close to the bed where her son was lying. 'I believe what you're saying,' she cried, tears running down her face. And then she asked the ICU nurse's permission for Vijay to pray for Maran. Vijay related how she had rebuked the spirit of death and broken the curses and bondages upon him. 'I released the Spirit of God over Maran,' she said 'to breathe life and healing into him.'

Following this she sat down with Mary and shared the gospel and her own story of healing that had taken place years before. 'I gave her my phone number,' she said, 'and asked her to call me. Keep saying, "Maran is healed in Jesus' name,"' she said.

The next day Mary called to say that Maran had opened his eyes and that strength had come back into his body.

That entire Hindu family has now come to accept Jesus. The sadness is gone. The house is filled with love and joy.

Maybe you have experienced miraculous healing like Vijay, maybe not. Maybe you have accepted Christ as she has. Perhaps this has not yet happened. Be assured that God can change your life. If you are willing to humble yourself before Him and call upon His name, you will be saved. Your life will be turned around. You will find a new identity in your Father God, which no man can take away. And by His Holy Spirit you will find peace, encouragement and power to live.

On the last day of our medical outreach to Battambong, we stood at dusk outside the small school which had served as our surgery that day, surrounded by a quarter of an acre of rice drying on tarpaulins. Some of us joined hands as Vijay was asked to pray over us. This was her prayer and I invite you to make it your prayer also.

'I pray for each and every one who stands before you now, O Lord. In the name of Jesus I commission them to do greater works than they have known. You are the light within them, Father. I pray that you will anoint them by Your Spirit and surround them with fire that they may grow strong in your Word and hear the calling upon their lives, O God. That they will have the desire to serve You, Father, and to serve *no* other god, that Your name alone will be glorified. That, by Your Spirit, these people will reach out to many, Father, far beyond what You will achieve in their lives alone. Lord, that they may see things in the spiritual realm because they belong to You. Surround them, O Father, with a pillar of cloud day and night. Be with them and guide them, O Father. In the name of Jesus.'

Vijay spent the first twenty years of her life under oppressive Hindu curses placed on her by her grandfather and in a state of progressive weakness as congenital heart disease took its toll on her health. But following God's intervention on her twenty-first birthday she was set free and totally healed. She now lives by the power of God's Spirit and releases that power over those in need. The final section of this book speaks of releasing God's power, of releasing the Lion within.

For the Lion of Judah shall break every chain,
And give us the vict'ry, again and again.[2]

Author's note

In July of the following year, 2015, the team once again visited Cambodia. The following is an account of an event that took place on 10 July at the town of Sisophon:

They called her 'Number 7' but she was anything but lucky. Permanently stooped by a 90-degree forward flexion of her thoracic spine, she had spent the last twenty years in pain, craning her head backwards just to see the way ahead. She was just one of the 227 patients who had presented to clinic that morning.

Triaged by Dr Malcolm, she was sent along to the general clinic for pain relief.

'I could see that there was nothing we could do to cure her condition,' he said. 'Even formal surgical correction would have been extremely difficult and fraught with danger.'

One of the doctors prescribed paracetamol and then directed Number 7 to a waiting team of Christians who counselled her and provided prayer support.

'Why can't we pray for her to be healed?' said one.

'We already have,' said another. At that stage her friend arrived to take her home on a motorcycle.

'Wait,' said Vijay. 'God can do a miracle for her.' Number 7 turned towards Vijay who laid her hand on the patient's back.

'Let's pray again,' she said. 'I command the bones to be straightened and I release the power of God.' The woman stood bolt upright as others watched and marvelled. The woman was overcome with joy.

'Throw away your stick,' said Vijay. She did, and then climbed onto the back of her friend's motorcycle to return to her village to share the news of what God had done that day.

Number 7 had become Number 1. Some of my Christian medical friends, including the surgeon and a dentist who had never before witnessed a miracle, saw it happen. Their lives would never be the same again.

'I saw it,' said the dentist. 'I was there.'

Part V

Releasing the Lion Within

Preface to Chapter 19

He gives power to the weak,
And to those who have no might He increases strength.

Even the youths shall faint and be weary,
And the young men shall utterly fall,

But those who wait on the LORD
Shall renew their strength;
They shall mount up with wings like eagles,
They shall run and not be weary,
They shall walk and not faint.

(Isa. 40:29–31)

It was such power that restored a heartbeat to young Elliott the Brave after three days and returned him to his family.

It was such power that raised a small, drowned boy from a waterhole in Australia's Arnhem Land following the faithful prayers of his small friends.

It was such power that protected Dr Jo as she served as the only doctor in a remote hospital in Somalia in peril of her life.

It was such power that rescued Ha-neul from the evil North Korean regime, carried him safely across the frozen Tumen River and introduced him to one who would save his people.

It was such power that delivered Zahir from the firing squad to become a leader of men.

It was such power that raised Vijay from her deathbed to minister God's healing power to the lives of many.

It *is* such power that is available to each of us irrespective of age, state of health or circumstance.

I can do all things through Christ who strengthens me.

(Phil. 4:13)

19

What We Do Now Echoes in Eternity

If we only achieve in this life everything that we are
capable of doing, we have failed.
For there is so much more. Go, with the wind of the
Spirit.

E.F.C.

The words of the title of this chapter were spoken by Marcus Aurelius to his men in preparation for battle. They are profoundly true and apply to us throughout life. Age and length of life are in themselves no barrier as to what might be achieved, and our actions have longstanding implications for family, friends and the world at large.

Life expectancy has increased dramatically during my professional career. I have witnessed the development of vaccines and powerful antibiotics, of coronary artery stenting, renal transplantation, even robotic cancer surgery. In my own field of medical imaging I have been privileged to work with men who developed modern ultrasound and nuclear medicine equipment. PET scanning[1] enables early detection and staging of malignancy; and MRI,[2] capable of displaying exquisite anatomical detail, has been dubbed the 'truth machine'. Our better understanding of the causes of illness, such as smoking, obesity, alcohol excess, has enabled the development of a modern approach to health maintenance.

In the Western world, life expectancy continues to rise. In Australia, a boy born in 2011–2013 can be expected to live to 80.1 years of age and a girl to 84.3 (cf. 47.2 and 50.8 respectively in 1881–1890).[3] In the United States, life expectancy for a male born in 2012 is 76.4 years and for a female 81.2.[4] The number of people living to 100 years of age in the UK has increased by 71 per cent over the last ten years and is currently 14,000 compared to 2,500 in 1980.[5]

Not only have advances in health care extended life expectancy but they have also improved quality of life. A patient recently came to me for a heart test. He was perfectly well but at 82 had decided that he needed a check-up.

'I'm off to New Zealand for a holiday next week, doc.'

'Great,' I said. 'Are you taking a coach tour?'

'No, it's a biking holiday.'

'What sort of bicycle will you be riding?' I ventured.

'Not sure yet, doc, either the Harley 1,200cc or my Yamaha.'

We may retire from business but we never retire from life. Sitting at home and watching television is simply not an option in the twenty-first century. So how should this increase in life expectancy impact us as Christians?

My friend Peter Irvine, after retiring from a career in advertising, purchased the Australian franchise to Gloria Jean's Coffees with his business partner. They began with one shop in Miranda Mall, south of Sydney. That business expanded to more than four hundred shops in Australia and eventually grew to encompass the world franchise. There was even a coffee booth in Baghdad.

Peter, now having moved on from the coffee business, helps others internationally with business development in a Christian context. He has been able to stand down from his own pursuits, and to step out into green fields, which God has laid before him. 'Always cast your seed into the fertile ground,' he says. 'That's where the benefit lies and where the growth will occur.'

My mentor, Pastor Noel Gibson, was one of the most remarkable men that I have ever known. Though short of stature he walked tall, rejoicing in the purpose that he found daily in serving his God.

Perfectly groomed with silver goatee, blazer and bow tie, he was the spitting image of Colonel Sanders and was often referred to as such by his friends. But his product was not for sale. It was a free gift to all that would receive it: spiritual freedom by the grace of God's Holy Spirit.

A New Zealander by birth, he spent his early years street preaching with Open Air Campaigners. His eloquence, sharp intellect, ready wit and booming voice made him a formidable presence on the streets of Sydney. Young would-be evangelists would seek anonymity in the shadows of those who gathered to listen. But many were called to take a stand, and his encouragement was the making of many young men and women.

As a personal friend he would often call me late at night.

'It's your spiritual stethoscope, doctor,' he would say.

'No,' I would reply. 'You are my spiritual scalpel.'

Noel had a serious heart problem for as long as I knew him. A leaking aortic valve put pressure on his heart, pushing him into heart failure. I performed echocardiography on him on a number of occasions and was appalled to see that his heart was as large as a football. Yet he maintained a punishing schedule of evangelism, personal ministry and counselling. He and his wife, Phyllis, established 'Freedom in Christ Ministries', which they operated from their condominium in Drummoyne, Sydney over many years, setting thousands free from addiction and other spiritual bondages.

Eventually Noel's heart disease caught up with him and his health deteriorated. I sat praying for him one morning.

'Lord, couldn't you give Noel just one more year?'

God responded immediately with that quiet inner voice, right out of left field.

'Yes, I could, but that would delay Phyll's ministry.'

Now Phyll was already 80 years of age and this did not make a great deal of sense to me, so I kept it to myself.

One year after Noel's passing, Phyll recommended ministry to others in her Drummoyne apartment. She continued until she herself went to be with her Father at 95 years of age. On the wall of her kitchen she had posted a handwritten note, which was her promise from God. It simply said: 'Trust me, Phyll. I have everything under control.' She dealt with the most serious problems of broken lives and lost dreams, honouring people and restoring hope and vision. Age had been no barrier to Noel or to Phyll.

Just the other day I met a patient of 76.

'Guess you're retired,' I said.

'No way,' he replied. 'I have an earth-moving business and I drive a Bobcat every day.' If a man of 76 can move tons of earth every day, we can move hearts and souls, just as Phyll continued to do until 95 years old.

And illness need not be a barrier. My friend Thomas recently alerted me to Ed's story.[6] Ed is an American pastor, family man, all-round good guy, whose great joy is to care for his people.

Ed noticed the progressive onset of muscle weakness and twitching, and after a series of investigations was devastated to learn that he had developed Lou Gehrig's or motor neurone disease. This condition affects 5 in 100,000 people worldwide. It does not affect sensation nor the ability to think or reason, but causes progressive muscle weakness, walking difficulty and eventually impaired breathing and swallowing. There is no known cure. The condition runs a progressive course with most people surviving three to five years. Ed was told that he had maybe two to five years.

Despite his debilitated condition, Ed was encouraged by his wife to attend the Christmas Festival of lights at his church. 'You have so much to share,' she said. Reluctantly, he set out in his pick-up through the snow and ice. His cell phone rang. It was his friend Billy with his high-pitched New York accent. Billy had a twenty-year history of heroin addiction, was HIV and Hepatitis B positive and also had a history of malignancy. He had watched his wife die in his arms and was unable to trace his son. He had every problem going.

'Ed,' he said, 'you need to be a Yogi Berra Christian.'[7]

'What do you mean?'

'I mean, Ed . . . "It ain't over till it's over".'

Ed perceived the voice of God through Billy that day. Alone in his truck on that icy road, those words changed his life. Every day became meaningful and filled with hope. He has now lived for ten years beyond diagnosis. He has walked his daughter down the aisle and witnessed the birth of his five grandchildren. Ed has well outlived his doctor's expectation. God gave him ministry, a mission and the time to devote himself to these and see them through to completion. Most of all, God has given Ed hope. God knows the number of our days and it is His purpose that we should live every one of them to the full:

> Your eyes saw my substance, being yet unformed. And in Your book they all were written, The days fashioned for me, When as yet there were none of them.
>
> (Ps. 139:16)

My doctor friend Doug whose story is written in *Nine Minutes Past Midnight* found himself in a similar position to Ed. Doug did not have motor neurone disease, but a rare form of neurological degeneration largely affecting the nerves in his arms and legs. He also had Type 1 diabetes. But he was not debilitated by these illnesses. Rather, he focused on them as a means of maintaining his wellbeing. 'Hypos are a problem, but I am managing them well,' he would say.[8]

When I first interviewed Dr Doug Penney, he was 71. The lines of his Bible were underscored and highlighted with yellow ink, but he pointed enthusiastically to words which had come to mean so much to him:

> The days of our lives are seventy years;
> And if by reason of strength they are eighty years,
> Yet their boast is only labor and sorrow . . .
>
> (Ps. 90:10)

I listened in astonishment. Most people of his age would find these words daunting. But Doug's take was different. 'I am 71,' he said, with a broad smile 'and this verse tells me that maybe I have ten years, and there is so much to do in that time.' I left Doug that day buoyed and greatly encouraged.

God uses people like Doug and Ed, and Ed's friend Billy, to speak directly into our hearts and minds. I treasure such people. They have suffered much, but in the depths of that suffering they have identified with Christ and have found hope and strength to bring to others.

Selwyn Hughes in *Every Day with Jesus* quotes Gabriel Marcel's marvellous definition of hope as 'the memory of the future'.[9] Hope sustains us by holding out promise for better days ahead, he says. He also quotes Norman Cousins as saying: 'The human body experiences a powerful gravitational pull in the direction of hope. That is why the patient's hopes are the physician's secret weapon. They are the hidden ingredient in any prescription.'[10]

In April 2013 I received an invitation from a UK radio network, Northsound 2, to be interviewed regarding *Nine Minutes Past Midnight*. The interview was to take place on the evening of Good Friday, Sydney time. It would be broadcast from Aberdeen across north-east Scotland. That afternoon I sat down to prepare. Ken Hancock, from Stained Glass Radio, Aberdeen, had sent me a list of possible questions, many of which I had anticipated. But there was something missing, something else that needed to be said.

'Lord, what do you want me to say tonight?'

The answer came quickly.

'Talk to Allen.'

Now, Allen was a dear friend who was in the terminal stages of acute myeloblastic leukaemia (AML), one of the most difficult forms to treat. Chemotherapy had failed and, despite the very best of medical treatment and on-going prayer support, Allen was dying. He was at home that afternoon but would be transferred to the palliative care unit the next day.

I found Allen reclining in a comfortable chair in the sitting room of his home. The sun streaming through the window highlighted his face perhaps for the last time. A true Aussie, Allan loved sun and surf and the last photo posted just a few weeks earlier on Facebook had shown him bracing for a wave on a Sydney beach. This was the nature and the character of the man. But he was now quite breathless and in some pain.

'Allen,' I said, 'I have a favour to ask of you.'

He looked at me in astonishment.

'How could *I* help you?' he responded.

'I have a radio interview with Scottish radio this evening and God has told me to ask you what I should say.'

Unbeknown to me, Allen had strong Scottish family ties.

'Oh yes!' he said. 'Yes, please tell them that I love them and want to bless them and that I miss the bagpipes . . . and read them Psalm 71:18.'

I hurried home to check out the verse. And there it was:

Yes, even when I am old and gray-headed, O God, forsake me not, [but keep me alive] until I have declared Your mighty strength to [this] generation, and Your might and power to all that are to come.

(Ps. 71:18, AMPC)

The broadcast went ahead. Allen's words went out over north-east Scotland and were well received. A week later he passed away quietly in his sleep.

As Allen's friends bore his casket from the church and the men formed a guard of honour, hands on hearts, it occurred to me then, and has since, that here was a man of immeasurable wealth who served his God to the very end of his life and would now spend eternity in His presence.

No one is too young to find God's purpose in his or her life and no one is too old. Each day is ordained and purposeful. The direction will change from time to time, depending on circumstances and the challenges to which we are called. We are not limited by our weakness but enabled by the enduring presence of His Holy Spirit.

Likewise, limited length of life does not determine the impact that we may have on those around us or on the world at large. In modern medicine, quality of life is valued perhaps more than length of life.

And in the spiritual realm it is quality of life that stands as a beacon to others, that dispels fear, engenders courage and hope.

In the next chapters I examine the impact of a young man whose life was cut short by execution. He spent his final years as a Christian in prison. During that time, he changed the world of those around him. And in death his heritage has global implications that are being realized daily.

Preface to Chapters 20 and 21

In 1867 Dwight L. Moody sat with his wife and friends in a public park in Dublin. Evangelist Henry Varley remarked, 'The world has yet to see what God will do with a man who is fully consecrated to him.'[1] That saying spoke to Moody's heart and he decided to be just that man. In a few short years, Moody, though not physically fit or robust, changed his world and the lives of generations to follow.

20

Behold the Man

*Of one hundred men, one will read the Bible
the ninety-nine will read the Christian.*

D.L. Moody

Nusakambangan Island, Central Java, 29 April 2015, 12:25 a.m. local time.

The shots that rang out were heard around the world. A paramilitary firing squad ended the lives of eight young men convicted of drug offences. Among those executed were Australian citizens Pastor Andrew Chan and artist Myuran Sukumaran.

Despite continuing appeals from the Australian government, impassioned pleas from six previous prime ministers and submissions from world leaders including Ban Ki-Moon, Secretary-General of the United Nations, the men were led to a killing field and summarily executed. Families and loved ones wept and prayed in the nearby town of Cilacap, and throughout Australia, thousands kept a candlelight vigil.

The men faced death bravely, without hoods or blindfolds. Andrew wore his spectacles as much as he disliked wearing them, so that he might look his executioners in the eye. As they were led from their cells to the site of execution, they sang 'Mighty to Save' and then 'Amazing Grace'. And when their voices waned, Andrew called to them, 'Come on, boys. We can sing better than this.' He embraced, in

turn, fifteen of the guards, who wept openly. The men had asked that
their hands not be tied so that they might raise them in an attitude of
praise and worship. But they were secured behind them with plastic
ties thrusting their chests forward.[1] In their final moments they were
heard to sing Matt Redman's song, '10,000 Reasons':

Whatever may pass
And whatever lies before me
Let me be singing
When the evening comes

Bless the Lord oh my soul
Oh my soul
Worship His Holy name
Sing like never before
Oh my soul

I'll worship Your Holy name

They managed to complete the first verse but halfway through the
second, they were taken.

As I sit writing in Sydney this Saturday morning, it is raining. The
heavens weep as the bodies of Andrew and Myu arrive at Sydney
airport. What a waste of young men's lives. But one fact is clear
that these men, and one in particular, achieved more in their short
lifespans and ultimate death than most ever do.

Andrew and Myu were convicted as part of the 'Bali Nine' of
attempted drug trafficking from Thailand to Australia via Indonesia in April 2005, and in February 2006 were condemned to death
by firing squad.[2,3] This was the first time that the Denpasar district
court had handed down the death penalty for drug trafficking. The
sentence was controversial in terms of possible court corruption at the
time.[4] The two remained in Kerobokan Prison throughout the presidency of Susilo Bambang Yudhoyono, a strong and compassionate
man, who proclaimed a moratorium on the death penalty, but with

the election of President Joko Widodo in 2014 the death penalty was reactivated and their fate was sealed.

Both men were totally rehabilitated during their years on death row. Myu, a gentle giant of a man, accomplished in martial arts but with a passion for painting, became a gifted artist in Kerobokan Prison under the watchful eye of Australian artist Ben Quilty who mentored him.[5] He established art classes for inmates. But these were more than art classes. They were a safe haven in a jungle of violence and discontent, allowing many young men and women to find purpose and re-establish lost hope.

But following transfer to Nusakambangan Island on 4 March 2015, all privileges were withdrawn. Myu and Andrew were locked down in the same cell where they remained for almost twenty-four hours per day. They were there for the sole purpose of execution and their guards maintained constant vigil, ensuring that members of the media were kept well away.

After two weeks Myu and Andrew were given separate cells, but all privileges remained suspended. Myu's world had been filled with interests and activities but these were now gone. He searched within himself for strength and purpose. He had been raised a Christian but he was a very private man who rarely discussed his faith with others. But in the last few weeks of his life he was remarkably transformed by the renewing of his faith. This was the direct result of intervention from a most unexpected quarter.

Ibu Yani lived alone on the island by a small chapel built from donations. A woman in her sixties, she spent her days caring for inmates of the several prisons on the island. Her whole life was spent visiting and ministering God's love. Myu had never met anyone who was so totally selfless. She would ride her motorcycle across the island to cross in the ferry to Cilacap. There she would buy food, returning home on the last ferry of the day. She would then cook meals and bring them to Myu and Andrew.

She pleaded with guards to allow Myu access to paints and brushes. 'No! No! No!' they would say, as the Indonesian Attorney General would not allow it. But little by little they yielded and Myu was able to paint again, producing remarkable works of art in his remaining days. His moving self-portraits flashed by media around the world were his final testimony and impacted the lives of many.

On 7 April, twenty-two days before execution, Andrew wrote these words to a dear friend: 'Myu said to me a few days ago that he was starting to like Christian songs . . . I just pray more and more that he talks to Jesus and has the sublime experience of God's ecstasy of love.' Just a week later Myu returned to his first love, Jesus, and entered into a deep and meaningful faith.

To that point Andrew and Myu had not been close. They lived in different worlds. But from that time on they became the best of friends, sharing a cell to their last days. Myu exhibited peace, confidence and a quiet joy that he had not been able to achieve through his own striving.

'When I saw him at Nusakambangan prison,' said Pastor Miranda Riddington, 'his face was alive and he was beaming. I could see such a difference in him.'

Myu did not want to die but as time passed he became impatient to meet his God. During the last few days, the prisoners and families were visited by the prosecutor from his case who wished to shake hands with family members. They bluntly refused. Myu's response was remarkable and gracious: 'If we want forgiveness we should be able to give it too. If Jesus can forgive them then so must we.'

The second person to impact Myu's life was Pastor Christie Buckingham from Melbourne, Australia. She had known Myu for years and had helped him with his art projects. As time moved on towards what seemed inevitable, they shared their faith on many occasions. In the last days Myu asked that Christie be his pastor during the final events. He needed someone strong enough to lead him through and to witness events on behalf of his family and loved ones.

On the night of execution, family members were asked to leave for the last time. I found myself in tears as this was revealed to me. As a father I could not possibly imagine the turmoil felt by loved ones at that time. Myu was to spend his last hours with Christie. They prayed, they praised and worshipped. There was writing on the walls of his cell. This, he explained, was his ongoing dialogue with God.

'You're an artist, Myu,' said Christie. 'Close your eyes and tell me what you see.'

There was a pause.

'I see Jesus,' he said, 'with His arms outstretched towards me.'

***

It was early during his imprisonment and during a stint in solitary confinement that Andrew Chan found faith in God. Here is his personal testimony:

I found myself in here. At first I thought it was no big deal, I'll get outta this. It wasn't until I ended up in solitary confinement that I realised I wasn't going to get outta this. In fact, I figured they were gonna kill me. I had never felt so hopeless and alone before, and decided that if they were going to kill me anyway, I'd just do it myself. I took my t-shirt off and made a noose, and then remembered the heaven/hell issue, and decided that if I was gonna kill myself I should make sure I ended up in heaven. I wasn't sure how to do that, but figured I should pray. I wasn't sure how to do that either, so I looked up and just said 'God if you're real . . .', and for the first time in my life I began to cry and ended up on my knees. I cried and cried and said, 'God if you're real, send someone who cares about me to see me.' I fell asleep like that. At 6.30 the next morning a guard woke me up. I woke up cursing him in my usual response, and he said 'Get up, you've got a visitor.' I said, 'I can't have a visitor, no one knows I'm here.' He took me to the visitor area and I saw my brother. I thought, my mum must have seen this on the news and sent my brother to see about me, because I knew my brother wouldn't just come – we don't like each other. We get along like cats and dogs.

When I got to him, he said, 'Andrew, no matter what happens or how long it takes, I'm gonna be here with you.' I told him to bring me a Bible. I started in Genesis when I got it and thought 'These are a lot of nice stories', but I got nothing out of it.

Someone else came to visit me who was a Christian, and I told him I was reading the Bible but didn't get much out of it, and he told me to read the New Testament. I didn't even know what that was and told him I didn't have one. He had to explain to me that it was a part of the Bible, and told me to start reading the Gospels of Matthew, Mark, Luke and John. I read through the New Testament a couple of times, but didn't really notice any change. I just didn't get it . . .

Just before my court date, I remember reading Mark 11:23–24, where it says that if you have enough faith you can say to this mountain, 'Be removed' and God will do it. So I said, 'God if you're real and if this is true, I want you to free me, and if you do I'll serve you every day for the rest of my life.' I went to my court hearing and they convicted me and gave me the death penalty. When I got back to my cell, I said, 'God, I asked you to set me free, not kill me.' God spoke to me and said, 'Andrew, I have set you free from the inside out, I have given you life!' From that moment on I haven't stopped worshipping Him. I had never sung before, never led worship, until Jesus set me free.[6]

Vicky Baird visited Andrew many times during his ten years of imprisonment. 'He became a totally rehabilitated and honourable man,' she said, completely given to the needs of others. There was a time when a prisoner in solitary confinement was extremely unwell. Andrew organized a roster with the other prisoners so that the man's needs could be taken care of. 'If not for Andrew,' she said, 'this man may not have survived.' She also recalled the countless times that Andrew had given mental and spiritual support to others and provided pastoral care. 'He sang with great passion: "Lord, I give You my heart, I give You my soul . . . have Your way in me".[7] He lived every moment he had to the glory of God,' she said.

Miranda Riddington recognized various stages of transition in Andrew during his imprisonment:

'I watched him go through his first trial,' she said, 'and come to realize that his life had now changed forever. He knew that when he gave his life to God that he had begun a new life. He knew when he was baptized in water that the old Andrew Chan was washed away and whatever he had done in life no longer defined him. He was free on the inside and it was out of that freedom that he lived.'

This new 'freedom' defined Andrew's life and ministry from that point forward. What he had so freely received he imparted to others until his final day.

This understanding was wonderfully expressed in the words of a song, which Andrew and his friends sang shortly before their deaths:

Everyone needs compassion
A love that's never ending
Let mercy fall on me

Everyone needs forgiveness
The kindness of a Saviour
The hope of nations.[8]

Miranda also observed Andrew's transition from prisoner to pastor: in the Gospel of Luke he read: 'The Spirit of the LORD is upon Me . . . To proclaim liberty to the captives' (Luke 4:18).

'This became his job description,' she said. 'He developed a heart for revival for Indonesia and this remained with him to his last night.' It was during those final moments that he was heard to call out with a loud voice: 'God bless Indonesia, God bless Indonesia, God bless Jokowi.'[9]

'Andrew had a unique way of teaching spiritual principles to the other inmates,' she explained. 'He would set up an obstacle course. He would then blindfold his fellow inmates and standing on the other side of the course would call them by name and guide them with his voice. This was to demonstrate how Jesus guides us. "We have to learn to trust his voice," he said.'

She also told of how he had gained permission to begin an English-speaking service in the prison and he was the pastor. 'An international church was birthed in that prison,' she said. 'He preached, led worship and quite often took up the offertory. He sang loud and strong and often was quite off key. But he was passionate.

He prayed for the inmates, preached to them, baptized them, fed them, treated their addictions and raised funds for them. He was the real deal. He said that he loved being a pastor in the prison as no one could leave. And as he said, his "cell group" *was* literally a cell group.'

Miranda observed a wonderful change in Andrew when Feby came into his life four years ago. 'They shared a common heart and passion for God,' she said, 'and with growing confidence he was able to complete his Bible college studies.' Just a few days before his execution they were married. As Miranda said, 'There was little time for marriage counselling but as Andrew put it, "Don't worry, we can work it out."'[10]

Just this week I spoke with Yudi, one of Andrew's friends.

'Two weeks before Andrew was taken to the execution island,' said Yudi, 'God spoke to me. "Go to the prison and tell Andrew to have no fear. Tell him My grace is sufficient for him. In my house there are plenty of rooms and My name *will* be glorified."

'But at that stage,' said Yudi, 'I had no access to the prison. Local and international media and the police were everywhere and I could not get in. But God told me to go and it was amazing. The gates just opened for me. I believe it was an angel and there I met a friend who said, "You won't have to wait, go directly to the tower and there you will meet Andrew." And there he was, sitting with his mum. They were crying.

'"Yudi," he called, "do you want to see me?"

'I gave him the message that the Father had given me. We prayed, we cried together. That was the last time I saw him. I miss him so much. But I am jealous of him as he is now with the Father.'

'No one could ever face death the way Andrew did,' said Feby at the funeral. 'He prayed "Father forgive them, they know not what they do" . . . He ended well. He ended well.

'On that last night they asked me if I wanted to write a letter to Andrew. You might think that I'm crazy but we both decided that whatever we did, whatever we said must bring glory to God. Our relationship began with God and we had to end it with God. I wrote to Andrew: "Don't worry about me, I'll be fine. But when you see Jesus, you can tell Him if you want to come back. If He allows you to come back, you can. But if you want to stay, then don't worry about me. Keep singing when they take you. Angels are with you. Jesus is closer than ever. Rejoice. I love you. Death cannot divide us."'

In one of his final letters to Feby, Andrew wrote:

'You will need to continue with the vision for the people on the island . . . I have found love for them through you. Continue the fight against injustice in this country.'

'I was with him when his appeal was rejected,' she said. 'I was so broken, but he said, "Don't worry, God is in control." And I was there with him when the message came through that he was to be executed at the end of the week. He said, "Don't worry, don't worry. Jesus is in control. Look up to Jesus."'

'There are so many questions in my heart,' she said. 'So many people prayed for a miracle and nothing seemed to happen. They said, "Lord, You gave me the promises." Every day I prayed together with him and we claimed all of God's promises. In the end I realized it happens. Today you might ask: how can someone facing death, like Andrew, say "forgive them"? How can someone have that courage and be so brave, to face death with open eyes?'

Shortly after Andrew's execution, Pastor Mark Soper's young daughter asked her mother:

'Mummy why are you sad?

'Because Andrew's gone.'

'Where has he gone?'

'He's gone to be with Jesus.'

The next day she asked again:

'Where is Andrew?'

'He has gone. He died.'

'Where is he, Mummy, Bali?'

'You know where he is. He's with Jesus.'

'If we FaceTime Andrew, Mummy, do you think we'll see Jesus?'

And as Pastor Soper said, 'If we could FaceTime Andrew, we *would* see Jesus.'

So take me as You find me, all my fears and failures,
And fill my life again

I give my life to follow everything I believe in
Now I surrender, now I surrender.[11]

On Sunday, 3 May 2015, four days following the executions, Pastor Lee Carlson of Global Church, Bali addressed his congregation. His topic: 'Empowered by The Holy Spirit.'[12]

He spoke with conviction of the supernatural peace available to those who embrace the empowering presence of God's Holy Spirit. Supernatural, because it far exceeds any peace that this world has to offer, supernatural because it defies understanding in times of tragedy. 'Supernatural,' he said, 'because it allows us to trust in the Father's good will, when we should be freaking out.'

Then with faltering voice and frequent pauses, he spoke of his good friends Myu and Andrew:

'Last Saturday they were given notice of their impending executions. They were given seventy-two hours to live. They were on the clock. There are not many people in this world that know the hour that they're going to die. Andrew and Myu knew the hour that they were going to die. In most people this would evoke emotions of fear and anxiety, but not for Andrew and Myu because the Holy Spirit dwelt in them and gave them supernatural peace and strength. When they should have been overcome with fear and anxiety they were filled with courage and peace and love.

'I can say this about these guys: prior to their death they showed me how to live life, especially Andrew. I became very close to him in partnership in the prison and helping him with the monthly prison service. One thing that Andrew taught me was how to live. See, when you're on death row, man, and death is knocking on the door, you approach each day a little differently. Paul's words in Philippians 1:21 became so real to me. "To live is Christ, and to die is gain." If I'm given another day that means living for Jesus Christ; if it's the moment for me to meet my maker, then praise Jesus, because that's better than anything this world has to offer. To live is Christ and to die is gain.

'In his last moments Andrew taught me another lesson. He taught me how to die well. He didn't just teach me how to live. He taught me how to die well. Even in their deaths these men's lives loudly proclaimed the gospel of Jesus Christ and perhaps it was in their final moments that their witness shined brighter than in all the previous time that they had been in Kerobokan Prison.'

The stories of Andrew Chan and Myu Sukamaran have impacted my life immensely. As a doctor experienced in the dramas of life, of death and suffering, I have found their courage and peaceful acceptance of what was to follow almost beyond understanding. Doctors battle to know how to broach the subject of death with patients, often approaching it in an oblique and cryptic manner. I once asked a prominent oncologist how he approached the subject with his patients. He said, 'I tell them I'm worried about them and I figure that if I'm worried, they should be also.'

So many of us live in the 'what if?' zone. What if this happens, what if that happens, knowing full well that most of the things that we worry about will never occur. Or we may live in the 'Why me?' zone, when the question should perhaps be, 'Why not me, Lord? After all, I am Your child and perhaps better able to face this imposition. You have the words of eternal life and Your Word says:

> Be anxious for nothing, but in everything by prayer and supplication, with thanksgiving, let your requests be made known to God; and the peace of God, which surpasses all understanding, will guard your hearts and minds through Christ Jesus.
>
> (Phil. 4:6,7)

To have observed Andrew and Myu's approach to impending execution has perhaps been my most humbling and inspiring experience. Their stories made such a profound impression on me that I travelled to Bali in August 2015, just months following their deaths, to speak with those who had been influenced by Andrew in particular, and to examine their heritage. I visited Kerobokan Prison, met with Matthew Norman whose sentence had been commuted from death to life imprisonment and saw how his life had been changed by personal acceptance of Jesus Christ into his life.

Here now is that story.

21

When Iron Gates Yield

The greatest act of a leader is mentoring . . .
What happens in your absence? That is your legacy.[1]

Kerobokan Prison, 27 August 2015

It was 8:50 a.m. precisely as our driver, Bayu, turned from the traffic chaos into the car park of Kerobokan Prison. We were thankfully on schedule and I watched as cars on the street beyond the razor wire inched past, hemmed in on all sides by hordes of motor scooters and bikes taking every conceivable shortcut. With Pastor Lee and his wife, Natalia we made our way through the entrance door to join scores of others patiently waiting to visit friends and family under the watchful eye of several guards.

A pin board for media was blank that day and another sign warned of attempting to take cameras, phones, handguns, cash or drugs into the prison. We surrendered our passports and cell phones to a waiting guard and were ushered through a grey steel door not more than 1.6 metres high. 'Watch your head,' they cautioned. The windowless room that we entered was about 6 square metres. Here we were searched, IDs were issued and a triangular prison logo stamped on our left forearms.

Then through security doors into what looked more like a park than a prison yard. There were Poinciana trees and bougainvilleas of every hue dotting the well-manicured lawns. Conifers in decorative pots, large rocks and ponds engendered an air of beauty and peace. Yet not 15 metres beyond the doors in ominous contrast stood 'Super Maximum Security', a cream single-storey, rounded building where Andrew and Myu had been housed and where Matthew continued to be incarcerated. The name was emblazoned across the front in large letters should anyone be in doubt of its purpose or identity. And above was a tower with a red roof, partially in ruins, and with green-framed windows, some with glass missing. The tower was said to be haunted and guards were reluctant to go there. Immediately behind 'Supermax' was a small building with a corrugated iron roof where twenty men were said to occupy the isolation cells. Ironic that twenty should be housed together in solitary confinement.

We made our way to the right past the tower, through a rusted revolving iron gate and then turned left along a path lined on both sides with gardens. Tomatoes thrived in a weedless vegetable patch and there were aviaries containing small birds flying to and fro in the wired enclosure, symbolizing what occurred around them on the greater scale. A single snow-white rooster sat confined in a small cage beside the path. I wondered what his purpose or fate might be. Then back past the mosque with the golden dome, and on to the right to a white building which sat alone. Words over the door read, 'Jesus is the head of this house'.

It was here that I met Matthew for the first time, a tall and muscu-lar Aussie lad from Quakers Hill with a clear and open face and ex-pression of anticipation. He wore a grey tee shirt and sported tattoos and a grey baseball cap. He gave us a warm welcome and with others we crowded into the church to be seated on red plastic chairs. It was a typical August Bali day, warm, dry and somewhat oppressive, but the overhead fans proffered a gentle breeze and I was reminded of the wind of the Spirit of God that had borne me to this island.

At the front of the church there were three paintings of Christ and beneath these sat the music team comprising three local men, one on keyboard, one on drums, another on guitar. They played up a storm as fifty to sixty people filed into the chapel. There were young men and women, mostly locals but with a smattering of foreigners. I met a

Frenchman who had been apprehended with drugs at the airport and several other European and Australian nationals.

The praise was better than I have heard for many years. Songs included 'Lord I Give You My Heart', 'I Exalt Thee' and 'Give Thanks with a Grateful Heart'. The enthusiasm of the inmates was unbounded and their words rang out through the open louvre windows and across the prison grounds to the cellblocks beyond.

We received a rousing welcome from the praise leader, himself an inmate; then Pastor Lee spoke on the power of praise. He quoted from Psalm 13:6:

I will sing the LORD's praise, for he has been good to me. (NIVUK)

Then he told of God's word to him, finishing with the challenge: 'What will your song be?'

I was given the opportunity to speak and brought a word that the Lord had given me. Of how identity based on worldly attributes of health, money, possessions, even freedom can be so quickly snatched away. But identity as a child of Father God can never be taken from us. 'Some of us,' I said, 'have been looking in the wrong mirrors all of our lives. We need to see ourselves as God sees us.'

At the conclusion of the service about one third of the congregation came streaming forward for prayer. No invitation had been given. It was entirely spontaneous. There were tears of joy, of repentance and reconciliation. I found myself hugging and praying for those who were ill, for a man on corruption charges, for another awaiting the result of an appeal, for others who just needed a touch from the Lord. These were people who had lost their freedom, some had lost everything, but they were finding new freedom in Christ. I was once again reminded of Jim Elliot's words:

He is no fool who gives what he cannot keep to gain what he cannot lose.[2]

Anwar showed me the small library which he and Andrew Chan had built, and across the yard, Myu's art studio continued to flourish.

Matthew showed us his plans for the church extension to house 100 people. The building pegs were already in place. He spoke of the classes that had been set up for inmates, including cooking, language etc. He himself was actively engaged in an Open University business course by correspondence from Australia.

'How long is your sentence?' I asked.

'Life,' he said, 'and here that means *life*.' We agreed to pray for a reduction of his life sentence and I would encourage all who read this to be in prayer for him also.

Matthew and Andrew had spent almost every day together for a ten-year period. They had been best mates and looked upon one another as brothers. I recalled his written eulogy for Andrew:

It is an honour and privilege for me to pay tribute to a very special person. In 2003 I met Andrew. It was while we were working at the Sydney cricket ground. We quickly became friends. We would always hang out; we shared lots of laughs and got up to lots of mischief as boys do. But in 2005 we made the biggest mistake of our lives. This mistake would eventually cost Andrew his life.

Through the whole court scene I was totally stressed out. But not Andrew, he was attending church regularly and had faith for whatever happened. He said that God doesn't give us any more than we can bear. Andrew was so carefree and even after being sentenced to death he did not complain or take pity on himself. He took it on the chin and carried on, changing his life and continuing to help others. When my sentence was upgraded to death Andrew was the first one to come to talk and pray with me. When I beat the death penalty Andrew was the first one to come and congratulate me. That's the type of person Andrew was. He cared so much for others and I respect him for that. He failed over and over in court but he never let it crush his feelings. He was always smiling and being cheeky.

I am so proud of the man that Andrew became and it didn't surprise me that Andrew sang and encouraged others in their final journey. It reminds me of Psalm 23. Andrew left his mark in the prison. He may have been labelled the kingpin. But no one here knew him as that. Everyone knew him as Pastor Chan the kind, caring guy that you could always talk to and always rely on. In the ten years that we were together here, I wouldn't be able to count the number of people that he helped.

He was doing God's work, bringing people to the Lord and that's what made him the happiest. Andrew had all of his own problems as well as the weight of other people's problems on his shoulders. He stood strong, never once complained. Andrew lived his life to the full and touched many people's lives during his time with us. I owe Andrew everything. He helped me to change my life. I am proud to have called him my brother. And I will be honoured to continue all of the programmes that Andrew started in Kerobokan.[3]

I spoke with another that day whom I shall not identify but rather call him Jamal. He was an educated man well versed in the Quran. Jamal had been jailed many times for political activism, for drug offences and marketing stolen goods. On one occasion he was arrested and placed in police solitary confinement. The room was small and dark, just 1.5 metres square. He slept on the cold concrete floor in his underwear. 'Sometimes the rats came,' he said. There was a hole in the floor which served as a toilet, and food was passed to him through a window. He remained there for three months. His friends did not know that he had been arrested or his whereabouts.

But during that time an event occurred which changed his life forever.

'Not sure of the date,' he said. 'It was July or August, but it was cold; that I can remember. I could hear the rain coming and you know, you can smell the water in the soil.' The door opened and a man robed in white entered and smiled at him.

'Follow me and you'll be free,' he said. This man appeared to him on six further occasions, once while he was watching a prison basketball match, each time uttering the same words. 'Follow me and you'll be free. Follow me and you'll be free.' Jamal had no idea of the identity of this man.

Eventually, fearing for his sanity, he approached Andrew Chan.

'What's up, mate?' said Andrew.

'Oh, nothing serious,' he said.

'Oh?' said Andrew. 'Your friend told me that you had a ghost come to you.'

'That wasn't a ghost,' said Jamal. 'If it was a ghost I would have run a mile.'

'If it was not a ghost,' said Andrew, 'what did he look like? What did he say?'

'He said, "Follow me and you'll be free." That's it.'

Andrew was confident. 'You know what, mate,' he said, 'that guy who came to you was Jesus.'

There followed a time of confusion and searching. Jamal returned to his studies of the Quran. Here he found Jesus and proved to himself once and for all that Jesus was God. The man appeared to him once more, in a dream. This time Jamal recognized him as Jesus who hugged him and spoke the words again, 'Follow me and you'll be free.'

The next day Jamal returned to Andrew.

'I give up,' he said.

'Why? Give up on what?' said Andrew.

'Your Jesus ruined my life.' He laughed. 'I give up, bro.'

'Why give up?'

'Because I now believe that Jesus is God and my Saviour.'

Andrew cried and hugged him. They prayed together.

As we made our way back through the maze of gates and checkpoints to the outside world I began to understand how important it was for us not to lose touch with Matthew and his friends who carry on the work commenced by Andrew. They need our prayer, our financial support, our friendship, and the constant reminder that they are not forgotten. God has commenced a remarkable work in Kerobokan Prison through Andrew Chan. And it continues through the efforts of Matthew and a band of faithful brothers and sisters, ably encouraged by such as Pastor Lee and his wife, Natalia. Their efforts impact the lives of thousands and will have far-reaching implications globally.

Later that day I signed myself into a Bali hotel to take time to listen to God and to write my experiences of the day. As I wrote and transcribed, God spoke to me so clearly: 'No prison walls shall restrain my mercy. No shackles will limit my grace. Iron gates will yield to the enduring presence of my Holy Spirit. And those who follow me shall be free.'[4]

> Now the Lord is the Spirit, and where the Spirit of the Lord is, there is freedom.
>
> (2 Cor. 3:17 NIVUK)

Preface to Chapter 22

Michelle Knight is one of three young women kidnapped in Cleveland, Ohio by Ariel Castro. She was 21 at the time of her kidnap in 2002, and was held for ten years. It's alleged that Castro starved and beat her so badly that she even miscarried his child during her imprisonment. When interviewed by Associated Press she made the following comments:

> I may have been through hell and back . . . I can walk with my head held high and my feet firmly on the ground . . . Walking hand in hand with my best friend I will not let the situation define who I am. We need to take a leap of faith and know that God is in control. God has a plan for all of us. The plan that He gave me was to help others that have been in the same situations that I have. To know that there is someone out there to lean on and to talk to.[1]

Michelle with her friends walked through deep and dark waters during her time of imprisonment by Ariel Castro. Yet God took her hand and led her through that dreadful time. By placing her trust in Him she found one who would never leave her or forsake her.

22

Trusting God

Have I not commanded you? Be strong and courageous.
Do not be afraid; do not be discouraged, for the LORD
your God will be with you wherever you go.
(Josh. 1:9, NIVUK)

Hospital rooms are hospital rooms, the world over. White ceilings, cream walls, featureless curtains and nondescript prints on the walls. And then there are those people who offer you tea and biscuits until they see the sign over your bed 'nil by mouth'. And that all-powerful control button which will summon the nurse, change the TV channel or dim the lights, if only you can find or reach it. And, of course, there is the nurse who appears hourly and who seems to have forgotten that she took your temperature earlier and it was fine.

In April 2012 I found myself in just such a situation, lying supine, intravenous line in each arm, staring at the ceiling, wondering, how did I ever get into this mess?

Lynne and I had been in Orange, a large country town 200 miles west of Sydney, where I had been speaking at a medical dinner. The next morning on the way to breakfast the pain struck and it was severe. My first thought was that I was having a heart attack. But no, maybe it was biliary. My host suggested that I might feel better after breakfast, bacon and eggs. I didn't. But through that day the pain eased, despite fish and chips for lunch and fried chicken for dinner.

At one o'clock the following morning the pain returned, big time, and this time it did not go away. A friendly intern at the base hospital

administered 10 mg of morphine intramuscularly, bringing some relief, and at 7 a.m. I was discharged to make my way back to Sydney.
I was scheduled to speak at a local church at 8 a.m. but my host was
sure that they would 'understand'. However I decided to give it my
best shot and, after several cups of hot coffee to stem the rigors,[1] and
still heavily under the influence of morphine, I went ahead. As Lynne
put it, I 'spoke with more conviction that morning than was normally
the case'.

By the time we reached Sydney the pain was extreme. It was
gall bladder pain and I had developed pancreatitis as a compli-
cation. So here I was in hospital, pancreatitis now under control,
waiting to have my gall bladder removed. The timing could not
have been worse. My book *Nine Minutes Past Midnight* was due
for US release and my editor, Kyle, needed the revised manuscript
'pronto'. I was seriously questioning God's purpose in this when a
friend arrived.

'Ern,' he said, 'I want to read you something. Guess you've heard
it before, Psalm 23.'

'Yes, of course, but thank you.'

It was as though I heard the words for the first time:

He makes me to lie down in green pastures;
He leads me beside the still waters.
He restores my soul . . .

(Ps. 23:2,3)

There it was again, the *rhema*[2] word of God reaching out as though
alive from the *logos* (written) word. This was no invitation to lie down
and rest, it was a command. In other words: 'I didn't cause this illness,
but I can use it. Lie down, son . . . I'm going to restore your soul.' I
stared out of the window and as far as I could see there were grassy
lawns, trees and beyond that, the blue waters of Sydney Harbour.

I had been working around the clock to meet deadlines and God
knew better than I that it was time for a break.

Surgery was successful and during the three weeks of convalescence I revised and submitted the manuscript, on schedule, before returning to medicine.

During a recent radio interview with Stephanie Riggs on *Divine Calling*, KRKS 94.7 FM Denver, a caller, Rudy, asked me: 'Shouldn't we expect God to answer our prayers straight away?' It was 2 p.m. Denver time, a warm summer's afternoon where the broadcast was live to air. In Sydney it was 6 a.m. on a cold winter's morning and I stood barefoot in the kitchen in my PJs thinking: 'How best can I respond to this man?'

But the answer was clear. Yes, God's response to prayer is not unduly delayed. But it is not always as we expect. He is Sovereign, He has the oversight and we can trust Him. Sometimes His answer will be to lift us directly out of a situation. Sometimes it will be to lead us through. That process may be complex and multi-layered, but it will be faith-building as each step is taken.

My understanding of a relationship with God has evolved over a lifetime and I remain on a steep learning curve. I became a Christian as a boy of 9 at Sunday school, later confirming that decision at age 14. Years later, as a medical resident in advanced training, I experienced the indwelling presence of God's Holy Spirit for the first time.[3] But it was not until I left my position as Director of Nuclear Medicine and Ultrasound at Westmead Hospital, aged 40, that I began to understand my true identity as a very much-loved son of Father God.

Most recently I've learned to trust God implicitly and to place my hope and faith completely in Him. This has been the greatest challenge of all, but it has allowed me to walk through pressing personal circumstances, through bereavement and illness, through good times and bad. I haven't always understood where God was leading me and I have often questioned His timing, His purpose and direction. But I am assured that He has the oversight and that He will lead me through whatever confronts me.[4]

On occasions we find ourselves in deep water that may not be as clean as we might like it to be. Naaman the leper was a great military leader in the army of the king of Aram. But he had leprosy. He was encouraged to visit the prophet of Israel who would cure his disease. With chariots and horses laden with gifts, he arrived at Elisha's house. Elisha did not even come out to meet him but sent a messenger with the instruction:

> Go, wash yourself seven times in the Jordan, and your flesh will be restored and you will be cleansed.
>
> (2 Kgs 5:7, NIVUK)

Naaman was enraged. He had not been received with honour and dignity and his prescription for healing was not acceptable.

'We have better rivers in Damascus,' he said. But when he was prevailed upon by his people to do as Elisha had advised, the Scriptures tell us that his flesh was restored and became clean like that of a young boy. He had not been healed instantly but had received instruction on how to proceed to achieve his healing. Furthermore, he had been required to bathe several times in dirty water.

Trusting God is one of the biggest challenges that we face. Yet one of the key elements in developing a personal relationship with God is learning to trust Him. In this book I have chronicled the progress of courageous men and women; of small boys in Arnhem Land who knelt in the mud to pray for their drowned friend; of Jo, a young medical graduate who stood her ground against death threats in Somalia – she was called prostitute and deceiver by those she had come to help. I have written of a young man in North Korea who crossed the frozen Tumen River at midnight to bring the good news of Jesus Christ to his people. Though family members and friends had been executed by the oppressive regime of Kim Jong-un, he found courage and resolve to complete his journey.

I have also written of Gladys Staines and her daughter, Esther, who found supernatural courage and strength to forgive those who brutally murdered their family members. All of these people learned to trust God implicitly and found strength in His provision to carry them through deep waters.

I have written also of Borin whose family was decimated by Pol Pot. He fell into a life of alcohol abuse and gambling but later became God's revolutionary in a Thai Cambodian border camp. And of Emeritus Professor Gordon Stokes who volunteered his services to the refugees of a Laotian border camp during one of the greatest humanitarian crises of our times. He developed typhoid and came close to forfeiting his life, but in that time experienced the presence of God in what may have been his darkest hour.

Some of these people were miraculously delivered from suffering and imminent death. Critical-care doctor Shane, as a schoolboy in deep depression, was about to throw himself under a truck on the Pacific Highway north of Sydney when he was rescued by the extraordinary sobering words of a drunken, homeless man. David, an Anglican pastor, was delivered from the hands of Congolese soldiers by a man who by all accounts, did not exist. Zahir was rescued from a firing squad by a man he had never met.

I began with the story of our own young Elliott the Brave. He survived for three days with no heartbeat to recover completely. Equally courageous were his parents, family and friends who stood firm through the storm which threatened his life. And I concluded with the account of Andrew Chan, executed in Bali, whose witness in the face of impending death was an inspiration to thousands and whose legacy will impact generations.

All of these people found safety and deliverance through a personal encounter with a God in whom they could trust implicitly.

Some found themselves in peril by their own resolve. General Ajai Masih was fired upon by Pakistani troops on the Siachen Glacier, 6,000 metres above sea level, in the highest battle ever fought. Pastor Chea narrowly escaped death on several occasions as a Cambodian foot soldier fighting Pol Pot's men. Yet God was there with him in the heat of battle.

There were others who faced death under circumstances over which they had no control at all, such as Vijay who lay dying of congenital heart disease. Her family built her a coffin as a 21st birthday present. And there was Rudy who was diagnosed with inoperable cancer.

These also found provision to carry them through. They found help in hopelessness and hope in helplessness.

And there were those who found themselves in the eye of the storm by following what they believed to be God's will and direction. Paul Dale, an Oxford Don, found himself out of favour with his church and unable to be ordained when he stood down from his exalted academic position to train for the ministry.

For security reasons I have not disclosed details of my friends in Cairo who have seen their friends crucified for their faith in this last year, or of two young families, one American, one Australian, currently moving to the Middle East to minister God's love to the persecuted and suffering. Their stories are continuing and are far too sensitive to relate.

Each of these people has recognized God as his or her silent partner. He did not send them into the storm. He went with them and at no stage left their sides, just as it was when Jesus calmed the storm on the Sea of Galilee.[5] He was there with them in the boat. And He was not fearful. In fact, He was asleep and they had to wake Him. First of all He rebuked and calmed the storm, and then He asked them why they were worried.

It should also be remembered that it was Jesus who led them into the storm.

'Let us cross over to the other side,' he said. His words were prophetic. The storm would not stop them. He would lead them through.

Life is not an easy passage and we are often called upon to be courageous.

'Courageous?' you say. 'But I'm not that kind of person.' Yes, courageous. And where does courage come from? From the very heart of God. Perfect love casts out fear and God *is* that perfect love.[6] When I asked Jo where her courage came from, she answered, 'I am in Christ.' When I asked Ha-neul, he referred to God as his 'love dad'. And the courage of Andrew Chan and Myu Sukamarin facing execution is almost beyond comprehension. That same courage is available to us all when we discover the love of God and find our identity in Him as His beloved child.

The Word of God tells us that to be courageous is not just a good idea. It's a command:

> Wait on the LORD; Be of good courage, And He shall strengthen your heart; Wait, I say, on the LORD!
>
> (Ps. 27:14)

There are many such verses, but the words must be quickened to us by the Spirit of God before we can effectively apply them to our own lives.

In the book of Mark we read where the Sadducees challenged Jesus.[7] They presented a hypothetical situation where a woman married each of seven brothers in turn after her previous husband had died. 'Whose wife will she be in the resurrection?' they asked. Jesus' response was scathing. 'You are mistaken,' he said because 'you don't know the Scriptures, and you don't know the power of God' (see Mark 12:24).

Many Christians today, though believing in the Word of God, fail to understand the power of the indwelling presence of God by His Holy Spirit. Both are vital to us as Christians. The Scriptures are the inspired spoken word of God. They bring direction, wisdom and guidance. It is the power of God that quickens that word within us that makes it alive. It is the power of God that enables Him to intervene in every situation. It is that same power that raised Jesus from the dead.[8] I have made it a habit each day before beginning my medical practice to draw upon the Spirit of God by asking Him to:

- strengthen my heart
- renew my mind
- refresh my spirit.

Without an understanding of the power of the indwelling presence of the Spirit of God we become fatalistic, accepting our lot as 'God's will'. We may fail to understand how He can use that circumstance to achieve His purpose or that He may wish to intervene to change that circumstance completely.[9]

When we decide to follow God and commit our way to Him, there is always a cost. We may be required to abandon personal pursuits so that we can follow the plan that He has for our life. Yet Jesus said:

> There is no one who has left house or brothers or sisters or father or mother or wife or children or lands, for My sake and the gospel's, who shall not receive a hundredfold now in this time . . . and in the age to come, eternal life.

(Mark 10:29,30)

The Scottish athlete Eric Liddell famously refused to run in the time trials of his favourite event, the 100-metre dash at the 1924 summer Olympics in Paris as they were to be held on a Sunday. Yet God rewarded him with the gold medal and a world record in the 400-metre final. His time stood as the European record for a period of twelve years. Through life, Liddell surrendered himself to God. His dying word in a Japanese internment camp in China, during World War Two was whispered to his young friend . . . The word was 'Surrender'. Eric Liddell's life has been an inspiration to generations of young people and will continue to be, both now and in the future.

The people whose lives are recorded in this book found themselves and their future in abandonment to God. They were prepared to step aside from all they had but were to find that God's rewards far surpassed all that they had surrendered.

Graham Staines and his boys were to pay the ultimate price in earthly terms, yet the international response to their deaths was to achieve far more in broadcasting the love of God to the people of India than Graham or his dear wife, Gladys or daughter, Esther could ever have imagined.

Life is transient and is well summed up in the words of Shakespeare's last play:

We are such stuff
As dreams are made on, and our little life
Is rounded with a sleep.[10]

When those dreams and aspirations are based on faith and trust in a God who will never fail or let us down, they find reality and fulfilment. They also find permanence and become a lasting legacy to those who follow.

Epilogue

William Sangster the great Welsh evangelist and writer died in 1960 of progressive neuronal atrophy. On Easter day shortly before he died, when he was unable to walk or speak, he wrote for his daughter: 'How terrible to wake up on Easter and have no voice to shout, "He is risen!" Far worse, to have a voice and not want to shout.'[1]

Lynne bought me a pair of shoes for Christmas, Rockport's. Very shmick, casuals, black with white stitching, size eleven. But they were tight across the midfoot. So . . .

I took them back.

No joy!

'Don't have your size, sir. Don't give refunds, not legally obliged to do so. Have a nice day!'

So I went downtown where they did have my size on sale and at half price. I came home with two pairs of shoes for the price of one, and two shoeboxes. Which got me thinking . . .

A close friend recently lost a brother to an aggressive malignancy. He was an ex US Olympian and had died in Paris. After the funeral, my friend returned home with two shoeboxes containing his brother's personal things. Not sure what was in them. Medals, I guess, maybe some letters, old photos, shadows of past times, perhaps some loose change.

Can a life be contained within a shoebox? The trappings, the treasures, maybe. The memories, friendships, life experience, faith in a creator God? I think not.

And when days are gone, what remains? The inheritance, the precious things soon to filter carelessly through the fingers of others. So what does remain? Is there anything of lasting value?

The legacy: values, caring, instilled wisdom, trust in God, far greater treasures. They are imparted to children and reborn in children's children. They cascade like a river down generations, finding their own expression. Unlike Yasmina Reza's downhill skier who appeared from the blizzard only to disappear, they re-emerge again and again.[2]

In the preface, I referenced the words of the philosopher John Paul Sartre who said that 'no finite point has meaning without an infinite reference point'. The stories of our lives, no matter how compelling, are transient and without meaning unless they are anchored in the infinite. And what is the infinite? The answer may be found in the book of Exodus where God said to Moses:

> I AM WHO I AM . . . you shall say to the children of Israel, 'I AM has sent me to you.'
>
> (Exod. 3:14)

Unless our lives are anchored in God, our stories are mere scratchings to be washed away with time.

What we are able to achieve in life is a mere extension of who we are. This will depend on whether we have found identity in God as our Father. It will also depend on whether we are able to trust Him completely and walk daily in the empowering presence of His Holy Spirit.

God has both plan and purpose. His *plan* will be achieved, no matter what our response. It was His plan that Jesus be born a man. It was His plan that Jesus die to save us from our sins and that He rise again from the dead, proclaiming victory over sin and death. It was also His plan that the Holy Spirit be poured out over all men and women.

His *purpose* is revealed to us, step by step, as we follow the path that He has set for us. It requires our trust, acceptance, obedience and availability. Not our ability. Whether or not we accept His purpose for our lives will determine whether we find fulfilment and whether we know the thrill, the peace and satisfaction of walking daily with Him.

We come into this world with nothing and leave with nothing (tangible, that is). What happens in the interim depends entirely as to whether we are prepared to accept His invitation to walk in His presence.

As Christians we do not journey alone. When we accept Jesus into our hearts He enters our lives and brings the Father also.[3] His Holy Spirit empowers, nurtures and comforts us if we allow Him to do so.[4] As we learn to relate to these three members of the Godhead and spend time daily in their presence, God becomes our constant companion, always by our side in every situation, in every circumstance.[5]

Even when oceans roar, He remains . . . our Silent Partner.

Were You There? is a popular afternoon radio segment on Sydney *Drive Time* radio 702. The announcer nominates a prominent event in recent history and invites people who were present to call in and share their experiences. On 9 September 2013, the topic was the Australian Billy Graham Crusade of 1959. I listened with interest, as it was on that occasion as a boy that I had recommitted my life to Christ, a decision that I have never since regretted.

A number of people recalled how they had been drawn to hear the great orator but had been astounded to find that God had spoken to them personally. An atheist praised Graham's oratory but said that he had remained unconvinced. Others told of how their lives had been changed from that time on by their decision to accept and follow Christ.

One woman who was 11 years old at the time told of how she felt the call of God on her life and when the invitation was given to accept Christ as her Saviour, she stood to her feet.

'Sit down, Cheryl,' snapped her mother. 'You are far too young to make a decision like that.'

'I obeyed my mother,' she said, 'and resumed my seat.'

The opportunity never presented itself to Cheryl again. That was fifty-six years ago.

Every man, woman and child has the call of God on their life.

What is your response?

To fall in love with God is the greatest romance;
to seek him the greatest adventure;
to find him, the greatest human achievement.[6]

Endnotes

Preface

1. Malcolm Muggeridge, 'Jesus' http://www.thewords.com/articles/mugger2.htm (accessed 17.8.16).
2. THE PROBLEM OF PAIN by CS Lewis © copyright CS Lewis Pte Ltd 1940.
3. Australian Broadcasting Corporation, 'Q&A. Adventures in Democracy', 4 November 2013.

Introduction

1. Ultrasonic assessment of the heart provides a moving image of the heart structures and allows the flow of blood through the chambers and valves to be assessed.
2. Don Richardson, *Eternity in Their Hearts* (Ventura, CA: Regal Books, 1981).
3. Geoffrey Blainey, *A Short History of Christianity* (New York: Viking, 2011).
4. Peter Craven, *The Australian*, 3 December 2011.
5. Malcolm Muggeridge, *Chronicles of Wasted Time*: *An Autobiography* (London: Collins, 1972).
6. Christopher Hitchens, *Mortality* (Crows Nest: Allen and Unwin, 2012). The brother of Peter Hitchens quoted in the Introduction.
7. See Acts 22:8.
8. See John 20:28.
9. See 1 Samuel 3:10.
10. One who might say, 'You can't prove that there is no God, so why bother?'

1. The Incredible Journey of Elliott the Brave

[1] A shunt between the main pumping chambers of the heart, which causes blood to be pumped backwards from the left to the right side of the heart.

[2] Intensive Care Unit.

[3] Extracorporeal membrane oxygenation.

[4] N. Grubb, *Rees Howells: Intercessor* (Cambridge: Lutterworth Press, 1986).

[5] Matty Crocker is a songwriter and praise leader at Hillsong Church.

[6] Michael and Naomi are both actively involved in Hillsong Church. Michael plays an integral role in music production and prior to that was a guitarist in the American groups Butch Walker's Let's-Go-Out-Tonite and The Academy Is.

[7] 'Oceans (Where Feet May Fail)', words and music by Matt Crocker, Joel Houston and Salomon Ligthelm © 2012 Hillsong Music Publishing. CCLI: 6428767. All rights reserved. International copyright secured. Used by permission.

[8] Starling's Law of the heart. As the left ventricle is distended so it must contract more forcefully to eject blood.

[9] See Zechariah 10:1.

[10] The general led the Indian troops against the Pakistanis on the Siachen Glacier. It was the highest battle ever fought. His story is told elsewhere in this book.

[11] Operating room.

[12] From a reflection by Sister Monica Joan in the BBC TV series *Call The Midwife* on the death of her friend. From Series 3, episode 8, written by Heidi Thomas, based on the memoirs of Jennifer Worth, first broadcast 9 March 2014.

[13] Graham Cooke, *Approaching the Heart of Prophecy* (Winston-Salem: Punch Press, 2006), p. 86.

[14] The story of Ginny and her husband is written in my previous book: *Nine Minutes Past Midnight* (Milton Keynes: Authentic Media, 2011). Ch. 7: China Syndrome.

[15] See Matthew 14:22–33.

[16] Neonatal Intensive Care Unit.

[17] 'Oceans (Where Feet May Fail)', words and music by Matt Crocker, Joel Houston and Salomon Ligthelm © 2012 Hillsong Music Publishing. CCLI: 6428767. All rights reserved. International copyright secured. Used by permission.

Preface to Chapter 2

¹ Martin H. Manser, *Westminster Collection of Christian Quotes*; Henry Krause (Louisville, KY: Westminster John Knox Press, 2001).

2. Resurrection

¹ The Rainbow Serpent is a common deity in the mythology of Aboriginal Australia.

² Oxygen saturation is measured by pulse oximetry, a simple means of measuring the level of hemoglobin that is oxygen saturated in the blood. A probe placed on a fingertip measures red and infrared rays to determine saturation. 90 per cent saturation on oxygen is dangerously low.

³ Maria Billias, '11-year-old saves toddler after seeing CPR on TV', *Northern Territory News* 6 March 2014, 1:47 p.m.

⁴ Uncontrollable shaking associated with fever. Lymphangitis is inflammation of the lymphatic channels seen as red streaky lines.

⁵ C-reactive protein levels in the blood are one indicator of the level of infection. Normally the level is <5mg/L

⁶ The serum creatinine level is an indicator of the level of renal function. The higher the level of retained creatinine the poorer the function.

⁷ When the eyes become painfully sensitive to light, often an indicator of central nervous system infection such as meningitis.

⁸ Stuart Piggin, 08, 'The Lord's Firestorms: God the Holy Trinity and the Experience of Religious Revival in Australia', *Lucas: An Evangelical History Review*, webjournals.ac.edu.au (accessed 31.8.16).

⁹ Ibid. p. 46.

¹⁰ An ancient custom among indigenous Australians whereby native plants are burned to produce smoke believed to have cleansing powers and ward off evil spirits.

¹¹ https://www.creativespirits.info/aboriginalculture/law/tribal-punishment-customary-law-payback (accessed 23.8.16). 'Payback' is perhaps the best known form of Aboriginal customary tribal law. One of the tribal punishments is spearing in the leg.

¹² See John 1:9.

Preface to Chapter 3

¹ S. Nade, and G. Warren, *The Care of Neuropathic Limbs: A Practical Manual* (Carnforth: Parthenon Publishing Group, 1999).

3. Mission Impossible

¹ British writer, broadcaster, activist. ABC *Drive* 702, 8 August 2014.
² http://www.dsto.defence.gov.au/page/3383/ (accessed 17.8.16). It was 1958, during an informal visit to ARL by Sir Robert Hardingham, the former British Air Vice-Marshal that the breakthrough occurred. Dave Warren was asked, during his lunchtime, to demonstrate his 'unofficial project'. Straight away Sir Robert saw the potential. Dave and his black box were almost immediately on a flight to England. The reception there was most encouraging. The Ministry of Aviation announced that the installation of the black box flight recorder for instrument readings might soon be made mandatory.
³ Grace's father had retired in 1931 and the family moved to Tasmania where he would work as a clergyman. But his retirement was interrupted two years later when three Japanese sea cucumber fishermen were killed by aboriginals in Arnhem Land. The authorities sent out a police patrol led by one Sgt. McColl. He was speared to death. The police planned to send out a punitive force, but the powers that be wanted to send someone who knew the people and spoke the language to find out what had really happened. 'That job fell to my father,' said Grace. 'He led a party of three. They soon discovered that the sergeant had interfered with aboriginal women and by aboriginal law had to be killed, as were the Japanese fishermen. The men responsible finally surrendered and were tried. One was found guilty of murder and sentenced to death, the other two were released. A high court challenge found in favour of the man who was subsequently released. He was never seen again. It's said that he was released late one evening after midnight and shot.'
⁴ The dura mater is the tough fibrous sheath, which covers the brain.
⁵ See www.britannica.com/biography/Saint-Damien-of-Molokai (accessed 31.8.16).
⁶ https://www.thecatholicthing.org/2009/07/15/we-lepers/ (accessed 23.8.16).
⁷ Bill and Jo Anne Dennett, *Unusual Marriage* (Forest Hill, Victoria: SPCK Australia, 2006).

Preface to Chapter 4

[1] Yasmina Reza, *Art* (trans. Christopher Hampton; London, Faber and Faber, 1996).

4. Reaching Out, Touching Eternity

[1] Pathological enlargement of the abdominal aorta to more than 1.5 times its normal diameter.
[2] Emergency room.
[3] Mortality of ruptured abdominal aortic aneurysm treated with open or endovascular repair Eric L. Verhoeven, MD, PhD, Marten R. Kapma, MD, Henk Groen, PhD, Ignace F. Tielliu, MD, Clark J. Zeebregts, MD, PhD, Foppe Bekkema, RN, MANP, Jan J. van den Dungen, MD, PhD.
[4] I found it interesting that the little boy who visited heaven and whose story is told in the book *Heaven is for Real* had no fear after that near death experience.
[5] A secondary tumour, which has spread by the blood stream from the primary lesion.
[6] 'I Heard the Voice of Jesus Say', Lutheran Hymnal, No. 277. Composer John B. Dykes, 1868.

Preface to Chapter 5

[1] See Acts 17:28.

5. Finding True Identity

[1] Gleeson score is the way in which a prostate cancer is graded for aggressiveness by the pathologist from biopsy results: 2-4 low, 5-6 moderate, 7 intermediate, 8-10 high.
[2] Distant spread to other organs via the bloodstream.
[3] See Isaiah 43: 'I have called you by your name; You are Mine.'
[4] See Romans 8:15.

[5] See Romans 8:38,39: 'For I am persuaded that neither death nor life, nor angels nor principalities nor powers, nor things present nor things to come, nor height nor depth, nor any other created thing, shall be able to separate us from the love of God which is in Christ Jesus our Lord.'

[6] US version.

[7] Grade Point Average based on course results ranging from 0 to 4.

[8] Doctors in that region were trained as specialists i.e. in cardiology, orthopedics, ophthalmology etc. They were not trained as general practitioner/family doctors.

[9] See Luke 15:22,23.

[10] Selwyn Hughes, 'His Story – Our Story', *Every Day With Jesus*, 16 October 2008.

[11] Graham Cooke. Presentation at Dayspring Church 20 November 2011.

6. The Man with No Name – But Known Unto God

[1] Russell and Kay Clark's story is told in my last book, *Nine Minutes Past Midnight*.

[2] The Bethlehem Babies Home was run by the British Government Protectorate in Palestine and managed on a day-to-day basis by matron who was a German citizen.

[3] Haile Selassie ruled as emperor of Ethiopia from 1930 to 1974, and his son Amha succeeded him as the last emperor of Ethiopia, a position handed down from the time of King Solomon.

[4] See http://www.gardentomb.com (accessed 31.8.16).

[5] 23 October–11 November 1942.

[6] Rommel returned to Germany supposedly on 'sick leave' five days following his resounding defeat by Eisenhower on 5 March 1943.

[7] U-boat 862 was the only German submarine to operate in the Pacific during World War Two. It was captained by Heinrich Timm and was credited with the sinking of seven allied ships totalling 42,374 tons. After Germany's surrender in 1945 it was commandeered by the Imperial Japanese Navy.

[8] David currently chairs groups such as the Heads of Churches Conference and the Human Rights Organization for Middle East, North Africa. He has edited the Lausanne series *A New Vision, a New Heart, a Renewed Call* and most recently *Islam, Human Rights and Public Policy*. He is also

Canon of All Saints Anglican Cathedral of Cairo and of St Andrew's Cathedral in Sydney.

9 Robyn is an evangelist and Bible teacher whose ministry takes her throughout Australia and abroad. As the Lausanne Movement's Honorary Senior Associate for women in world evangelization, she has developed an international network of over two thousand women who are committed to telling others about Jesus in a variety of ways and ministries.

She chaired for many years the Australian Lausanne Committee with its particular focus on training Christian leaders; She has established a young women's network for encouragement and sharing, leading a fortnightly women's Bible study at St Andrew's Cathedral in Sydney; preaching from time to time at the cathedral and in other churches and speaking at conferences and conventions throughout the country.

Robyn Claydon is also a licensed lay reader/preacher with the Anglican Sydney Diocese and was a member of the Council of Moore Theological College. As an educator for over twenty-five years, Robyn is a Fellow of the Australian College of Education, has been a contributing author to books and journals on education, was one of the pioneers of Personal Development as a subject in schools, has written a text book to encourage teenagers' self-esteem and, until 1990, was deputy headmistress of Abbotsleigh girls' school in Sydney.

10 See Proverbs 3:5,6: 'Trust in the LORD with all your heart, And lean not on your own understanding; In all your ways acknowledge Him, And He shall direct your paths.'

11 In India and Pakistan, a gang of roving criminals who commit violent robbery.

12 Missionary Aviation Fellowship.

13 Canon Andrew White has had a remarkable career spanning some forty years, firstly in the field of medicine in London and later as a priest of the Anglican Church. He has worked tirelessly for peace and reconciliation in many of the Middle East's hotspots. As one of his friends has said, 'Andrew has a talent for being in the wrong place at the wrong time . . . Whether it's an Intifada in Palestine or terrorism in Baghdad, there he is.' He has counted among his friends such as Yasser Arafat.

In November 2014 he was instructed by the Archbishop of Canterbury to leave Baghdad as it was too dangerous for him to remain in Iraq. Today he continues his work from Israel and Palestine.

14 Andrew White, *My Journey So Far* (Oxford: Lion Hudson, 2015).

15 White, *My Journey So Far*.

[16] See 1 Kings 17:14: 'For this is what the LORD, the God of Israel, says: "The jar of flour will not be used up and the jug of oil will not run dry until the day the LORD sends rain on the land"' (NIVUK).

7. Father to the Fatherless

[1] See Mark 8:24.

[2] This is a simple visual aid used by the Navigators to explain our relationship with God as Christians. www.navigators.org (accessed 17.8.16).

[3] This is the term used when a sponsoring bishop gives permission to an overseas bishop to ordain on his behalf.

[4] An Ironman Triathlon is one of a series of long-distance triathlon races organized by the World Triathlon Corporation (WTC) consisting of a 2.4-mile (3.86 km) swim, a 112-mile (180.25 km) bicycle ride and a marathon 26.2-mile (42.2 km) run, raced in that order and without a break. Most Ironman events have a strict time limit of seventeen hours to complete the race. The Ironman race starts at 7:00 a.m.; the mandatory swim cut off for the 2.4-mile (3.9 km) swim is 9:20 a.m. (two hours twenty minutes), the mandatory bike cut-off time is 5:30 p.m. (eight hours ten minutes), and the mandatory marathon cut-off is midnight (six hours thirty minutes). Any participant that manages to complete the triathlon within these timings becomes an Ironman.

[5] Paul was one of the two unmarried rectors in the Sydney Diocese at the time.

[6] A malignancy of the plasma cells within the blood, which deal with immunity.

[7] Paul meets with the bereaved relatives and friends of those who have died as the result of violent crimes.

Preface to Chapter 8

[1] http://www.youtube.com/watch?v=o5VZKWcgw6c (accessed 17.8.16).

[2] Chapin, 'Cat's in the Cradle', p. 60.

8. Thomas

[1] The Siachen Glacier at 6,000 metres has been the site of an ongoing war between India and Pakistan for almost thirty years. Read more about this war in the chapter 'The General'.

[2] Abbottabad was named after General Abbott of the British Armed Forces. Though not related, Thomas said that his name was often good for a cheap meal at the local hotel.

[3] The official Protestant Church of the People's Republic of China established and sanctioned by the Three Self Patriotic Movement to practise self-governance, self-support and self-propagation. The Church remains patriotic to the Chinese government and is not affiliated with home churches.

[4] Eugene Peterson, *The Pastor* (New York: HarperCollins, 2011).

[5] David Rohde www.nytimes.com/2002/08/06/world/gunmen-kill-6-at-a-christian-school-in-pakistan (accessed 17.8.16).

[6] See Malachi 4:6: He will turn the hearts of the parents to their children, and the hearts of the children to their parents; or else I will come and strike the land with total destruction' (NIVUK).

[7] See Luke 1:17: 'And he will go on before the Lord, in the spirit and power of Elijah, to turn the hearts of the parents to their children and the disobedient to the wisdom of the righteous – to make ready a people prepared for the Lord' (NIVUK).

[8] Jennifer Worth wrote 'midwifery is the very stuff of drama' in the preface to her book *Call the Midwife* (London: Phoenix, 2008).

[9] UNICEF.

9. Twice Blessed

[1] Spanish, meaning pilgrim.

[2] With the fall of Saigon in April 1975, the CIA withdrew their support for the 'Secret Army' of 30,000 Hmong people in Laos who had been recruited to fight the North Vietnamese. Vang Pao, one of the Hmong leaders, was called before the prime minister of Laos and ordered to cooperate with the communist Pathet Lao. He refused, tore the general's stars from his collar and strutted from the room. Days later an order was issued for his extermination. Jerry Daniels who was Vang Pao's CIA case officer arranged for evacuation of several thousand

Hmong leaders. Tens of thousands of Hmong, together with other tribal people, fled west to the Mekong on the Thai Laotian border. Many died in transit at the hands of pursuing communist troops and many drowned as they attempted to cross the Mekong. It's said that 50,000 died of chemical poisoning and 45,000 from starvation and disease. Children died of drug overdose as their parents attempted to sedate them to prevent their cries which might alert enemy troops.

3   Sadly, Dr Catherine Maddox died later that year in the UK of lymphoma.

4   Known commercially as Tylenol and Panadol.

5   These are flat rose-colored spots up to 4 mm in diameter that develop on the skin of patients with typhoid and paratyphoid fever.

6   The child's blood pressure was more than twice normal even for an adult. Malignant hypertension is uncontrollable rapidly rising blood pressure. Status epilepticus is a condition of continuing grand mal epileptic seizures.

7   ACE inhibitors are now the most common form of drug used to control hypertension. They prevent an enzyme in the body from producing Angiotensin II, which raises blood pressure.

8   A serious condition affecting 5-10 per cent of pregnancies and characterized by high blood pressure, protein in the urine and soft tissue swelling (oedema). If not controlled, it threatens the lives of both mother and baby.

9   A congenital condition where the abdominal contents herniate into the chest cavity through a defect in the diaphragm. Often the lungs fail to develop properly.

Preface to Chapter 10

1   We need three 'quiets' in our lives: a quiet time to seek God daily, a quiet place to commune with Him, and a quiet friend with whom to pray and share our experiences.

2   Andrew White, *My Journey So Far* (Oxford: Lion Hudson, 2015).

10. Stepping Out – The Interface

1   http://www.smh.com.au/world/daredevil-wallenda-walks-across-grand-canyon-20130624-2oryr.html (accessed 31.8.16).

2   *Sydney Morning Herald*, 24 June 2013.

³ These are paramedics trained to the highest level.
⁴ Cardiopulmonary resuscitation.
⁵ The terminal respiratory efforts of a dying person.
⁶ '000' is the telephone call for emergency in Australia.
⁷ The normal dose would be less than 1 mg.
⁸ Contaminated drinking water resulted in a severe infection eventually resulting in a rare form of meningitis where the bodies own cells attack the covering of the spinal cord.
⁹ See Ecclesiastes 1:2 (NIVUK).
¹⁰ ABC *Foreign Correspondent*, 8 October 2013. 'Coming Home Part 2', Sally Sara correspondent.

11. God's Liberator

¹ Youth With A Mission.
² The name is translated Sky/Heaven.
³ The present situation in North Korea is no better. Kim Jong-un recently ordered an army officer to be blown to pieces by mortar shells, so that no trace would be left of him, for drinking alcohol during the official period of mourning for his father Kim Jong-il.
⁴ http://www.globalsecurity.org/military/world/war/china-norkor.htm (accessed 17.8.16).
⁵ BBC News, Olenka Frenkiel 29 May 2008, http://news.bbc.co.uk/2/hi/asia-pacific/7423994.stm (accessed 17.08.16).
⁶ Jenna Yoojin Yun, *The Guardian* (Australia), Friday, 5 February 2016. 'Thirty thousand children born to North Korean mothers who had fled to China said to be without access to schooling, healthcare or citizenship.' https://www.theguardian.com/world/2016/feb/05/north-koreas-stateless-children (accessed 31.8.16).

12. The General

¹ Dehradun Military Academy is a sister to Sandhurst and West Point. It had trained princes.
² The term '*mandir*' refers to a Hindu temple.
³ Kargil campaign.

[4] The flash-bang interval is one method used to evaluate the distance of artillery. The flash is seen almost immediately whereas the bang travels at the speed of sound. The distance is calculated by dividing the time by the speed of sound.

[5] One of the most inspiring sermons of all time is Oral Robert's 'The Fourth Man'. A segment is archived on the web. It is well worth the watching: https://www.youtube.com/watch?v=UqQYpSqtM40 (accessed 31.8.16).

13. God's Freedom Fighter

[1] Both were founded on Islam and under the control of Field Marshall Ayub Khan.

[2] See Matthew 13:45,46: 'Again, the kingdom of heaven is like a merchant seeking beautiful pearls, who, when he had found one pearl of great price, went and sold all that he had and bought it.'

14. Never Alone

[1] One of the Munda peoples living in Orissa and West Bengal. They worship a court of spirits who must be placated with prayers, offerings and sacrifices to ward off evil influences. joshuaproject.net/people_groups/14743/IN (accessed 31.8.16).

[2] Now known as Odisha.

[3] The Voice of the Martyrs, *Hearts of Fire: Eight Women in the Underground Church and Their Stories of Costly Faith* (Nashville, TN: Thomas Nelson, 2003).

[4] http://www.hindunet.org/hvk/specialrepo/wadhwa/Preliminary.htm (accessed 17.8.16).

[5] British House of Commons, bound vol. Hansard, 10 February 1999, column 441.

[6] Extract taken from the song 'Because He Lives' by G Gaither and W J Gaither. Copyright © 1971 Gaither Music Company.*

[7] Locals were astounded. In Hindu tradition, forgiveness of others was the privilege afforded to deities alone. To forgive these men elevated Gladys and Esther into a spiritual realm in the minds of the people.

8   Dara Singh was initially sentenced to death by Khurda District and Sessions court on 22 September 2003, but the Orissa High Court on 19 May 2005 commuted the death penalty to life imprisonment after he appealed against the district court verdict.

9   The Supreme Court judges stated: 'though Graham Staines and his two sons were burned to death while they were sleeping inside a station wagon at Manohorpur the intention was to teach a lesson to Graham Staines about his religious activities of converting poor tribals to Christianity', *The Statesman*, 25 January 2011.

10 V. Mangalwadi et al., *Burnt Alive, The Staines and the God They Loved* (Mumbai: GLS Publishing, 1999).

11 www.dawn.com/news/1169844 (accessed 17.8.16).

12 Excerpt from *Our Daily Bread*, 7 January 1999: William Sangster (1900–1960), the noted English preacher, visited a young girl in the hospital at a time when doctors were struggling in vain to keep her from becoming blind. With sadness she said to him, 'God is going to take away my sight.' He listened but at first made no reply. Then he answered compassionately, 'Don't let Him, Jessie. Give it to Him.' 'I don't understand,' she responded. So he explained, 'Try to pray this prayer: "Father, if I must lose my sight, help me to give it to You."'

13 *The Lancet*, 29 March 2003.

14 See Hebrews 11:4.

15 A full account and media references are available in my previous book: *Nine Minutes Past Midnight*.

16 The story is told in detail in *Nine Minutes Past Midnight*. And it is clear from the stories of the survivors that many more would have been killed if God had not intervened.

17 Hebrews 13:5: 'I will never leave you or forsake you.'

18 God TV Summer Celebration Plymouth 2014. (Andrew White) www.god.tv/the-god-tv-team/video/summer-celebration/canon-andrew-white (accessed 5.9.16).

19 Mark 16:7: 'He is going ahead of you into Galilee. There you will see him, just as he told you' (NIVUK).

Preface to Chapter 15

1   World Hope Network had been my friend Daniel's vision to honour and bring hope to third world people. The vision had now become reality and as a small team we were to visit Cambodia.

[2] Stanley Smith of the Cambridge Seven. From his farewell address, Exeter Hall, London, 4 February 1885. B. Broomhill, *Evangelism of the World, A Missionary Band: A Record of Consecration and Appeal* (1889).

15. Cambodia

[1] John 10:27: 'My sheep hear My voice, and I know them, and they follow Me.'

[2] It was Air Asia flight QZ8501 that went down in the Java Sea on Sunday, 28 December 2014 with loss of all lives.

[3] A pterygium is a fleshy growth of the conjunctiva that grows from the nasal side of the eye. It is thought to result from excessive UV light exposure. It causes irritation and may affect vision.

[4] A mandibular block is something with which we are all familiar. It involves the rather uncomfortable injection of local anaesthetic close to the mandibular nerve near the back of the mandible to anaesthetize the lower jaw.

[5] It was reckoned at the time that 63,000 people in Cambodia were HIV positive. The incidence of Hepatitis B was significantly higher.

16. God's Revolutionary

[1] In 2013, thirty-four years later, Borin and his family returned to his father's gravesite to erect a memorial.

[2] Bill Bright, *Come Help Change the World* (Orlando, FL: New Life Publications, 1999); first published 1979.

[3] I had met that man and had observed for myself the powerful mantle of evangelism that rested upon him.

17. Good Morning Vietnam

[1] On a rest day we visited the famous Angkor Wat temple. There was a strong spiritual presence, however, similar to that I had experienced visiting Buddhist temples in China and I was content to observe from the outside.

2 http://www.news.com.au/world/cambodias-clothes-makers-being-killed-after-protesting-for-a-pay-rise-to-make-clothes-for-nike-gap/story-fndir2ev-1226797612232 (accessed 17.8.16).

3 An overactive thyroid gland.

4 No prescriptions were required.

5 Formerly known as Saigon.

6 Words to the verse by Isaac Watts. *Hymns and Spiritual Songs Book II*, 1707–09 and ironically sung to the tune: 'Martyrdom' by Hugh Wilson, 1800. The refrain was written by Ralph E. Hudson in 1885.

18. Vijay

1 This is called central cyanosis and refers to the blue colouring of the skin and mucous membranes due to reduced oxygen levels in the blood. In Vijay's case it appears to have related to a reversal of the shunt in her heart. It is likely that the shunt carried blood from the high pressure left side of her heart back to the right side placing an additional load on the heart and lungs. When resistance to flow in her lungs increased, so the shunt was reversed and blood was not oxygenated.

2 Hymn, 'The Lion of Judah' by H.Q. Wilson.

19. What We Do Now Echoes in Eternity

1 Use of positron emitting radiopharmaceuticals to map images of bodily function.

2 Magnetic resonance imaging.

3 aihw.gov.au Australian government. Australian Institute of Health and Welfare.

4 http://www.usatoday.com/story/news/nation/2014/10/08/us-life-expectancy-hits-record-high/16874039/ (accessed 17.8.16).

5 http://www.dailymail.co.uk/sciencetech/article-2802895 (accessed 17.8.16).

6 Ed finally passed away on Christmas Day, 25 December 2015. You can read more about this wonderful man and his ministry at http://edsstory.com (accessed 17.8.16).

7 Yogi Berra was a famous American Major League baseball player who for almost his entire career played for the New York Yankees. He was also famous for his quotations.

[8] 'Hypo' is a term used to describe the symptoms associated with low blood sugar levels.

[9] Gabriel Marcel, *Homo Viator: Introduction to a Metaphysic of Hope* (Chicago, IL: H. Regnery Co., 1951).

[10] S. Hughes, 'Finding yourself in the Psalms', *Every Day With Jesus* (Farnham: CWR, July/August 2000).

Preface to Chapters 20 and 21

[1] Lyle Dorsett, *A Passion For Souls: The Life of D.L. Moody* (Chicago, IL: Moody Publishers, 2003).

20. Behold the Man

[1] This made for a better target for the riflemen. The guards had ensured, however, that the ties were not too tight. (Information from Andrew's wife, Feby.)

[2] Four other members of the Bali 9: Martin Stephens, Renae Lawrence, Scott Rush and Michael Czugai were apprehended at Denpasar Airport with packages of heroin strapped to their bodies. Si Yi Chen, Tan Duc Than Nguyen and Matthew Norman were arrested at a hotel in Kuta Beach also in possession of heroin.

[3] www.abc.net.au/news/2015-02-12/bali-nine-timeline.../6085190 (accessed 17.8.16).

[4] http://www.smh.com.au/world/bali-nine-executions-investigation-into-bribery-allegations-completed-by-judicial-commission-20150428-1mv3sq.html (accessed 17.8.16).

[5] Ben Quilty is a celebrated Australian artist living in Sydney who won the 2014 Prudential Eye Award, 2011 Archibald Prize and the 2009 Doug Moran national portrait prize.

[6] As given to Chris Makin from Leading the Way http://www.biblesociety.org.au/news/following-jesus-on-death-row (accessed 16.8.16).

[7] 'I Give You My Heart', Words and Music by Reuben Morgan © 1995 Hillsong Music Publishing (APRA) CCLI: 1866132. All rights reserved. International copyright secured. Used by permission.

[8] 'Mighty To Save', Words and Music by Ben Fielding and Reuben Morgan © 2006 Hillsong Music Publishing (APRA) CCLI: 4591782. All rights reserved. International copyright secured. Used by permission.

9   The shortened version of the name of President Joko Widodo.

10 Words of Pastor Miranda Riddington spoken at Andrew's funeral. Printed with permission.

11 'Mighty To Save', Words and Music by Ben Fielding and Reuben Morgan © 2006 Hillsong Music Publishing (APRA) CCLI: 4591782. All rights reserved. International copyright secured. Used by permission.

12 https://soundcloud.com/globalchurch/empowered-by-the-holy-spirit (accessed 31.8.16).

21. When Iron Gates Yield

1   These were Myles Munroe's final words before he died in a plane crash with his wife and several others. https://www.sajigroup.com/leadership-success/the-greatest-act-of-true-leaders/ (accessed 17.8.16).

2   Jim Elliot was one of five American missionaries who were massacred by the Huaorani tribe of eastern Ecuador in September 1955. His story is told in the book written by his wife, Elisabeth, *Through Gates of Splendor*, first published by Harper Brothers, 1957. These words were written in pencil in his diary shortly before his death. Elisabeth passed away 15 June 2015.

3   With permission from Matthew Norman at Kerobokan Prison 26 August 2015.

4   The title of this chapter is taken from a book written by missionary Geoffrey Bull and published in 1955 regarding his imprisonment in Tibet as a spy at the time of Tibetan Independence.

Preface to Chapter 22

1   http://www.nbcnews.com/news/us-news/i-am-strong-enough-walk-through-hell-smile-cleveland-kidnap (accessed 17.8.6). Castro was sentenced to life in prison plus 1,000 years on his guilty plea to 937 counts, including kidnapping and rape. He was found dead in his cell on 3 September 2013 after apparently hanging himself.

22. Trusting God

[1] Rigors are the violent tremors that often accompanies a fever and are not uncommon in diseases of the biliary tract.

[2] The *Logos* is the written word of God but I also discerned this as His *rhema* spiritually revealed word for me at that moment.

[3] The story is told in my first book: *Nine Minutes Past Midnight*.

[4] See Deuteronomy 31:6b: 'For the LORD your God, He is the One who goes with you. He will not leave you nor forsake you.'

[5] See Mark 4:35–41.

[6] See 1 John 4:18: 'There is no fear in love; but perfect love casts out fear . . .'

[7] Sadducees did not believe in resurrection of the dead.

[8] See Romans 8:11.

[9] See Romans 8:28: 'And we know that all things work together for good to those who love God, to those who are the called according to *His* purpose.' (my italics)

[10] William Shakespeare, *The Tempest*, Act 4, Scene 1.

Epilogue

[1] © 2008 Lenya Heitzig, Penny Pierce Rose. *Live Fearlessly: A Study in the Book of Joshua* is published by David C Cook. All rights reserved.

[2] Heitzig, Rose, *Live Fearlessly*, p. 59.

[3] See John 14:23.

[4] See John 14:16.

[5] See Psalm 16:8: 'I have set the LORD always before me; Because He is at my right hand I shall not be moved.'

[6] Augustine of Hippo, http://www.catholic.org/news/national/story.php?id=33940 (accessed 31.8.16).